D1388215

THE MILLS OF GOD

The State and African Labour in South Africa
1918 - 1948

THE MILLS OF GOD

The State and African Labour in South Africa
1918 - 1948

DAVID DUNCAN

WITWATERSRAND UNIVERSITY PRESS

Witwatersrand University Press
1 Jan Smuts Avenue
2001 Johannesburg
South Africa

ISBN 1 86814 227 2

First published 1995

Typeset by Photoprint, Cape Town

Printed and bound by Creda Press

CONTENTS

ACKNOWLEDGEMENTS

Many people have helped me in the research and writing of this book. In particular, I would like to thank Professor Alan Jeeves of Queen's University, who supervised the original thesis. Without his constant advice, encouragement and generosity, the project would not have been possible.

In South Africa, many thanks are due to Anna Cunningham and Michelle Pickover of Historical and Literary Papers, University of the Witwatersrand and to the staff of the State Archives, Pretoria. I am also grateful to Professor Bruce Murray for his friendship, guidance and support, on and off the tennis court. Professor Charles van Onselen kindly extended the hospitality of his African Studies Institute from 1989-90.

Financially, I received support from Queen's University, the Canadian Commonwealth Scholarship Fund, the Reid Trust and, latterly, as a Visiting Research Fellow at the University of the Witwatersrand.

Finally, I would like to thank my mother and father for their love and support. The book is dedicated to them.

ABBREVIATIONS

ACDWU	African Commercial and Distributive Workers' Union
ACL	Advisory Council of Labour
AMWU	African Mine Workers' Union
ANC	African National Congress
CCATU	Co-ordinating Committee of African Trade Unions
CHB	Central Housing Board
CNETU	Council of Non-European Trade Unions
CPSA	Communist Party of South Africa
DNL	Director of Native Labour
FCI	Federated Chamber of Industries
FNETU	Federation of Non-European Trade Unions
GNLB	Government Native Labour Bureau
GPC	Gold Producers' Committee
IC	Industrial Conciliation
ICU	Industrial and Commercial Workers' Union
IFL	Inspector of Farm Labourers
ILO	International Labour Organisation
INL	Inspector of Native Labourers
JCATU	Joint Council of African Trade Unions
NAC	Native Affairs Commission
NAD	Native Affairs Department
NC	Native Commissioner
NHPC	National Housing and Planning Commission
NLR	Native Labour Regulation
NMWIU	National Milling Workers' Industrial Union
NRC	Native Recruiting Corporation
NSC	Native Service Contract
SAAU	South African Agricultural Union
SAIRR	South African Institute of Race Relations
SAMWU	South African Mine Workers' Union
SAP	South African Party
SATLC	South African Trades and Labour Council

SEPC	Social and Economic Planning Council
SNA	Secretary for Native Affairs
TAMWU	Transvaal African Milling Workers' Union
TAU	Transvaal Agricultural Union
TCM	Transvaal Chamber of Mines
WC	Workmen's Compensation
WNLA	Witwatersrand Native Labour Association

...the Native Affairs Department is a body which is regarded by the Africans not as their friend but as someone who is merely carrying out the duty imposed on it by a distant, ruling government.
Pauline Podbrey
Cape Town Trades and Labour Council

May I suggest that you have a discovery yet to make, namely that there are men who have given every ounce of their energy to see that conditions are improved and that are faced with what you perhaps do not appreciate, namely two grades of civilisation. We have been told that the mills of God grind slowly but they grind exceedingly small, and we are apt to take the whole thing on our shoulders and to forget that this is a matter of working out your salvation over a period of years. I would invite you earnestly to remember that these things cannot be done overnight and that you are dealing with a situation which calls for all the wisdom and all the grace that is going in this world.
Alexander Simpson Welsh, K.C.
Member of Native Laws Commission

Evidence to the Native Laws (Fagan)
Commission, Cape Town, 24 Sep. 1946.

1

INTRODUCTION

Prologue

In recent years, the state has been partly dislodged from the centre of South African historiography. Its place has been taken by a rich and evocative social history focusing on experiential and cultural issues, often at the local level. This has helped to balance the previous concentration on national politics and the state. The social history school developed in part as a reaction against the tradition pre-eminent in 1970s South African historiography, which appropriated neo-Marxist, structuralist theories of class struggle and the function of the state. An over-adherence to concepts not directly applicable to the South African context encouraged members of the structuralist school to twist the evidence to fit their preferred interpretation. The more recent social history 'tradition' has studiously avoided this trap. Local histories are usually well versed in empirical data. However, the focus on other, narrower subjects, can produce an equally distorted image of the state, more through lack of interest than wilful manipulation of the evidence. There is a danger of simplifying government interventions to the point where the state becomes a reified, monolithic force, gathering momentum down the decades, undeterred from its path of repression and discrimination.

A further problem with the recent historiography is its lack of attention to labour issues. There are, of course, notable exceptions: among them, Helen Bradford on the Industrial and Commercial Workers' Union and Baruch Hirson's recent book on class and community struggles in the 1930s and 1940s.[1] Jon Lewis has written a book on the Trades and Labour Council, and Iris Berger has produced an important study on the Garment Workers' Union.[2] Nevertheless, there remain large gaps in our knowledge of South African labour history. Historians have defined their subjects more by the places they live in and the cultural and ethnic groups they belong to, than by the jobs they do. In part, this reflects the complexity and diversity of South African society; but we suffer from a dearth of understanding of worker consciousness and experience, and of the extent and impact of state control.

This book examines the South African state and the evolution of labour regulation for Africans between 1918 and 1948. Special attention is given to officials in the seven or so departments which had primary responsibility for African workers. The main departments examined are Native Affairs, Labour, Public Health, Social Welfare, Justice, Agriculture and Mines. It is not 'labour history' in the pure sense of the term. Rather, it deals with the crucial nexus of relationships between the state, capital and black labour. For several reasons 1918 is taken as the starting date. Most obviously, it was the end of World War I and the departure point for a new period of peacetime politics and economic development. Secondly, it marked the beginning of a new period of growth for the civil service, in terms of departments, personnel and responsibilities. An important part of these duties concerned the regulation of African labour. While black mineworkers were already subject to official control by 1918, it was only after that date that successive governments extended their powers to encompass every sector of the economy and almost every material aspect of working class life. The period from the end of the Great War until the National Party victory in 1948 saw an unprecedented expansion of the state's interventions in this area. Simultaneously, the centrality of black labour to the future prosperity of white South Africa gained official recognition. The civil service played a central role in formulating and implementing legislation, and in mediating between the government and the mass of black workers. The attitudes of central state administrators, the ways they affected policies, the impact of those policies, and relations between bureaucrats and workers, form the major themes of this study.

Although this diverges from the social history school, it employs some of the approaches developed there. In particular, it seeks to come to terms with the social, cultural and political milieu within which these largely middle class, English-speaking officials, operated. A sensitivity to factors which contributed to their outlook is essential in explaining state-labour relations in this period. Bureaucrats in pre-1948 South Africa were not the mere instruments of a higher will. To borrow an English writer's term, these were the 'Ruling Servants', their official position belying their ever-increasing significance in public life.[3]

At the same time, this study draws on Marxist, liberal and Weberian political theory, which, together with the secondary literature on the period, is discussed briefly in the following section. Political theory provides useful ways of looking at the South African state. It draws attention to the nature of class struggle and the relationship between class struggle and the political and administrative spheres. It also allows us to identify those areas in which the racial mould of class relations in South Africa produced unique situations and those where South Africa merely replicated what had happened in other forms, overseas.

The disparate nature of civil service duties with regard to black workers provoked conflict and ambiguity among and within government departments. The book's title – *The Mills of God* – highlights this ambiguity. When AS Welsh used the phrase I have quoted, he was defending the administrators' work in helping Africans towards a higher grade of 'civilisation'. In fact the civil service's work could also be seen in a very different light, as grinding African workers down in the mills of restrictive legislation. One of the tasks of this study is to analyse the tension between the repressive and welfare functions of labour regulation, and between the departments which applied them. In so doing, the book measures the degree to which the bureaucracy fitted together to apply a coherent policy, and posits a reconceptualisation of the state.

In discussing the South African state, there is a danger of becoming too refined – of underplaying the rapacity and cruelty of white supremacist rule. In the Union before 1948, the state denied workers basic rights and prescribed heavy penalties for breaking exploitative contracts. It spied on, harassed, imprisoned and assaulted African workers who tried to stand up for themselves. But, the state's attitudes towards black labour were full of contradictions. The origins and nature of those contradictions must be exposed to achieve a fuller understanding of the state and African labour in pre-apartheid South Africa.

Historiography and Theory

A number of works published over the last fifty years have broached the topic under discussion. The following section does not constitute a comprehensive critique of the literature on the state and labour in South Africa. It seeks merely to sketch the broad outlines of how far the historiography has taken us in understanding this important subject, and where the present study fits into the literature.[4]

*   *   *   *

At least until the early 1970s, South African historiography was dominated by liberal interpretations of the country's past. The basic premise of liberal historians is that South African economic development has been hampered by racially discriminatory policies sponsored by the state. According to this argument, many of the state's interventions in African labour regulation have been unsound, for both moral and economic reasons.

The first major work to tackle the question head-on was WM

Macmillan's *Complex South Africa: An Economic Foot-Note to History*, published in 1930. Macmillan believed the segregation 'popularly preached on political platforms' had three main purposes: to preserve jobs for whites, protect the supply of African labour for white farms and, most importantly, to entrench the political domination of the white electorate. To these ends, the state sought to develop the reserves, limit the influx of Africans to the towns and remove enfranchised Cape Africans from the common voters' roll.[5] Similar views were expressed by CW de Kiewiet and ST van der Horst.[6] All three writers stressed the centrality of black labour to all sectors of the economy. They saw a solution to the 'native problem' in lifting blacks to the same standard as whites and treating them accordingly. The advantages of this course to employers and the country as a whole, were based on the principle of equality of opportunity.

In the post-war era, a new and more hardline breed of liberal dominated the study of the South African economy. They were more inclined to see the economic system as working against racial inequity, which they regarded as the product of non-economic forces. Lacking the greater empirical and historical orientation of some of their predecessors, they took a more deterministic approach to economic development, arguing that race discrimination was inevitably inimical to business interests. They also emphasised the potential liberalising effects of economic growth much more strongly than Macmillan, De Kiewiet and Van der Horst.

Of these later works, perhaps the most influential have been those of GV Doxey and D Hobart Houghton.[7] For the latter, the migrant labour system and growing rigidities in the labour market are seen as anachronistic hindrances to national productivity.[8] His goal is to explain how South Africa can achieve greater maturity as a modern industrial economy. Hobart Houghton's work has been complemented by that of other members of the liberal school, notably WH Hutt, R Horwitz and, more recently, Merle Lipton.[9] Lipton sets out specifically to refute accusations by Marxist and revisionist academics that discriminatory labour legislation arose from capital's needs rather than from the interests of the white electorate. Her purpose is to show that apartheid was a hindrance to the more dynamic sectors of capital (mining and manufacturing) and was maintained only through the political alliance of white agriculture and white labour.

The early liberal historiography lacked an understanding of the workings of the capitalist system and its relationship to the South African state. This was corrected in post-war liberal works, but here, the desire to defend the free market system has led successive writers to take the utterances of business interests at face value. For example, while Lipton recognises the importance of the state/capital relationship, she fails to appreciate the way power has been manipulated both inside and outside the state at the political and bureaucratic levels. The present study aims to recover the historically nuanced perceptions of the pre-war writers, but to ground the analysis in a clearer perception of the political economy and the many facets of state power.

The application of Marxist theory to twentieth century South African history has trodden a long and winding path over the last twenty years. In broad terms, the historiography has evolved from a crude assault on liberal history to a more sophisticated 'neo-Marxist' analysis of state and capitalist power. More recent works have extended the scope of radical scholarship to the subject of African resistance. In the process, we have seen the flowering of the school of social history. The social historians have explored the experiences and cultural practices of ordinary working people, whom they see as having a significant impact on the development and implementation of state policy.

The Marxist view of the state places it firmly in the context of the existing social structure. Marx describes the state as evolving out of the conflict between competing class interests, reflecting in 'illusory form' the struggles of different classes. The state operates to prevent conflict between the classes, thus preserving the *status quo*. In the modern age, this allows the capitalist class, that is the owners of the means of production, to continue to exploit wage labour.[10]

South African historiography has been particularly influenced by Marxist structuralist writers who analyse the structure of society in accordance with basic Marxist principles. The most significant theorists for the South African debate are Louis Althusser and Nicos Poulantzas. Althusser argues for the autonomy of ideology and politics, and seeks to understand the ways in which ideological apparatuses ensure the reproduction of existing modes of production. For Althusser, ideology is 'the imaginary relationship of individuals to their real conditions of existence'.[11] He assumes that the state has primary responsibility for maintaining the ideological apparatus and reproducing existing relations of production. In connection with this, he divides the state theoretically into ideological and repressive apparatuses.

Poulantzas attempts to explain the different roles played by the bourgeoisie and the proletariat in a capitalist economy. Following Marx, he treats the state as a product of those class relations. The state keeps power in the hands of the ruling classes by legal and political apparatuses which prevent workers from coming together as a class. The state conceals from workers their class position, and thus keeps the working class divided. At the same time, the state makes use of its 'relative autonomy' from the bourgeoisie to mediate conflicting interests (often termed 'fractions of capital') within the ruling classes.[12] For Poulantzas, politics in a capitalist society is the struggle between different groups within the dominant economic class for control of the state.

Harold Wolpe makes partial use of these theories in his pioneering article, 'Capitalism and Cheap Labour Power: From Segregation to Apartheid'.[13] Wolpe sets out to prove that major shifts in state policy are dependent on change and conflict in the mode of production. He sees the state as an instrument of class rule, as opposed to a mere tool of white oppression of blacks. The undermining of the reserve economy before 1948 threatened the interests of the ruling classes by diminishing the reserves' ability to reproduce a migrant labour force. The late 1940s also saw a

renewed militancy among black workers and political movements. The state could only go two ways: improve economic
conditions for blacks or reinforce its coercive powers to preserve
the cheap labour system. The latter option was dictated by an
alliance of white workers, who feared competition from African
labour, and Afrikaner capital, which was 'struggling against the
dominance of English monopoly capital'.[14]

Subsequent writers have built on Wolpe's work. Marian Lacey
argues that the state systematically built up a system of 'super-
exploitation', with each government adding to the work of its
predecessor.[15] The Native Economic Commission (1930-2) and
the Fusion of South African and National Parties (1934) are taken
as central events in this process. The first paved the way for the
solution of the 'native labour problem' and the second represented its acceptance by the two major power blocs (mining and
national capital) within the ruling classes. Rob Davies, David
Kaplan, Mike Morris and Dan O'Meara made a further attempt
at the same sort of analysis in their Class Struggle and the
Periodisation of the State in South Africa.[16] The state is portrayed
as dominated until 1924 by imperial mining capital. This domination ended with the National/Labour Party victory, which
brought protection for South African manufacturing and subsidies for agriculture. 'National capital' sought to shore up the
power bloc by alliances with the white working class and petty
bourgeoisie. The state 'held the ring' between the economic policies of different fractions of capital through the South African
Party/Hertzogite coalition. But national capital retained its hegemony, with taxes on gold profits increasing from 1933. The hege-
monic structure took the strain during the war, but broke
between 1945 and 1948, when the nationalists won agriculture
over and captured the state with the support of farmers and the
petty bourgeoisie.

In 1976, FA Johnstone published his study of class relations on
the gold mines.[17] Johnstone argues that racial discrimination
arose from the specific problems and interests of the two white
groups – the white workers and the mineowners – in the gold

mining industry. White workers countenanced 'exploitation colour bars' developed by mining companies and the state to ensure an 'ultra-exploitable' pool of black labour. Johnstone shows the contradictory position of white workers, at once threatened and made more secure by their fellow miners.[18] He sees the Rand Revolt of 1922 as representing the mineowners' victory over white labour, whereas the election of the Pact government in 1924 ensured the protection of white workers through state measures.

Likewise, Rob Davies, in his study of *Capital, State and White Labour in South Africa, 1900-1960,* is anxious to identify capitalist enterprises as responsible for racial prejudice, rather than seeking a broader social or narrowly political explanation. His work has been heavily criticised by David Yudelman in his grandly-named book, *The Emergence of Modern South Africa,* more accurately defined as a study of mining houses, white miners and the state from 1902-39.[19] Yudelman teaches salutary lessons about those who regard 1924 as a major turning-point in South African history. As he explains, the mineowners did not suffer greatly under the Pact or Fusion governments, nor (as Labour Party Cabinet Minister FHP Creswell knew) did white workers make any major gains through state interventions. His treatment of the state is also helpful as he recognises the autonomy which allowed the government to address the long term requirements of legitimation and accumulation. However, the book is not as great a departure as the author claims. His debts to previous Marxist writers (especially Davies) are considerable, and his analysis of the state is not so profound as to encompass its constituent parts.

A more sophisticated understanding is contained in Stanley Greenberg's *Race and State in Capitalist Development.*[20] While the state was 'elaborated as a simple instrument of class needs', it 'evolved beyond mere labour repression'.[21] It 'began representing and managing the increasing formalisation of race lines'. In the process, bureaucratic machinery acquired a degree of autonomy. Greenberg expands on this in a later work, which points to the inefficiencies and contradictions inherent in the bureaucratic system.[22] Greenberg's observations on the pre-apartheid period are scanty, but his insights into the functioning of bureaucracy are most useful. For example, he contrasts the conflicts which exist within the bureaucracy today with the...

> ...ascendant unity which characterized the central bureaucracy in apartheid's heyday. The officials at all levels seemed extravagant in their elaboration of the State and their receptivity to the lead of politicians.[23]

Staff purges of wayward thinkers and the dissemination of a coherent, dominant ideology in the 1960s, produced a clarity of purpose within the state which was not present before 1948 or after 1979. As the following chapters show, however, this clarity did not exclude the influence of the attitudes and prejudices which civil servants brought to work with them each day on the development and implementation of government policy in the pre-apartheid era.

Strikingly absent from the literature discussed so far is a coherent treatment of African labour and its role in the political economy. Although such a book has yet to be written, several works have explored salient themes in South African labour history which are germane to this study. Three books by Alan Jeeves, Jonathan Crush and David Yudelman have focused attention on the centrality of the migrant labour system in sustaining South Africa's gold mining economy.[24] Their work, published together and separately, provides a richly textured analysis of the mines' recruiting system, the factors which stimulated Africans to take up employment and the wider ramifications of large scale labour migration. As they show, the mines battled to secure and protect their labour supply against other employers. Moreover, as Yudelman's earlier book also stressed, the Chamber of Mines' close working relationship with the government developed slowly, as a marriage of convenience rather than the subordination of one party to the other. Chapters 2 to 4 of the present study both draw on and complement the findings of these works.

In the manufacturing sector, Eddie Webster's *Cast in a Racial Mould* examines the history of the all-white Ironmoulders' Society, which excluded Africans from semi-skilled and skilled work in the metal industry in the face of technological advances and deskilling.[25] Jon Lewis's work on the Trades and Labour Council, covering the 1920s to 1950s, shows the other side of the coin.[26] He demonstrates how the predominantly white industrial unions in the SATLC resisted the segregationist labour legislation of the 1920s and 1930s and continued to admit Africans as members of organised parallel unions until the late 1940s. Finally, Baruch Hirson explores elements of urbanised African resistance to poor living and working conditions on the Rand in the 1930s and 1940s.[27] All three works provide useful background for the present study, though Lewis tends to whitewash the SATLC, an organisation which, in fact, did little to assist black unionisation or narrow the wage gap between white and black workers. None of the three works attempts to paint the whole picture: Hirson is the only writer to focus primarily on black workers, and even then, his work is heavily flavoured by his own Trotskyite leanings.

While the literature on African labour has not advanced very far, there has been some movement in analyses of the South African state in recent years. Belinda Bozzoli focuses on class formation and ideologies, especially those of 'national capital' (local, non-mining financial interests), which overtook mining capital in importance in the 1920s.[28] She develops the concept of the 'narrow' and 'wide' state, meaning on the one hand, the political and administrative organs of coercion and repression, and on the other, bourgeois hegemony as a whole, which dominated South Africa at the social, political and ideological levels. Bozzoli's analysis draws heavily on Marxist structuralist theory. The idea that the state is completely subsumed by the interests of one fraction of a class is difficult to sustain. Nevertheless, it does open a useful avenue of approach to the South African state, and to the means by which capitalist interests sought to extend and legitimate their power.

DC Hindson is more concerned in his *Pass Controls and the Urban African Proletariat* with the state's concrete efforts to mediate between the interests of 'successive ruling classes'.[29] Hindson's original thesis explains the development of pass controls from the nineteenth century to 1980. His main point is that 'the pass control system played a crucial role in containing contradictions which arose from the concentration of capital, and an industrial reserve army in the urban areas'.[30] This is more than half true, but Hindson underplays the social reasons for passes. He exaggerates the coherence of the 'system', as well as its success in tackling the labour supply's unevenness. It seems unwise to focus only on 'passes', given the twin difficulties of explaining what the term means and taking into account the full range of factors affecting the labour supply.

Saul Dubow takes a more subtle approach[31] and makes a valuable attempt to disaggregate the ideological, administrative and political dimensions of segregation. In the process, he goes a long way to explaining the contradictory role of the Native Affairs Department. The NAD was on the front line of defending white supremacy; it was also supposed to be the 'protector' of African interests.[32] As Dubow shows, the department depended on segregation for its administrative power-base, re-arming itself with status lost during the 1922 public service reorganisation, through the strongly segregationist 1927 Native Administration Act. The major weakness in Dubow's work is the explicit exclusion of the NAD's handling of labour issues. These occupied a central role in the department's duties and were crucial in determining its ambiguous position *vis-a-vis* the government's segregation policy. Dubow also excludes other departments of state which played key roles in the evolution of segregationist ideology and policy during this period. The inclusion of *The Origins of Apartheid* in the title is grossly misleading, given that the book does not extend beyond 1936, even though the relevant state archival material was freely available for years before the date of publication. As the present study shows, it was in the crucial period from 1937-48 that the state struggled to make sense of Hertzog's Acts, driven by the war effort and pressed by unprecedented industrialisation and urbanisation. The state's failure to reconcile these different pressures was the central reason why the Malanite nationalist challenge gained momentum.

The latest book to tackle the topic of the South African state and African labour is Deborah Posel's *The Making of Apartheid, 1948-1961*.[33] Posel focuses on the history of influx control, which she sees as having had a 'critical role to play within the wider Apartheid project'.[34] Like Dubow, she concentrates on the Native Affairs Department as the central institution involved in the formation and application of state policy towards Africans. As Posel herself states, the book is an examination of but one aspect of the 'making of apartheid', where a full treatment would involve a consideration of a much broader range of topics than merely controls over movement. Again, the author does not utilise the thousands of post-1948 NAD files which have been accessible for over five years. However, the book has much to commend it. The author shows how apartheid was…

> …forged through a series of struggles within and beyond the state, which forced the architects of state policy to adapt and revise many of their original strategies. Uncertainties, conflicts, failures, and deviations, although often less visible than the continuities and triumphs of Apartheid, were fundamental to its development.[35]

The same could be said with even more conviction for the pre-apartheid era, when different political groupings, trade unions and departments of state fought over the meaning of segregation as it applied to African workers. The present study highlights the range of voices and issues with which the state had to deal before 1948, and the ways in which officialdom responded to the task at hand.

As Marks and Trapido have written, 'Recent turbulence in South Africa makes the study of its racially divided social order and its national and ethnic heterogeneity an urgent intellectual and political task.'[36] At present, this task is proceeding on several fronts, with historians at the forefront in delineating the origins of South Africa's contemporary problems. The Marxist and neo-Marxist critique of traditional, liberal economic history has shed light on the state's role in that process. In the last ten years, social historians have examined the impact of the state on black South Africans and the survival and transmutation of oppressed communities in the economic and cultural spheres. Others have analysed the ideological forces which underpinned white supremacy and the linguistic, health and educational dimensions of that process. This study of the state and labour regulation takes in many of these themes, while also drawing on the ongoing debate about the nature of the state and its position in the political economy. As South Africa enters a new and uncertain phase, the emerging historiography is fluid, reaching into uncharted territory. The following chapters seek to map out a small part of that difficult terrain.

Politics and Political Economy, 1918-1948

The chapters which follow are primarily concerned with the administration of labour legislation; they are not intended as a reappraisal of South Africa's entire political and economic history. However, the broad policies implemented by successive governments were crucial in determining the role civil servants played in labour regulation. A short outline of the main trends in both the political and economic spheres is thus necessary to contextualise the thoughts and actions of the administrators.

In the political arena, the period was dominated by two of the giants of twentieth century South Africa, Generals JC Smuts and JBM Hertzog. Although both had distinguished themselves fighting the British in the Anglo-Boer War (1899-1902), they represented differing tendencies and traditions in South African politics. Smuts succeeded General Louis Botha who, as leader of the South African Party and Prime Minister from Union in 1910 until his death in 1919, had accepted South Africa's position as a dominion within the British Empire.[37] Smuts supported Botha's policy of full involvement on the Allied side in World War I. He was Prime Minister from 1919-24 and throughout his subsequent career, maintained a keen interest in South Africa's position in the world. An anglicised Afrikaner, he relished South Africa's important contribution in both world wars and felt deep ties of loyalty to England and the British Commonwealth.

At home, Smuts was a ruthless and highly effective political leader. In 1920, he and his party merged with the largely English-speaking Unionists (led by Sir Thomas Smartt), in order to hold on to power in a hung parliament.[38] Smuts was not greatly interested in labour issues and African policy, though his ideas on those subjects acquired more definition between 1919 and 1924. In relation to labour matters – whether black or white – he was generally reactionary, taking a personal hand in suppressing the white miners strikes of 1913 and 1922 and later, the black miners strike of 1946. As shown in Chapter 7 Smuts's lack of sympathy for trade unions affected the relationship between the Native Affairs and Labour Departments and organised black labour.

His perspective on 'native' policy was more complex. Fundamentally, he believed that Africans could not and should not be drawn into the same political and economic structures as whites. To quote his famous speech to the Royal Colonial Society in 1917:

> We have realised that political ideas which apply to our White civilization generally do not apply to the administration of Native affairs ... In land ownership, settlement and forms of government we are trying to keep them apart and in that way laying down in outline a general policy which it may take a hundred years to work out, but which in the end may be the solution of our Native problem.[39]

Smuts tempered his adherence to the principles of segregation in two ways. Firstly, he was essentially a pragmatic man, ready to adapt to circumstances which prevented him from adhering to a segregationist policy. In the words of his biographer, WK Hancock, '... Smuts did not push his advocacy of that doctrine to the limit. His attitude to it was experimental and pragmatic: if collisions should occur between the doctrine and the facts, he would be prepared to modify the doctrine'.[40] Secondly, he asserted the notion of 'trusteeship', involving whites maintaining their political domination over Africans while administering to them in an even-handed manner.[41] The outcome of this principle, which Smuts shared with many civil servants, can be seen in statutes and regulations which eschewed the harsher, more repressive measures favoured by many Afrikaner nationalists between 1918 and 1948.

Unlike Smuts, Hertzog, who was Prime Minister from 1924-39, concerned himself primarily with domestic affairs. He had broken away from Prime Minister Botha in 1912 over the issue of relations with Britain, taking the view that South Africa could never achieve nationhood while so closely tied to the British Empire. As leader of the ruling National Party (founded 1914), he supported compulsory bilingualism in white schools to raise the status of the Afrikaans-speaking community.[42] He opposed South Africa's involvement in the Great War and, as Prime Minister, backed the white dominions' drive for greater sovereignty in the British Commonwealth.

From 1924-31, the National Party ruled through an alliance with the Labour Party. The latter organisation, founded in 1909, was led by FHP Creswell. It stood for the protection of white workers' interests. The Labour Party was very much the junior partner in the Pact government. Despite the legislation it passed to protect white wages and to extend the employment of whites in secondary industry and the civil service, Hertzog's government remained dependent on revenues from the gold mining industry. It therefore avoided policies which might have had a serious impact on mining profits.[43]

Hertzog's policy towards Africans was more systematic than

Smuts's, though it was largely based on the same principles. Hertzog first aired his segregation bills in 1926; they were finally passed as the Representation of Natives Act and Native Trust and Land Act of 1936, and the Native Laws Amendment Act of 1937. The Acts defined the parameters of government policy towards Africans in this period. They reflected a broad consensus within the white community that a rapidly urbanising and industrialising South Africa required a more rigid, legal expression of white supremacy in the economic, social and political spheres. Although the Acts retained vestiges of older, more paternalistic, protectionist perspectives on race relations overall, they strengthened the repressive and racially discriminatory tendencies of the Act of Union (1909), the Natives Land Act (1913) and the Natives (Urban Areas) Act (1923).

Three years after the collapse of the Nationalist/Labour Pact in 1931, Hertzog and Smuts buried their differences and formed the United South African National Party under Hertzog's leadership. The new Fusion government agreed on seven main points: South Africa's constitutional status as defined in the Statute of Westminster; the South African national flag; equal status for the Afrikaans and English languages; maintaining a 'sound rural population'; a 'white labour' policy; political separation of the races and the preservation of white civilisation; and the safeguarding of South Africa's currency and assets.[44]

Some National Party members, rejecting Fusion as compromising their National Party principles, split off to form the Purified National Party under DF Malan in 1934. Col CF Stallard, meanwhile, refused to follow Smuts into coalition with the anti-British Hertzogites and formed the Dominion Party. Fusion itself lasted only five years, for in 1939, a crisis arose over South Africa's participation in the war against Nazi Germany. Hertzog favoured neutrality but lost the vote in the House of Assembly. He then resigned and the Governor-General, Sir Patrick Duncan, asked Smuts to form a coalition government. This comprised mainly pro-war members of the Fusion government, supported by the Labour and Dominion Parties. Smuts held the coalition together until 1948, despite growing pressure through the war years from the Malanite nationalists, who played heavily on white fears of being overwhelmed by the rising numbers of urbanised Africans. In the 1948 election, Malan took power with the support of the tiny, Hertzogite Afrikaner Party. This gave him an overall majority of eight in the House of Assembly.[45]

The course of politics between 1918 and 1948 can thus be divided into four periods: 1918-24, when the South African Party, under Botha and Smuts, governed; the Pact government years, from 1924 to the early 1930s; the Fusion period, 1933-9; and the war and post-war rule of Smuts's coalition. In the administrative sphere, civil servants and the policies they implemented were naturally affected by changes in government, but the impact of these changes was limited for several reasons. The long-serving nature of the Smuts and Hertzog ministries prevented sudden reversals in policy, and the lack of major differences in their respective African policies helped to minimise shifts in policy after 1924 and 1939. The administrators' continuity in office was also significant. Rarely did a new government replace a senior civil servant for political reasons. The British tradition of apolitical administrators was maintained.

*   *   *   *

As we have seen Davies, Kaplan, Morris and O'Meara have attempted to explain South Africa's economic history in accordance with the aforementioned changes in government. More recently, historians such as David Yudelman have placed more emphasis on the similarities between the various governments' economic strategies than on their differences. The three main identifiable economic watersheds are World War I, which brought about the real beginnings of local manufacturing; South Africa's departure from the Gold Standard at the end of 1932, which provoked further growth in manufacturing and mining; and the onset of World War II, which brought yet more expansion in primary and secondary industry.

Of course, the story of South Africa's economic development and of the forms of labour regulation which accompanied it, goes back much further. The first non-agricultural, planned labour process began to take shape on the Kimberley diamond fields in the 1870s.[46] By the time gold was discovered on the Reef in 1886, certain key labour practices had already been tried and tested: using blacks for spade and shovel work under white supervisors, recruiting migrant labour for fixed contracts, and compounding African workers to maximise control and productivity. The drive to keep working costs down, appalling conditions and continued African resistance to proletarianisation, led to continuing labour shortages into the 1930s. In the 1900s, the Randlords almost abandoned African labour as they sought the answer to their labour problems in mainland China.[47] By 1910, it was clear that gold mining profitability would depend, for the foreseeable future, on securing adequate supplies of well-regulated African migrants. The newly unified state recognised this by regulating recruiting and living and working conditions under the Native Labour Regulation and Mines and Works Acts of 1911. Important questions remained to be fought over, such as the precise role of white workers in gold mining, and the geographical area from which the mines could draw their unskilled labour. Some whites were retrenched in the 1920s, while the mines preserved their access to Mozambican labour in 1929 and renewed their acquaintance with labour from other parts of the subcontinent in the 1930s (see appendix 5). But the principles of state policy towards black mineworkers were established by the start of our period. The government would maintain the migrant labour system, keep wages low and prevent unionisation. This remained state policy right through the 1946 strike and beyond.

On the farms, state intervention before 1910 was largely confined to masters and servants and pass laws. The 1913 Natives Land Act laid the foundations for future legislation on segregation of landholding throughout the country. The vast bulk of the land would be preserved for white ownership. Blacks would fulfil the role of farm labourers, except in specially demarcated reserve areas. It was only after 1924, when the National/Labour Pact government came to power, that state ministers and officials began to think coherently about helping farmers find labour and deploy it more efficiently. From the 1930s, more traditional forms of farming, using squatters, sharecroppers and labour tenants – all of which involved blacks living and farming on 'white' land other than as mere paid employees – fell out of favour in state circles. But another three decades were to pass before the state could finally eliminate independent black peasants outside the reserves.[48] In the meantime, more immediate solutions to farm labour shortages had to be found. The whole question was inextricably linked to land segregation, financial and technical aid for white farmers, and the expansion of the mining and industrial economy. Juggling these issues was a major problem for administrators between 1924 and 1948.

Before 1918, the relative insignificance of manufacturing and commerce as employers was reflected in the lack of state intervention in these areas. This changed after the Factories Act of 1918 and the advent of efforts to promote employment for whites under the 'civilised labour' policy from 1924. With the Industrial Conciliation and Wage Acts of 1924 and 1925, the government became more involved in regulating industrial and commercial undertakings. The state's role expanded through amendments to the Acts in the 1930s, further legislation on working conditions in 1939 and 1941, and a series of war measures in the early 1940s. At first, legislation was intended primarily to benefit whites, but as the state soon discovered, it was impossible to administer to one section of the population without taking other races into account. Manufacturing interests, which had minimal influence on government policy before 1918, also grew in stature, though manufacturers never enjoyed the political pre-eminence of farmers and mineowners.

The rising importance of secondary industry and commerce was based on their rapid expansion during the Great War. This ground to a halt around 1919-20, but picked up again at a moderate pace through the 1920s. The worst of the Depression in

South Africa, between 1929 and 1932, ended when Pretoria came off the Gold Standard at the close of 1932. From 1933-9, secondary industry and gold mining saw unprecedented growth, making even greater progress under the special conditions of World War II. Gold mining output rose from R98m in 1932, to a pre-1948 peak of R242m in 1941.[49] In private industry, the number of workers grew from 123 975 in 1918-19 (of whom 80 081 were classified as 'non-white'), to 423 824 in 1945-6 (of whom 295 009 were so-called 'non-whites').[50] Special areas of expansion included chemicals, food, beverages and tobacco products. In addition, the founding of Iscor as a state-owned company in 1928 laid the foundations of an iron and steel industry. Employment in metal products and engineering increased by 1 000 per cent between 1925 and 1955.[51] Inevitably, industrial expansion accentuated the drift to the towns. In the inter-war years adult, black males predominated in this movement. As appendix 3 shows, by 1951 the urban African population was 2 328 000 out of a total African population of 8 560 083. Whereas fourteen per cent of Africans lived in urban areas in 1921, 27,2 per cent did so by 1951. Agriculture was slower to modernise; per capita production grew only gradually between the wars, despite state assistance of about R15m per annum through the 1930s.[52] Farmers remained dependent on large numbers of very poorly paid black labourers. By 1947-8, agriculture (including the reserves) tied up thirty-six per cent of the economically active population while contributing only about fourteen per cent of the national income.[53]

State and Bureaucracy

The position of the South African bureaucracy and its implications for our understanding of the state have not previously been explored in any detail, either from a theoretical or an empirical perspective. This section attempts three things. Firstly it outlines the theories of Durkheim and Weber and explains their importance in analysing the bureaucratic functions of government.

Secondly it explains the present writer's understanding of the state bureaucracy, drawing partially on the insights of Raymond Williams. Finally it provides background information on the structure and personnel of the South African civil service in this period.

*   *   *   *

Writing in the late nineteenth and early twentieth century, the French theorist, Emile Durkheim, redefines his brand of political liberalism in response to perceived threats from socialism and a rejuvenated conservatism.[54] As society becomes increasingly complex, power must be in the hands of what Anthony Giddens has interpreted as a 'differentiated political agency'.[55] According to Durkheim, the state must avoid the two extremes of absolutism on the one hand, and on the other, following in an immediate, unthinking way, what it believes is the general will. To retain the state's 'government consciousness' while forestalling dictatorship, Durkheim advocates a bureaucratic state in which officialdom forms the link between the government and differentiated society at large. The *corps intermédiaires* act as a crucial stabilising force. They offset the worst excesses of vacillation within the political sphere and limit the effects of contradictions and shifts of opinion among the public. The South African civil service can be seen as fulfilling this function before 1948: it absorbed pressures from all sectors of society on every issue of labour regulation. It also kept the administration of African workers ticking over, even when the government was unclear on policy, as during World War II. A further point raised by Giddens is worth mentioning. He argues that the bureaucracy is more likely to possess real power, which it uses to preserve the *status quo*, when the government is weak.[56] By contrast, in an absolutist state, the bureaucracy becomes a mere instrument of the ruling oligarchy. Something along these lines occurred in South Africa: whereas before 1948, the bureaucracy was significant in formulating and interpreting legislation, its role under Verwoerd (both as Minister of Native Affairs and as Prime Minister) was more clearly subordinated to National Party policy. We will return to this theme in considering Raymond Williams on dominant and residual cultures.

In his *Economy and Society* and *The Theory of Social and Economic Organisation*, Max Weber paints a much less positive picture of bureaucracy than does Durkheim.[57] Weber bases his ideal bureaucracy on the principles of rationality, stability and legality. The administration should be divided according to skill and authority. Each office should be independent of its occupant; the office should be permanent while the staff changes. Authority and responsibility should be centralised and defined by legal and administrative regulation. Written legal records should be maintained for the sake of organisational continuity.[58] Weber sees the development of a bureaucratised apparatus as essential for the growth of capitalism and industrialisation. Bureaucracy, with its pyramidal hierarchy of authority and salaried, full time officials, is an integral part of the formal, codified legal system. But he fears the unintended consequences of such a system: the concentration of power in the hands of a small minority; the ritualistic over-emphasis on rules; specialisation carried to extremes; self-protection for the sake of personal career advancement.

Weber's criticisms of bureaucracy, especially state bureaucracy, in part reflect the thinking of ordinary citizens, in the former communist bloc as much as in the West, and in ex-colonies as much as in industrialised nations. Despite efforts by the academic discipline of 'public administration' to rehabilitate the image of civil servants as being highly efficient professionals, the public tends to perceive what one writer describes as ...

... a system of administration so marked by its officialism, red tape, and fixed, almost arbitrary, rules and procedures that it sometimes seems to exist only for perpetuation of the bureaucracy's or bureaucrat's own sake.[59]

The South African civil service produced its full share of inefficiencies, as this book shows. Yet the contradictions and ambiguities of labour regulation cannot be explained solely in terms
of a malfunctioning bureaucracy. One must situate the history
of state/black labour relations within the economic, political
and social processes of the time. To understand the bureaucracy's place in these processes, one must achieve a more
nuanced definition of the state and, in particular, its administrative apparatus. The following paragraphs, in brief outline,
describe the state and bureaucracy as they appear in Chapters 2
to 8.

*   *   *   *

At one level, the South African state operated, in the classic
Marxist sense, as a straightforward relation of production. The
state existed to create the conditions in which capitalism could
thrive. It took steps to provide employers with the forms of
labour demanded by their respective production processes and
cost imperatives. It also looked to the longer term interests of
capital in ways which employers could not, by tackling working
conditions, housing, health and social welfare issues. However,
one cannot explain every state intervention in the labour market
in terms of a response to the needs of capital. Rivalries between
white political parties and the need to appease politically important sections of the population must be considered.

At the same time, the state developed interests of its own
alongside those of groups of employers and industries, and
political parties. Pre-eminent among these was the preservation
of state authority itself, a factor which transcended the interests
of any one government or political party. In ideological terms,
this meant ensuring the legitimacy of the state among the voting
public and achieving at least a grudging respect for its powers
among the rest of the population. Closely linked to this was the
need to preserve the physical security of the state, a priority
which invoked the phrase 'law and order'. The third element

involved the state's financial viability, which was sustained through taxation, either of business enterprises or individuals (following Claus Offe, Posel talks of the state's ' "institutional self-interest" in furthering the accumulation process').[60] For the most part, these interests could be safeguarded in harmony with those of the 'ruling classes' as a whole, but they were nonetheless considered distinct by those who saw themselves as holding the well-being of the state at heart.

Frequently, it was not the politicians but the civil servants who saw themselves as giving expression to the state's interests. From Union in 1910 to the advent of apartheid in 1948, the state bureaucracy grew considerably. During these years, parliament tended to frame legislation in very general terms, leaving it to the administrators to guide their ministers by adding long schedules to the acts. The Social and Economic Planning Council's review of the Public Service sums this up:

> The customary legalistic approach of the administrator is, therefore, superseded by purposive social and economic engineering, based (or so it ought to be) not on predilections or trial and error methods but on research into actual conditions. For this investigational work and study, the responsible Ministers obviously have not the time. They must rely largely on the findings of administrative officials who, in fact, become important instigators of legislation... The Council is, indeed, of the opinion that, especially in the field of agricultural marketing, industrial legislation, the creation of quasi-public corporations and possibly in certain aspects of Native Administration, the delegation of regulatory powers may already sometimes have proceeded beyond the desirable limits ... It is, furthermore, imperative that the public be safeguarded against arbitrary bureaucratic decisions and autocratic functioning of the administrative machine. As has been

explained, much of the administrative work has lost
its purely executive or passive character.[61]

The rules could be changed at short notice and without reference
to the House of Assembly. They represented a considerable delegation of the powers of parliament. Nowhere were civil servants
given more latitude than in the field of 'native administration',
both in the reserves and in urban and industrial areas.

In addition to the grand interests of the state, officials were
moved by the more immediate worries which are a feature of
any large bureaucratic organisation. Procedure, power, prestige
and principles – these concerns were central to the way administrators performed their duties. Under procedure, one must consider the adherence to codes of regulation which could take on a
life of their own in the minds of officials and hinder the introduction of new administrative measures. In addition administrators
concerned with their own careers and with the wider reputation
of their branch of the civil service, were often preoccupied with
departmental power and prestige – a 'lightening of the load' was
always feared, while the ultimate bogey was professional embarrassment. As the SEPC Report observed:

> The administrative machine is characterised by
> strict demarcation of duties between departments.
> These duties are very readily converted into jeal-
> ously guarded vested rights, which are exercised
> with but little reference to other Departments. As
> long as the public service fulfilled purely executive
> functions, this was no great weakness: the advan-
> tages of specialisation were paramount. But now
> that the Departments, acting through Ministers,
> have assumed policy-shaping and sub-legislative
> functions, the result is that in one governing body
> there are several legislative units of equal rank. This
> makes a unified social and economic policy imposs-
> ible. Open warfare between Departments is rela-

tively rare; but concealed discord and lack of co-operation are common.[62]

The idea that some officials were moved by principles or morals is more difficult to understand as a systematic process, but a sense of trusteeship – of a duty to protect Africans from the adverse effects of contact with the white man – was still a part of the administrative psyche, at least in the NAD. To an extent, this attitude may be traced to the British concept of 'service', which Raymond Williams identified in his *Culture and Society*:

> This is much more a characteristic than a training for leadership, as the stress on conformity and respect for authority shows. In so far as it is, by definition, the training of upper servants, it includes, of course, the instilling of that kind of confidence which will enable the upper servants to supervise and direct the lower servants. Order must be maintained there, by good management, and in this respect the function is not service but government. Yet the upper servant is not to look to his own interests. He must subordinate these to a larger good, which is called the Queen's peace, or national security, or law and order, or the public weal. This has been the charter of many thousands of devoted lives, and it is necessary to respect it even if we cannot agree with it.[63]

For some South African administrators, the principle of service (or the common weal) could only be advanced if the worst abuses against African workers were curbed.

Another of Williams's theories which is illuminating in this context is that of the relation between residual, dominant and emergent cultures. In South Africa between the wars, the residual could be seen as paternalist trusteeship, the dominant as segregation, and the emergent as the more hard line policy of apartheid. As Williams suggests, though, it is ...

> ... necessary to distinguish between the active mani-
> festation of the residual which may have been
> wholly or largely incorporated into the dominant
> culture, and that aspect of the residual which may
> have an alternative or even oppositional relation-
> ship to the dominant.[64]

Along with some white liberals, the NAD upheld segregation as one answer to South Africa's immense social, economic and political problems in an age of rapid industrialisation. The residual element of trusteeship at times functioned as a 'neutralising or ratifying component', softening the harsh edges of discrimination without tackling root grievances. Governments between 1910 and 1948 tolerated the NAD's more paternalistic traditions in order to neutralise some of the resentment felt by black South Africans. At times, officials moved by this residual element assumed oppositional tendencies, defying the most overtly repressive intentions of government ministers – either by lobbying against changes in the law or by neglecting to implement legislation to its fullest extent. As the following chapters show, however, there were limits to the civil servants' autonomy: while the administrative structure allowed them a degree of latitude (especially in 'native administration'), the cabinet set the broad policy objectives, and held the public purse.

Increasingly in the 1940s, Smuts's coalition struggled to meet the challenge of the emergent culture of apartheid orchestrated by the Malanite nationalists. This further weakened the power of the residual element, which gradually disappeared after 1948.

*   *   *   *

In this section I shall consider more practical aspects of the bureaucracy. The Union administration was based largely on the Cape civil service. A much less important influence was the cadre of officials who joined the imperial Governor, Lord Milner, to run his 'model' administration in the Transvaal after the

Anglo-Boer War.[65] Both adhered to the British ideal of a professional, apolitical public service, serving the government of the day without prejudice. Even so, the vast majority of civil servants were English speaking and many were antagonistic towards the Afrikaner Nationalist Party formed under General Hertzog in 1914. Hertzog was far from happy with this situation. When he took power ten years later, he raised the number of Afrikaners in the public service and enforced the principle of bilingualism.[66] Henceforth, senior officials had to be able to speak both languages. Yet despite Hertzog's efforts, English remained the *lingua franca* of the public service. A large number of monolingual English-speakers kept their positions in the lower administrative and clerical grades. The public service continued to be dominated by English-speakers and anglicised Afrikaners, especially in the NAD, Labour and Public Health Departments.

To explain briefly the origins of individual departments, a Mines Division was already functioning under Kruger and networks of Magistrates existed in the South African Republic and the Free State. As Dubow shows, the Native Affairs Department developed out of existing organisations in the Cape, Natal and Transvaal (the Free State NAD was abolished in 1908). Cape officials dominated the NAD until 1934, when DL Smit was transferred from the Justice Department to become Secretary for Native Affairs.[67] The powers of the Native Labour Bureau, established between 1907 and 1908 to assist the mines in replacing Chinese with African labour, were formalised under the Native Labour Regulation Act of 1911. Several departments involved in regulating African labour were founded in the three decades after World War I. In 1918, the government created a Factories Division in the Department of Mines and Industries. The division passed to the Department of Labour when it was founded under the Pact government in 1924. The Public Health Act of 1919 established a Public Health Department, whose functions were previously undertaken by the Department of the Interior. Meanwhile, the NAD received major shake-ups from 1921-23 and again in 1927 under the Native Administration Act. The

1920s also saw the expansion of the Department of Agriculture, and in particular, its Marketing and Economics Division. The bureaucracy was further augmented by subsidiary official bodies, made up partly of civil servants and politicians, and partly of lay 'experts', such as the Advisory Council of Labour and the Native Affairs Commission.

The basic structure of labour-regulating departments was thus in place by 1929. From the late 1930s through the war, the state extended its intervention in the labour market via new structures. In 1937, a Department of Social Welfare was established to aid, in a rudimentary way, the disadvantaged and handicapped of all races. In the early 1940s, the government began planning the country's post-war future through the Social and Economic Planning Council and other quasi-governmental bodies. It was as if the state, under the unique pressures of war, was beginning to test its enormous potential for shaping and re-shaping South African society.

At the end of World War I, there were 23 963 public servants. This figure includes 631 NAD officials, 1 334 Justice Department officials and 7 154 officers in South African Police. Over the next thirty years, the civil service expanded considerably. By 1948, the total figure stood at 85 321, an increase of 356 per cent.[68] This figure is deceptive, given that it includes relief works and sheltered employment for 'poor whites'. Nonetheless, the NAD's staff complement had risen by 692 per cent to 4 369. Justice had grown by 113 per cent to 1 502, and the police by 234 per cent to 16 797. A number of commentators regarded the consequent expansion in Union taxation and expenditure with dismay. Surveying state finances in 1927, the economist MH de Kock, wrote: 'The moral to be stated... is, therefore, that the Union and Provincial Governments should make an earnest endeavour to check as far as possible any further increase in administrative expenditure...'.[69] The government did not heed his warning and the size and power of the civil service continued to grow.

Ever since the Public Service and Pensions Act of 1912, there had been a running battle between the Treasury and the Public

Service Commission over control of the civil service. In 1920, the Graham Commission Report on the public service produced recommendations designed to make the civil service more 'businesslike'.[70] The report proposed that the Public Service Commission be reconstituted with increased status and wider duties; that the Treasury's control over the minutiae of departmental functions be curtailed and that senior departmental officers 'assume more responsibility in keeping with their positions'.[71] The PSC was reorganised between 1921 and 1923, and given control over appointments and promotions, grading, and efficiency.[72] However, its functions were never entirely free from political interference.

Despite the new, streamlined hierarchy, the PSC and Treasury continued to clash, most notably over the upgrading of posts in 1937. The government considered altering the structure in 1939, but the matter was dropped, largely because of opposition from the PSC, which feared a diminution of its role. In the meantime, two major problems had developed. The first was the growth of devolved, administrative responsibility, discussed above in section (iii). This led in 1949 to a series of Select Committee Reports on Delegated Legislation, though these did not produce concrete results until the ruling National Party began to assert greater control over the civil service in the 1950s.[73] The second problem concerned the selection and training of civil servants. The civil service comprised three main divisions: clerical, administrative, and technical. The technical branch which demanded professional qualifications such as medical and agricultural science degrees generally functioned satisfactorily.[74] On the other hand, the vast majority of officials entered the civil service via the clerical grades. The chief requirement was a pass in the matriculation or equivalent examination. From 1913-22, the Public Service Examination provided an alternative means of entry, but this produced few successful candidates and was discontinued. Over the next thirteen years, the waiting list of applicants for clerical posts grew and grew, until it became impossible for the PSC to judge prospective civil servants on achievement.[75] An open, selective examination, supplementing matriculation, was reintroduced in 1935 and made compulsory in the mid-1940s. From this, the PSC drew up a short list of candidates for interview. The successful interviewee then began a period of probation designed to weed out the unethical and inefficient.[76]

Almost all the civil servants who appear in subsequent chapters occupied administrative grades, that is, those holding the position of senior (chief) clerk and above. Very rarely was an 'outsider' appointed to an administrative grade. The fact that senior officers had 'come up through the ranks' was supposed to ensure a good grounding of experience, as well as to provide avenues of advancement for clerks.[77] This contrasts sharply with the British civil service which to this day, strongly favours Oxford and Cambridge graduates as administrative trainees.

Both the SEPC and the Centlivres Commission were unimpressed by the selection procedures. They argued that advertising of positions was unimaginative and that 'active propaganda' was needed in schools and universities. Passes in English and Afrikaans had been compulsory since 1934, but there were still many officers who could not function in one or other medium.[78] The entrance examination did not include commercial arithmetic, accounting, bookkeeping or economics and there was no attempt to use aptitude tests. The problem extended to training of recruits – there was a lack of supervision of new officers and they were not moved around sufficiently frequently to test their skills in various sections. The Centlivres Report called for a Director of Training, with officers in each branch appointed to supervise new recruits.[79]

The negative side to recruiting administrators from the clerical grades was that few graduates were attracted to the civil service. The SEPC Report noted an 'animus against degree men in the administrative division'.[80] To counteract this, the Centlivres Report favoured giving graduates 'special notching' with the prospect of rapid promotion to higher office.[81] Promising clerks should also be given the opportunity to take university courses in public administration. The lack of qualifications was especially apparent in the Justice and Native Affairs Departments. Many magistrates had not passed the Civil Service Higher Law Examination and very few had an LLB of 696 second-grade clerical assistants in the magisterial branch in 1946, only twenty had passed the Lower Law Examination.[82] Things were no better in the NAD. Few Native Affairs officers had passed the law exams, learnt African languages or acquired diplomas and degrees in 'bantu studies'. The NAD was further plagued by the lack of courtesy its officers frequently showed to Africans and by the tendency to move officers around too frequently, with a consequent lack of expertise in relation to particular districts.[83]

The shortcomings in selection procedure and the paucity of education and training remained unsolved by the end of the period, and Smuts fell from power before the reports of the mid-1940s could be effected. The one problem which his government did try to tackle involved the allegiance of senior members of the civil service to the Afrikaner Broederbond. Founded in 1918, the Bond was a secret, middle class, republican, nationalist organisation, wedded to achieving and holding power on behalf of the Afrikaner people.[84] The exact number of Broeders in the civil service will never be known. The English writer Henry Gibbs, recording his impressions of his 1949 visit to South Africa, reproduced a current opinion that several senior public servants in the 1930s and 1940s, including Dr J van Rensburg (Secretary for Justice), Dr GAC Kuschke (Secretary for Social Welfare), J Combrink (Secretary of the National Housing and Planning Commission), Dr PR Viljoen (Secretary for Agriculture) and Dr JE Holloway (Secretary for Finance), were members.[85] Following investigations into its civil servants' membership of this secret organisation towards the end of the war, the government dismissed two officials from the Treasury and the Department of External Affairs. A few others resigned to avoid facing trial.[86] The extent of their influence on labour regulation is also very difficult to measure. The fact that the Broeders were pledged to support strict racial segregation may have exerted some pressure in that direction, though they could hardly have affected the predominantly English-speaking Departments of Labour and Native Affairs. All this was to change with the rise of the Nationalists, who brought with them a determination to purge the state and fashion it anew in their own image.

Plan of Chapters

This study, given its wide scope could profitably be approached from a number of angles. The seven main departments involved in labour regulation could be discussed in turn, or the thirty year period covered could be divided up according to changes in the government, or in line with booms and slumps in the economy. However, these plans would lead to repetition of the same themes in different periods and to a reappraisal of the same material as it pertained to various branches of the civil service. To avoid this, Chapters 2 to 7 tackle each major aspect of labour regulation in turn. At certain points, the same ground is surveyed from different vantage points, as in the chapters on wage regulation and trade unions. At others, I have separated themes which are inextricably intertwined, as in the sections on urban areas and passes. The reader's patience is begged in these concessions to the writer's art.

In theory, state interventions can be seen as a balance between procedures which purported to protect workers, and those designed to control them. In reality, it is impossible to divide the two neatly, largely because the state sought to disguise repression by including measures which would benefit labour in most laws. That said, Chapters 2 and 3, concentrating on the state's welfare functions, fit well together. Chapter 2 compares the efforts of inspectors from the Mines, Native Affairs and Labour Departments to enforce minimum standards in factories, mines and compounds. Chapter 3 moves from specific attention to the workplace to broader questions of Health and Welfare, in the process introducing the Public Health and Social Welfare Departments. The main issues covered are workers' compensation, housing, and health care. Most of the development in these areas came in the later 1930s and 1940s, though the chapter traces the origins of welfare in theory and practice from before 1918.

Chapter 4, on Control over Movement, maintains the breadth and scope of the previous chapter, but addresses the state's more oppressive actions. Prevention and regulation of travel from one part of the country to another was not new in the 1920s and 1930s, but it was during this period that the state tried to create a coherent system under the banner of 'segregation'. The elaboration and impact of passes and urban areas laws is explained and the related question of recruiting, as regulated by the NAD's sub-department of Native Labour is considered. This is complemented by Chapter 5, which focuses more narrowly on farm labour. The link between state aid for farmers and the broader question of control over movement is discussed. This encompasses developments in the policy debate between the Departments of Native Affairs, Agriculture and Justice from 1924 to 1948.

Having dealt with the welfare and repressive sides of labour regulation as distinct, though interlinked, themes the study addresses the general labour problems arising from the growth of an industrial economy from the 1920s to the 1940s. Chapters 6 and 7 analyse labour relations in industrial areas, focusing on wage regulation and the state and African trade unions. These two subjects are closely connected, as the degree of participation for black workers under the Wage and Industrial Conciliation Acts hinged, to a large extent, on the government's policy towards African trade unions. The main player here is the Labour Department, with a significant supporting role for the NAD. Chapter 8 summarises the study's main findings and outlines the situation as it was in 1948.

2

REGULATION OF WORKING CONDITIONS FOR AFRICANS

Introduction

One of the most notable areas in which the state bureaucracy developed its contact with African workers between 1918 and 1948 was in the regulation of working conditions. As the South African economy expanded and diversified, it developed different labour processes in each sector. In every sphere of labour regulation, the state then evolved separate administrative divisions to regulate and control working conditions. The main goal was to ensure the long term viability of primary and secondary industry by preventing clashes between workers and management and by minimising loss of human life. On the mines, officials who enforced the regulations were also expected to contribute to the efficiency of the enterprise by advising the government and the industry on appropriate changes.

These were the aims behind the appointment of mines inspectors on the Rand in the 1890s and, in part, behind the creation of the Government Native Labour Bureau (GNLB) (1907-8), which became a sub-department of the NAD in 1910. (The GNLB was also intended to control the recruitment of migrant labourers. This is discussed in Chapter 4.)[1] However, in the course of their operations, both branches of the state bureaucracy found themselves subject to a variety of pressures arising from their structural position within the state and developments in the economy and labour process as well as the interests of business, white and black labour organisations, and political parties. From the start, the two departments internalised some of these pressures, which were subsequently passed on to successive officers as part of the 'administrative ethos', or guiding principles, on which each department operated.

Much of this is also true for the factory inspectorate, founded in 1918. This was originally intended by the state to more directly improve conditions and apply health and safety regulations. The reason for this, its affect on the working principles of the Factory Inspectors and the ways in which those principles changed over time, are crucially important in explaining the state's relationship with labour in mines and industry.

The following section deals with the mines inspectorate, the next examines the work of the NAD's Inspectors of Native Labourers and the final section focuses on the factory inspectorate.

Down the Mines

The state's powers of control over working conditions in the mines were defined in the Mines and Works Act of 1911. This laid down certain basic standards – no women or boys under sixteen to work underground; no work to be done on Sundays, except maintenance, emergencies and milling of ore in mills established before 1911; a maximum working day of eight hours and a maximum working week of forty-eight hours.[2] It was left to the Department of Mines to draw up regulations pertaining to the duties of managers and overseers; the safety and health of employees in mines and works; provision of ambulances and medical aid; and the granting of certificates for blasting, engine driving, engineering, overseeing, surveying and management. The notorious 'colour bar', enshrined in Regulation 285, reserved these jobs for white workers.

The Act was administered by the Mines Division of the Department of Mines and Industries. This was split into three sections: the Mining Commissioners and the Registrar of Mining Titles, who issued licences for prospecting and mining titles; the Geological Survey and the engineering branch, headed by the Government Mining Engineer (GME). His authority extended over the Inspectors of Mines, Machinery and Explosives, the last of whom came under the Explosives Act of 1911. Unlike the factory inspectorate, the GME had twofold responsibilities: to ensure the physical safety of those working on the mines or using machinery and explosives and to advise the government on technical mining matters. He was thus placed in the potentially awkward position of serving two masters – the immediate demands of health and safety and the wider requirements of the state in its relationship with the mining industry.

The crux of the argument in this section is that the GME and his inspectors did indeed take both imperatives into account. Their work was complicated by the fact that the industry was hugely important in the political arena, much more so for most of this period than secondary industry. Their problems were exacerbated by the peculiar nature of the production process in mining, with its many, varied and constantly changing points of production underground, and its *ad hoc* approach to geological, financial and labour-related problems. Inspectors of Mines could not concentrate solely on the task of ensuring the physical well-being of workers, since even the most basic health and safety issues had immediate political and economic overtones.

The key figures in the 1920s and 1930s were the two GMEs, Sir Robert Kotze (1908-26) and Dr Hans Pirow (1926-37). Both appointments were politically motivated: Kotze's by his old friend, General Smuts, and Pirow's through unnamed members of the Pact government.[3] Kotze was highly significant in the development of state policy towards the mining industry. He played a key role in opposing the white labour policy of Creswell and the white trade unions in the 1910s and 1920s.[4] He also blocked improvements in underground working conditions used his considerable authority to promote the profitability of the big mining companies.

Kotze's talent in doing business with the Randlords was most strikingly illustrated when he chaired the Low Grade Mines Commission in 1919-20. William Gemmill and Evelyn Wallers, respectively joint secretary and president of the Transvaal Chamber of Mines, were also members. The Commission considered ways of dealing with unprofitable low grade mines and of alleviating the shortage of cheap black labour on the goldfields. The idea of raising African wages was roundly condemned. The report showed uncharacteristic concern for secondary industry in this regard, arguing that increasing black mineworkers' wages would draw labour away from other sectors and precipitate an industrial crisis.[5] On the other hand, the Commission recommended lifting the 'colour bar' to allow management more room to manoeuvre in its organisation of the labour process.[6] Here again, the report sounded spuriously pious, appealing to principles of 'abstract justice' on behalf of black workers. The third major proposal – that of opening up further catchment areas for recruiting migrant labour – was again guaranteed to outrage white workers. The Commission also bolstered the mineowners' case by arguing that it would be no bad thing if some low grade mines closed down.[7]

On the related question of the increasing rate of accidents underground in the early 1920s, Kotze initially denied that it was due to changes in the ratio of Whites, that is supervisors, to Blacks, but was then forced to agree that the reduction in supervision over jackhammer teams contributed to a rising number of misfire accidents. He accepted, under pressure, that fewer accidents would occur if there were more inspectors, but did not demand a larger staff.[8] The total number of accidents underground increased more rapidly than the expansion of the industry as a whole: 3 314 accidents in 1920, 9 070 in 1930, and 17 909 in 1940, while the number of mineworkers grew from 306 554 in 1920, to 502 008 in 1940 (see appendix 5).[9]

Despite a background which included years of safety-related research in England, Pirow was as unconcerned about safety as Kotze had been.[10] In 1930, Pirow drew up suggestions for the

Low Grade Ore Commission which would have done his old boss proud. Pirow argued that removing as many whites from underground as possible was the best way to save money and make millions of tons of low grade ore profitable. White miners who had worked for ten years would be given surface work. This move would cut down the incidence of phthisis and save money in compensation. The flow of migrant labour would also be augmented as underground labourers would fill more semi-skilled positions, thereby having the opportunity of earning higher wages – though obviously not as high as those paid to whites.[11]

Although the Kotze Commission opposed the legalised 'colour bar', both GMEs excused overt discrimination on the mines by referring to the crude, racist stereotypes common in society at that time. For example, Kotze stated that Africans had reached the limit of their abilities doing semi-skilled work on the coal mines.[12] Pirow later argued that two white men had to be present when precious metals were handled, as a white employee was more likely to be honest than a black one. While such prejudices certainly existed among members of other state departments, it is unusual to find them used so blatantly as arguments in official documents. Kotze's and Pirow's contemptuous, utilitarian attitudes towards black workers were of a sharper, more vicious order than those of most civil servants of the period.

The perspectives of more lowly Department of Mines officials were exposed in disputes over staff ratios in the mid-1920s. From 1924, the presence in the cabinet of several Labour Party members triggered renewed efforts by white miners to reverse the trend towards fewer white overseers and falling real wages. The South African Mine Workers Union supported the findings of the Mining Regulations Commission of 1924, which attributed the rising accident rate to the white miners' increasing responsibilities.[13] The miners took their stand on the issue of health and safety, and condemned the record of the Inspectors of Mines:

The Deputation then remarked on the futility of the inspection conducted by the Mining Engineering Department. It is useless and quite ineffective. The number of inspectors is quite insufficient and there is too much sympathy between the mine management and the inspectorate who have no sympathy with the miner.[14]

Colonel Creswell then took up the struggle, calling for a report on the dismissal of white miners and urging the use of the inspectorate to prevent the emasculation of underground supervisory staff.[15] Most inspectors responded that there was no appreciable diminution of the white staff and that the general practice was not to overload men with work. However, Charles Gray, Inspector of Mines for Johannesburg, admitted that supervision of drilling had fallen off and that the greatly increased speed of drilling was causing an increase in misfire accidents.[16] He went on to describe his job as being almost impossible. Overlapping shifts made it extremely difficult to tell what a particular miner's job was. Conditions down the mine varied from day to day and the inspector received little support from the workers, who were afraid of gaining a bad reputation with mine officials. In any case, as there were no objective standards, it was left up to the inspector to decide whether or not a work load was reasonable. This involved weighing efficiency against safety, neither of which had been defined. Gray's evidence was borne out by a deputation from the Witwatersrand White Miners Association to the Ministers of Mines and Labour in 1925. Representing the miners, TC Hynd claimed he knew of cases where one man supervised sixteen drilling machines on several levels at once, and had the task of charging up to 150 holes in an hour. He agreed that the inspector's job was made more difficult by the fact that miners generally knew when an inspector was coming so the official rarely saw a mine working normally.[17]

Gray's outburst suggests one reason why working conditions underground were not regulated as carefully as they were in secondary industry. The shifting nature of the work and the many points of production rendered the mine inspector's task much more difficult than that of the factory inspectorate. Yet for the most part, inspectors of mines did not complain about their duties. They busied themselves with promoting the efficient working of the mine and presented accident rate statistics in the best possible light. They avoided disputes over the ratio of supervisors to labourers and did not call for more inspectors to make their jobs easier. In general, they supported the policies of mine management against the protests of Creswell and the white trade union movement. They acted, in a sense, as a Trojan horse for the mining industry within the state.

By comparison, the inspectors of factories were less likely to sacrifice safety for profitability. There are several possible reasons why these two departments saw the needs of the state (or, to take a more crudely Marxist line, those of the 'ruling classes') so differently. One can argue that the difference was related to the relative strengths of various 'fractions' of capital. Others would see it more in terms of the pre-eminent position of the gold-mining industry in the economy.[18] The weakened position of white workers after the Rand Revolt allowed the mineowners to extend their retrenchment of white labour. The election of the Pact government in 1924 brought little relief for white miners despite the Labour and National Parties' promises. One should also take into account the comparative strengths of organised workers in the two sectors in the 1920s and their differing capacities to insist on better working conditions. Or again, there were the differences in the production process, the exigencies of profit-making at near impossible depths beneath the ground and the question of competition with cheap foreign imports.

All these factors are important in analysing the ways in which administrators approached the issue of workplace regulation. However, in the mines division as in other departments one must look to the social background and attitudes of the administrators to understand why they supported a particular policy and how they reacted to external pressures. In the case of the

GME and his staff, it was not simply a question of blindly obeying government directives. Both Kotze and Pirow actively participated in drawing up strategies to improve productivity and circumvent opposition from white labour. In doing so, they interpreted very broadly their administrative function of advising the Government on technical mining matters.

In part, their close association with the drive to improve efficiency may be explained by their background as engineers and scientists. The GME's staff held professional qualifications. If they had not found posts in the civil service, they would have worked for the same mines they inspected. Their training as engineers led them to seek ways to overcome technical difficulties and in the department they were encouraged to apply their knowledge for the good of the mining industry. The issue of how to deploy labour was so important for the industry and was so bound up with the more technical and mechanical matters that, inevitably, inspectors found themselves dealing with questions which directly affected pay, staffing levels and working conditions. At the same time, the state did not encourage inspectors of mines to think like social workers. Unlike their colleagues in the factory inspectorate, they were not privy to the nineteenth century British reformist tradition that caring for the material comfort of labourers was a worthy goal in its own right. The Mines Division had been established in the days of the Kruger Republic, at a time when state intervention in working conditions had been minimal. This division had struggled alongside the mineowners and their managers and technical staff to overcome the huge physical obstacles which threatened to prevent profitable deep level mining. The close, if not symbiotic relationship between this branch of the state and the representatives of mining capital grew out of this common experience of the geophysical, technological and bureaucratic difficulties ranged against mining. The shared experience and interest made it unlikely that inspectors of mines would formulate and implement stringent regulations which might drive some businesses under. On the other hand, it was not so surprising that Kotze, on leaving the civil service, became a director of De Beers Consolidated Mines Ltd, while Pirow was appointed consultant by another leading mining firm, Corner House.[19]

Working Conditions and the
Native Labour Regulation Act

> I must naturally keep in touch with native labour conditions from the four points of view from which I have to approach it; in the first place I advise the Government on matters of policy in connection with labour; I have to see that the mining industry and employers of labour who employ agents get fair play from their employees in so far as it comes under Government control, and I have to see that the labour agent's interests in so far as they are legitimate are properly protected, and to ensure that the native labourer gets a square deal from the two.[20]

The Native Labour Regulation Act of 1911 was passed to help ensure an adequate supply of migrant labour for the gold mines and to centralise state control over African workers in industrial areas. The act empowered the Director of Native Labour (DNL) to issue licences to labour recruiters and employers of recruited labour. Compound managers who supervised large numbers of Africans on mines and 'works' (where machinery was used) were also obliged to obtain licences. The DNL was in charge of inspectors of Native labour (INL), who were to act as the 'protectors' of labourers, inquiring into grievances but also fining workers whom they judged not to be fulfilling their contracts. Contracts were to be attested before an officer of the NAD who would ensure that workers understood the terms. Most INLs operated in the Transvaal, though others were appointed for Kimberley and Barkly West (river diggings), Natal (coal and sugar areas), and the Free State (diamond and coal mines). Labour districts were proclaimed under the Act, again mostly in the Transvaal, in which tighter pass laws were applied. Special regulations for housing, feeding and hospital treatment existed in these areas. Municipalities had the power to operate their own regulations for compounding under the Native (Urban Areas) Act of 1923.[21] The DNL retained his powers of inspection in places where machinery was used.[22]

The role of the NAD's sub-department of Native Labour (the GNLB) became increasingly important between the wars, although by 1948, the DNL was enforcing substantially the same regulations as in 1918. The GNLB received a major shake-up along with the rest of the department in 1923, at the hands of the Public Service Commission. The thrust of the Commission's report was that the DNL's staff should be cut.[23] The old command structure did not permit proper supervision of staff, and left INLs and Pass Officers working independently of each other. In any case, the report argued, close control over mine labourers' working conditions was no longer necessary. Mining operations had shrunk and employers now treated their workers much more sympathetically. The report recommended cutting the number of labour districts on the Rand from eight to four, with a net saving of £2 568 per annum. The DNL's salary would be cut from £1 500 to £950 and his office combined with that of the Johannesburg sub-Native Commissioner and the Native Commissioner for the Witwatersrand.[24]

The hardliners within the South African Party felt that the 'old guard' administrators in the NAD were too lenient on Africans to be able to deal with post-war militancy and to apply repressive countermeasures.[25] This sentiment was by no means universal; cuts to the NAD faced widespread opposition, notably in a series of articles on African administration by the future 'native' senator EH Brookes.[26] From within the state, the outgoing SNA Edward Barrett fought a bitter but ineffectual battle to keep his position. Yet the GNLB did not attempt a similar defence of its operations. The chief reason for this was that the DNL, Colonel Pritchard, wanted to take early retirement.[27] Pritchard gave the commission the evidence it needed to reduce the sub-department's staff. He then took credit for raising the efficiency of his operation and allowing sweeping economies.[28] The Public Service Commission permitted him to retire in January 1924. It then appointed Herbert Cooke as DNL and Chief Native Commissioner for the Rand.[29]

Cooke held the office for eight years. He was well suited to a system which kept black workers firmly in place, while contending that the entire structure was to their benefit. Before the Mills and Holloway Commissions, Cooke painted a very rosy picture of the GNLB's services to Africans. He argued that NAD officials were becoming more and more sensitive to the needs of the African worker.[30] The department's officers remitted money which was urgently needed by distressed families back in the reserves. They handled the estates of deceased migrant workers, instituted enquiries for men worried about their relatives and even induced employers to 'liberate' a worker if his wife was seriously ill.[31] In 1931, Cooke presented the Native Economic Commission with a memorandum listing the advantages for Africans of the Act. Under cross-examination, he claimed triumphantly that strikes and disputes were a thing of the past: labourers now had so much confidence in NAD officials that they counted on them to settle grievances amicably and equitably.[32] Before both commissions the DNL was given considerable latitude by the SNA, Major Herbst, whose opinions were generally similar to Cooke's.

A combination of personal and departmental prestige were at stake here. The DNL may have exaggerated his role to counter the image of the NAD as the poor sister of the civil service, a department of cranks and liberals which served no real purpose other than to complicate the higher work of Justice, Mines and Agriculture Department officials. He may also have felt the need to defend himself from the more progressive elements on both commissions, especially Bill Andrews (a communist and white trade unionist) and Frank Lucas (Chairman of the Wage Board) in 1925, and the latter again in 1931. Likewise, the wider image of the NAD as an organisation which coupled paternalistic care

with even-handed administration of severely restrictive legislation, was always important to its members. Whatever his reasons, Cooke also made clear his acceptance of the whole
apparatus of state control (including pass laws, masters and servants laws, compulsory compounding and repatriation on the
completion of a contract) and his opposition to major changes in
the migrant labour system. In this, he appears to have been
moved in equal measure by concern for mining profits, fear of
the social consequences of an ever-increasing urban African population and anxiety at how the NAD could deal with mine
labour in administrative terms.

If African mineworkers were stabilised on the Rand with their
families, he argued, it would put up working costs. It would also
promote venereal disease and the sale of illicit liquor, which
would bring down productivity.[33] The wider problem was that
when an industry closed down, the urbanised African and his
family had nowhere to go. Missionary education lifted Africans
above the level of the labouring class but left them without any
marketable skills. Thus, the NAD was left to deal with large
numbers of unemployed people who lived by their wits. Migrant
labour was the lesser of two evils; its only drawback was the
'unnatural vice' it encouraged among mineworkers.[34]

Unlike the inspectors of factories and mines, INLs were primarily concerned with the living conditions provided by
employers. Periodic inspections were a factor in the steady
improvement of health and living conditions for black mineworkers between 1911 and 1939. Death rates from respiratory
diseases were reduced and nutrition and hygiene much
enhanced. This did not mean, though, that the inspectors placed
an intolerable burden on the employers. On the Simmer and Jack
Mine in 1932, for example, the DNL only took action when the
Tuberculosis Research Committee pointed out that poor facilities
for Africans could rebound on the white workers' health.[35] The
local MP, C Potgieter, protested that the NAD had no right to
allow Africans to be employed under such degrading conditions
and that profits should not take precedence over health.

The main problems on Simmer and Jack were overcrowding and the long distance labourers had to walk to the mine shaft. The DNL ignored evidence that the mine was easily profitable, and took the part of the mineowners. He argued (against the GME) that there was a danger that the company would close the mine if forced to invest in new housing accommodation. 'You will readily realise that Mining companies are averse to spending money on new compounds for which in a few years they may have no use,' he pleaded to the SNA.[36] A report by a Public Health Department officer showing that conditions in the compound were 'very unhygienic', and complaints to the Minister of Native Affairs, finally forced the DNL to approve a plan for eighty additional rooms. But the company was able to stall until 1934 when the manager won acceptance from the new DNL AL Barrett, for a much reduced plan for twenty-five rooms.[37] At no point did the DNL invoke his powers to force the mineowners' compliance under the regulations of 1911.[38] By the time the work was underway, countless thousands of mineworkers had passed through the compound, enduring slum conditions off duty and then having to walk miles to work each day. The mine produced profits of £198 095 in 1931 alone, of which £41 604 was distributed as dividends.

Besides political pressure from workers and interested whites, the other major factor which galvanised the DNL to improve compound conditions was the effect this had on the labour supply. The DNL inspected the Natal sugar and cotton estates in the late 1910s, after which inspectors were appointed to supervise housing and feeding.[39] Despite this, plantation owners responded only slowly and grudgingly. Much of the work of persuading them was left to the Public Health Department.[40] The NAD took no real interest in the situation until the mid-1930s, when sugar estates were struggling to keep up their labour complements. On the basis of a departmental report, the DNL blamed the shortage on conditions and wages on smaller estates. He then pressured a few employers to improve conditions for the sake of the industry's reputation among prospective workers.

On the mines, INLs occasionally stepped into the GME's arena to protect black miners from physical violence. Each month the DNL drew up a table of assaults on labourers by white miners and the punishment inflicted on the latter. These usually involved fines of a few shillings or pounds – in most cases the mine did not discharge the culprits.[41] The vast majority of assaults went unreported and a regime of subordination built on fear of the overseers was maintained. Most inspectors appear genuinely to have regarded violence as unnecessary and counter-productive in controlling black workers. When the courts found mines policemen, *indunas* and even compound managers guilty of such behaviour, the INLs normally called for their dismissal. GNLB officials accepted violence as a last resort, as in the many cases in the later 1930s and 1940s when they called in the South African Police with fixed bayonets. But for the most part, the INLs favoured the compound manager who retained at least a modicum of the respect of his charges, beyond merely dreading his appearance with a sjambok.[42]

Underground though, the INLs' capacity to limit violence was minimal. Beatings of labourers by 'boss-boys' and white supervisors were everyday occurrences, a part of the labour process by which supervisors drove black miners to fulfil the day's work quota. GNLB officials neither understood this process nor had easy access to it. They received little help from the inspectors of mines or from management and preferred to play down the incidents they encountered. It was left up to the labourers to protect themselves from attacks as best they could, with little help from the law or their supposed 'protectors'.[43]

The task of 'controlling' black workers by preventing them from disrupting production in mines and works or antagonising the white population was fundamental to the very existence of the GNLB. This was not a function which concerned either the GME or the factory inspectorate whose duties related primarily to white workers, for whom 'civilised' standards were supposed to be their own restraints. African workers were not supposed to possess those advantages and consequently, had to be hedged around with various repressive measures to keep their minds on the job. In addition, the lack of political power of the African workers allowed the state to apply legislation which employers, at least in the wake of the Rand Revolt of 1922, might have been happy to see extended to all employees. These measures included penalties contained in the Masters and Servants laws, the Native Labour Regulation Act, the Urban Areas Act and the Native Service Contract Act for African workers who broke their contracts, whether by striking, desertion or otherwise. The GNLB was responsible for enforcing Section Fifteen of the Native Labour Regulation Act. This prescribed two months with hard labour or a £10 fine for breach of contract by a 'native labourer'.[44]

The importance of compounds in the minds of GNLB officers can hardly be underestimated. The cheap labour policy, which kept hundreds of thousands of so-called 'raw natives' with numerous legitimate grievances on the Rand, could only continue as long as African mineworkers were kept as isolated as possible from white residents. Moreover, as Cooke explained to successive commissions between 1924 and 1932, compounding was the only way to avoid desertions, falling efficiency and the 'contamination' of black mineworkers through unlicensed access to drink and women. Workers could and did leave the compounds when off shift, but management could deny access to outsiders (as they did to African Mine Workers Union organisers in the 1940s), and could close the compounds completely in times of crisis. The mines provided unparalleled opportunities to control and coerce migrant workers in a way that superintendents of urban locations could only dream about. Van Onselen has gone so far as to argue that 'it was the compound as an institution which provided the framework for the total exploitation of black workers.'[45] Of course, the system also encouraged the development of a community of feeling amongst the workers, as highlighted in the labour disputes of 1920 and 1946.[46] In the 1987 strike, workers turned the compound itself to their advantage (though, significantly, not until Anglo American and several other large companies had allowed union organisers onto their premises). But in the 1918-48 period, the DNL and his staff were there to prevent such a shift in the power balance. Their public image and professional status within the civil service depended on their self-projection as experts who were intimately aware of the climate of opinion in the compounds, ready to step in, mediate and pre-empt major problems before they mushroomed. The mineowners generally tolerated the INLs where they did not expose serious maltreatment of the workers and where demands on the mineowners' resources were minimal.[47] To them, the INLs served a purpose which they could not perform for themselves. The GNLB's interference was also infinitely preferable to direct, formalised representation for the workers.

From 1932 through 1948, the office of DNL changed hands every few years. The sub-department's importance may have been partially diminished in this period. The growing significance for black workers of authorities such as the municipalities and the Department of Labour and the much-discussed idea of giving recognition to African trade unions, may have proportionately reduced the GNLB's influence. Moreover, it is possible that EW Lowe and CP Alport, successive DNLs between 1940 and 1946, did not enjoy the SNA's full confidence. This is borne out by the SNA Douglas Smit's demand that he be informed immediately of all confrontations between black workers and their employers.

A further reason for the apparent declining importance of the DNL lies in the increasing direct involvement of politicians. As the industrial sector expanded and a new militancy took root amongst African workers, the task of handling this threat was more frequently taken up by Smuts himself. However, this did not mean that the DNL was any less busy in the late 1930s and 1940s, nor did it imply a complete rejection of the policy of governing African workers through a separate, powerful, strongly paternalistic administrative structure. Whatever the notions being debated in the 1940s, the period closed with the migrant labour system and the body administering it still intact.

Factories, Shops and Offices.

In 1937, the Department of Labour set out its view of its responsibilities:

> The two principal interests concerned, those of employers and employees respectively, are frequently in conflict and the Department, when called upon in the course of its statutory activities to decide a thorny point, must endeavour to choose a course of action calculated to promote the objects of the law and the well-being of those concerned.[48]

State supervision of the workplace in secondary industry was as thorny an issue as it was on the mines. Employers weighed every interference by state officials in terms of how it affected their profits, and resisted legislation which would force compulsory improvements. At the local level, ingrained habits of cutting corners and evading rules meant that inspectors of factories had to be constantly on their guard against minor infringements, especially given the huge expansion of secondary industry in this period.

Factory inspectors were further preoccupied by two other considerations. From 1924, the government's express policy was to promote the employment of 'civilised' (that is white) labour in secondary industry. Faced with the need to augment job opportunities, the Department of Labour's enthusiasm for enforcing unpopular regulations too strictly was reduced. Officials were concerned that by scrutinising working conditions too closely and by enforcing its regulations too rigorously, they would force many newly created manufacturing firms out of business, with the consequent loss of 'civilised' jobs. On the other hand, an increasingly vocal white trade union movement was pushing the department to take action against wayward employers and to improve conditions. This led to head-on conflicts between unionists and administrators in the Labour Department, who liked to think of themselves as doing their best for the working man. In his 1937 report, the Secretary for Labour complained about '…a stream of abuse which not only does disservice to the workers' cause, but inevitably raises doubts as to the sincerity of any future representations from that same source'.[49]

Despite this hostility, the Labour Department took protests from organised white labour seriously. It investigated their complaints in full and reported back to the trade unions concerned.

The development of legislation for South Africa's industrial workplace began later than that for the mines, with the long overdue Factory Act of 1918. This provided for the appointment of a cadre of inspectors of factories under a chief inspector, with powers of entry to any factory.[50] All factories had to be registered within six months of the Act coming into force. The Act laid down standards for ventilation, sanitation, lighting, statutory holidays and the employment of juveniles and pregnant women. The maximum working week for adults was fifty hours (reduced by the Factories (Amendment) Act of 1931 to forty-eight hours). Pay for overtime was at time-and-a-quarter. The minister could grant exemptions to the above regulations if the factory worked seasonally or if it was subject to intermittent supplies of raw materials. Voluminous regulations were published in December 1918, with further instalments in subsequent years.[51]

The Factories Act came at a time when governments around the world were beginning to compare the treatment of workers in different countries and to set international standards. The International Labour Organisation, which arose out of the Treaty of Versailles and whose conferences were normally attended by South African delegates, helped to focus the Union Government's attention on factory conditions. The 1918 Act, although based on the British principles of centralisation and specialisation of the inspectorate, did not go as far as Britain's Police, Factories (Miscellaneous Provisions) Act of 1916, which was another stimulus behind the South African legislation. In another sense, the whole Victorian tradition of state regulation of working conditions, stretching back to Britain's Factories Acts of 1844 and

1847, was behind this Act.[52] South African inspectors lacked the experience of their British counterparts. On the positive side, they were conscious of not having to cope with antiquated, dangerous plants dating back fifty or a hundred years. The bulk of the Union's industrial development still lay ahead of it.

In 1924, the Act came under the jurisdiction of the newly-established Department of Labour. This does not appear to have aroused much animosity among inspectors. Their work was largely separate from the rest of the Mines Department, so there was little chance of losing out on promotions within the department. The old Deputy Chief Inspector HC Fowler, became Chief Inspector under the Secretary for Labour, CW Cousins.[53] The inspectorate's powers were further increased in 1931. In that year, the regulation of machinery under the Mines and Works Act was divided between the Mines, Labour and Agriculture Departments.[54]

This accretion in the duties of inspectors of factories, coupled with rapid growth in the industrial sector after 1933, helped to broaden the inspectorate's experience. In the process, the inspectorate embellished its image as an organisation of experts entrusted with the noble task of safeguarding life and limb and in general, promoting the care and welfare of the workforce. Departmental reports portrayed the inspectors as scrupulously fair-minded and objective. The Secretary for Labour, Ivan Walker argued in 1941 (in terms that could have come straight from the pages of Weber's *Theory of Social and Economic Organization*),[55] that inspectors were perfectly capable of handling the abnormally high level of delegated responsibility to be introduced as departmental regulations under the new Act of 1941:

> Without wishing to cross swords with those who view with disapproval the modern tendency to govern by regulation, I must point out that this 'modern tendency' arises from the necessities of the present day world, and not from any desire on the part of civil servants to exercise their brief authority.[56]

The critics who troubled Walker hailed from both right and left. For Afrikaner Nationalists, the state's declared policy of non-discrimination in the application of the Factories Act was an easy rallying point for raising race-consciousness. In the 1930s and 1940s, Women's Congresses affiliated to the Provincial Agricultural Unions passed resolutions against Asians employing white women, Africans working in the same room as white women and Africans being employed in enterprises which manufactured foodstuffs. This last point they linked to a concern for health and hygiene – it would be much safer, the Women's Congresses claimed, to reserve jobs in abattoirs, dairies and bakeries for whites.[57] This would also promote the 'civilised labour' policy. The Department of Labour dismissed their arguments on two grounds. Most importantly, neither Hertzog nor Smuts would agree to overloading secondary industry at one blow with a more expensive and untrained white labour force. Industrialists rejected such a policy out of hand, arguing that it would drive into bankruptcy many businesses which already employed a percentage of white workers. In any case, such a move would have derailed the government's longer term strategy of raising industrial wages very gradually through the Wage Board.[58]

Secondly, any shift towards government-sponsored racial demarcation in factories would have encountered fierce opposition from the left in South Africa and from overseas. It would have exposed the department's pretence (thin as it was at times) of being non-discriminatory in its administration of labour legislation. In the inter-war years, Department of Labour officials were anxious to avoid being accused of breaking up what little working class solidarity there was. By the same token, they could not be seen to be creating the conditions for a low wage policy in industry, based on the exploitation of cheap, black labour. The department, after all, had been established in part to persuade white workers of the Pact Government's commitment to their welfare and advancement. To this end, Labour Department officers went to great lengths to present themselves as unbiased. They even denied knowledge of any racial bias in the application

of labour legislation other than in the 1911 Mines and Works Act
– 'which I understand', wrote Walker disingenuously in 1944,
'contains a colour bar'.[59]

Labour Department officials tried to fend off the right wing by
pointing to the immense practical difficulties involved in keeping whites and blacks in separate rooms. The department argued
that this would ultimately limit the scope of employment for
whites. The final compromise came in the Factories, Machinery
and Building Work Act of 1941. To appease both right and left,
section fifty-one allowed the Governor-General to insist on
segregated rest rooms, eating areas and so on for the different
races. As Walker insisted in a letter to a white trade union:

> The Minister wishes me to point out that the Bill
> does not contain any provision under which any
> class of labour could be excluded from any occupa-
> tion on the grounds of race or colour and it is, there-
> fore, considered incorrect to refer to the Act as
> containing a colour bar.[60]

The white unions were not only concerned about the prospect of
being undercut by black workers, they also criticised the department over the general operation of the Factories Act. In 1939, the
general secretary of the South African Trades and Labour Council (SATLC) claimed that the failure to pass a new Factory Act
that year was a blow to thousands of workers. The Act was out
of date, he argued. Employers openly flouted it and inspectors
were too willing to grant exemptions. There was an urgent need
for new provisions for annual leave, rest periods, night work,
childbirth, breaks in employment and protection for the young.[61]

Labour Department officials were piqued by the implication
that they were not doing their job properly. In response to the
SATLC's protest, an in-house investigation was carried out in all
major industrial centres to prove that inspectors were administering the regulations fairly. However, South African industry
had undergone major changes since 1918. Of 5 754 factories

registered under the Act in 1939, 3 597 had been established since 1933.[62] In the same period, the number of workers employed in private industry had risen from 176 510 to 282 779, of whom 130 597 were Africans (see Appendix 6). The report indicated serious problems to do with overtime regulations, visiting factories in outlying areas and the powers given to management once exemptions had been granted. These difficulties, plus the passing of the British Factories Act of 1937, encouraged departmental officials to lend their full support to the Factories, Machinery and Building Work Act of 1941.

The British Act extended the definition of 'factory'. It also expanded welfare services for workers and enlarged the inspectorate.[63] South African legislation moved in a similar direction, though in some respects at a slower pace. The 1941 Act extended the definition of a factory, reduced ordinary hours of work to forty-six per week and raised overtime pay to time-and-a-third. Paid holidays were introduced and the minimum age for employment rose from fourteen to fifteen. The Act also tightened up a range of other general safety measures concerning the operation of machinery, the fencing of electrical apparatus, floor space, ventilation and lighting.

The new Factories Act took its place alongside the Shops and Offices Act of 1939, which extended similar protection to workers in those sectors for the first time.[64] Again, the Act left the Department of Labour with wide powers to be defined under administrative regulations, approved at ministerial level. Both pieces of legislation looked impressive on paper and they were certainly considerable, if belated, steps in the right direction. But the impact of the new laws on black workers was limited for several reasons. In the first place, the 1941 Factories Act was not applied until September 1945.[65] This was intended to allow industry to work unimpeded for the war effort and may well have been the result of personal interference from Smuts.[66] The benefits of the new Act for African workers were further reduced by regulations drawn up under section fifty-one. Blacks and whites working at the same benches were supposed to be as far

apart as possible and employers had to provide separate con-
veniences.[67] Finally, the Act excluded labourers working within
the precincts of a factory (such as packers and handlers), the vast
majority of whom were Africans.[68]

In these ways, the Department of Labour operated laws which
treated white and black workers differently, while maintaining
that their administration was free from discrimination. The purpose behind the non-discrimination principle was something
more than public relations. As in any sphere of industrial relations, to push special regulations for whites too far would cause
wholesale displacement of whites by blacks who, already in the
1930s and 1940s, were gaining a foothold in semi-skilled positions. This was coupled with the state's commitment to promoting the profitability of industrial capital and, from 1939, to
maintaining productivity during the war.

It is tempting to see regulations enforcing racial and gender
segregation at the workplace as strategies both of the Afrikaner
nationalists who demanded them and by the Labour Department which enforced them to forestall the development of a
united proletariat. Yet the idea that the Labour Department was
party to a conspiracy of this nature does not fit with its wider
policy statements on labour legislation. The original Industrial
Conciliation and Wage Acts of 1924 to 1925 had been intended to
buy off the white working class, but the department had soon
found how difficult it was to exclude black workers.[69] It was
much easier for Labour Department officials to encourage the
incorporation of blacks into the white trade unions and the IC
Act, rather than to make completely separate provision for them
and then face opposition from the Left and from employers. The
Factories Act had never really been intended to apply discrimi-
nately, except where public pressure – particularly that stirred up
by Afrikaner nationalists – made some form of segregation a
political necessity. The fact that the Government in its legislation
and the Department of Labour in its regulations, bowed to that
pressure in the 1940s, is more a reflection of prevailing social
values and their manipulation for political ends than proof that

this branch of the capitalist state was hell-bent on the bifurcation of the working classes.

Conclusion

> At the present time where a matter concerns one Department that Department gets to work and handles it, but you have things which concern more than one Department, and each Department is liable to look after its own affairs, and to busily engage in them without that intimate touch with other Departments interested in the same matter which is usual and necessary in industrial life.[70]

There were, naturally, certain features of the regulation of working conditions which were common to all branches of the state bureaucracy. In broad terms, they acted as the *corps intermédiaires* which Durkheim identified as necessary in modern society. Their actions and the principles for which they stood provided a stabilising force in an age of conflict and change. More narrowly, officials of the various departments all administered regulations which were drawn up in consultation with industry and which they designed to protect the life and limb of the labour force. Each department divided its staff territorially under a senior officer. Inspectors were encouraged to become regional experts and to remain in close touch with local employers. Given the paucity of staff members and the large regions they had to cover, these officials had to be allowed a considerable degree of autonomy. Yet there is evidence that inspectors in the same division shared many of the same attitudes to their work. The explanation for this lies in the sense of *esprit de corps* or commonality of purpose which developed within each division. It also relates to the wider concerns of the state for the viability of key economic sectors.

On the other hand, we have seen how variations in the attitudes of officials in different divisions were significant. Efforts made by the average inspector of factories to improve working

conditions were of quite a different order to those of his counter-
part in the Mines Division. The reason for this lies partly in the
position of the respective sectors in terms of economic and political muscle. Throughout the period, the gold mines were of primary importance to the material welfare of the state and the
country as a whole. Mineowners exercised their political
influence more concertedly and more effectively than the cap-
tains of secondary industry. The Randlords therefore had the
power to block any attempt to enforce decent standards in working conditions if the state ever attempted to do so. When, in the
1970s and 1980s, major changes did at last come in working conditions on the mines, it was the companies themselves that over-
came individual mine managers' opposition to cost-raising
initiatives.

The differences in the production processes in mining and
secondary industry are also significant. It is easier to make life
safer and more pleasant in a factory, shop or dormitory than
thousands of feet below the ground, where the point of production constantly shifts. The inspector of factories and INL's tasks
were much more straightforward than that of the mines inspector, whose arrival at the many different points of production was
known to mine managers well in advance. This helps to explain
the significant improvements in factory and compound conditions, compared to conditions underground.

A third argument, put on occasion by the DNL himself, was
that the cost structure of the gold mines could not support the
luxury of mollycoddling its workers, either underground or on
the surface. Both the industry and the state were committed to
maximum exploitation of ore bodies, including those of a lower
gold content where the profit margin was minimal. This drove
down the overall pay limit and put pressure on cost minimisa-
tion strategies. With this constraint in view, mining companies
were not prepared to consider alternatives to a bounded, poorly
paid migrant workforce, even on relatively high grade mines
where this might have been possible.

A further reason why inspectors in the Mines, Labour and

Native Affairs Departments operated differently involves their understanding of their function. They were under no illusions that they were there to help the gold mines produce ore cheaply, efficiently and safely. Inspectors of factories, by contrast, believed their first duty was to white workers. This does not imply that they wanted to hand the means of production over to labour lock, stock and barrel. They accepted the broad structure of the capitalist system in which they operated. But they did not think in terms of forestalling revolution by partial concessions. They believed their regulations made a meaningful contribution to the well-being of the white working classes.

The first constituency of the GNLB was the African labourer, and the sub-department's attitudes to him largely determined its performance as an inspectorate. The NAD generally held that Africans would not perform responsibly as employees unless they were subject to a degree of control. In addition, the most degrading and exploitative conditions had to be eliminated in order to improve efficiency, prevent resistance and satisfy moral compunction. This task continued through the first four decades of Union. At the same time, there were limits to what the white man could be expected to do for the socially and intellectually inferior black worker and that consideration restrained GNLB officials from taking action beyond a certain point. These factors were reinforced by the knowledge that African labourers were not the only constituency with which the NAD had to deal. These dilemmas were a very real part of the *Weltanschauung* of the NAD official in every field. As we shall see, they were equally to the fore in the administration of health and welfare, which is the focus of the next chapter.

3

HEALTH AND WELFARE

Introduction

The living and working conditions of the industrial proletariat cannot be considered independently.[1] The exigencies of profit-making spill over from one to the other, compelling capital interests to interfere in areas not directly controlled by the production process. To understand the full scope of black labour regulation in South Africa, it is necessary to examine the extent of health and welfare provisions in society at large, and the way in which they complemented state control of health and safety at the actual workplace.[2] In the 1930s and 1940s, groups ranging from Afrikaans nationalist organisations to African trade unions pressed the government with demands for social welfare. Within state structures the Department of Labour, the Industrial and Agricultural Requirements Commission, the National Housing and Planning Commission, the Social and Economic Planning Commission, the Social Services Commission and the National Health Services Commission recommended a social security system fit for a prosperous, post-war industrial economy. World War II also brought greater contact with Britain and the United States, where state intervention and social planning were already well established. The impact of these factors on Smuts's wartime coalition government can be seen in several areas.

Workmen's Compensation and Miners' Phthisis

The most prominent health and welfare provisions for African workers were contained in the compensation laws covering industrial injuries and diseases. As in other aspects of labour regulation, the development of state policy was uneven and complex. Originally, black workers were administered under the Native Labour Regulation Act (1911), the Workmen's Compensation Act (1914) and the Miners' Phthisis Act (1919).[3] Throughout the period between 1918 and 1948, the state amended and redrafted these laws to streamline the organisation of payments and to increase the value of compensation. In the process, compensation became a battleground between officials of different departments. They were concerned with both the wider effects of the legislation on employers and workers, and with the repercussions inside the bureaucracy of successive changes in administrative organisation. The government's initiatives encouraged the mines to take disease prevention and health care more seriously. Anxious to avoid paying compensation to incapacitated workers, the mines, especially between 1910 and 1930, improved their medical facilities. Their efforts helped to reduce the number of mineworkers who fell victim to respiratory diseases. Yet in health and welfare compensation, the cost imperatives of big business had a more immediate impact on the state than in many other areas of labour regulation. This tended to limit the scope of legislation and to restrict administrative discretion.[4]

The law was intended to serve several purposes. Compensation was supposed to bolster the impression among prospective migrant workers that they would be well looked after in the mines and labour areas. In particular, lump sums paid out to sick and injured migrants were expected to encourage young men anxious to save money for *lobola* to present themselves for recruitment.

They would also counter fears of living out a useless life in miserable penury after sustaining an injury or contracting an incurable disease. Compensation would thus have a positive effect on the labour supply in general. This was linked to the need to satisfy Portuguese authorities who controlled recruiting in Mozambique, and British officials in the High Commission Territories, that they were getting a fair return for permitting labour migration.

More generally, the South African state was concerned to show at least a degree of commitment to protecting the health of black workers. The government had set out clear provisions for whites under the 1914 and 1919 Acts. By including Africans under these Acts while at the same time keeping the NLR Act and laying down lower rates for black mineworkers, the government sought a middle course between a completely segregated administration for Africans and the equal treatment of Africans before the law – a course of action that would have undermined the entire cheap labour system. The former would have antagonised black workers and political organisations, white trade unions and liberals; the latter would have been unacceptable to the big mining companies, as they struggled to monopsonise migrant labour.[5]

Another impulse behind the Act, stated in successive Select Committee Reports was to 'facilitate the introduction of sound schemes for the prevention of accidents and industrial diseases and the rehabilitation of disabled workmen'.[6] The state and the Chamber of Mines were deeply worried about the high attrition rate among black workers caused by illnesses such as tuberculosis and pneumonia. In the first three decades of the twentieth century they began to seek solutions through medical research and surveys of those at risk.[7] But Dr AJ Orenstein, chief medical officer for the Corner House group, better expressed the underlying motivation of both the state and the mining industry in his address to the Medical Congress in 1922:

> It could not be seriously disputed that in its six or seven millions of natives, this country had an asset of great value, if it were not indeed, the most valuable asset. If this premise was conceded, it followed

that whatever threatened to undermine the health or diminish the numbers of the natives, became a matter of the deepest concern to the European population, even on economic grounds alone.[8]

The compensation laws developed in the decade after Union were therefore a cornerstone in the state's attempts to limit the 'violence' which the capitalist class inflicts upon the working class, and in the process preserves what David Harvey has called the 'happiness, docility and efficiency of labour'.[9] Official ideology presented these laws as promoting all three at once. However, as officials themselves tacitly admitted over the next few years, the law afforded only a minimum of relief to black mineworkers. Despite the force of Orenstein's appeal to capitalist self-interest, he and others had to labour long before state and industry fully accepted the basic principle of protecting human resources.

The Native Labour Regulation Act of 1911 made the DNL responsible for assessing compensation for personal injury to 'native labourers'. Between £1 and £20 was awarded for partial temporary incapacitation (inability to resume work due to injury), £30 to £50 for permanent, total incapacitation and £10 for death. No compensation was payable where the accident was due to 'serious or wilful misconduct' on the part of the injured man. It was left up to the DNL to decide how payment would be made to the labourer or his dependents.[10]

The Workmen's Compensation Act of 1914, which replaced provincial legislation in Natal, the Cape and the Transvaal, covered Africans who did not qualify as 'native labourers' under the NLR Act.[11] Workers had the choice of either suing the employer under common law or instituting proceedings under the 1914 Act. The latter course involved delivering a written statement of the case to the magistrate's court (if the applicant was illiterate, the clerk of the court was supposed to complete this). Compensation was based on loss of wages and the assessment and method of payment were left to the magistrate's discretion. The Department of Mines and Industries administered the Act until 1924, when it was passed to the Labour Department.

The problem of silicosis from mineral dust was dealt with in the Miners Phthisis Act of 1919, which consolidated previous legislation. A new Miners Phthisis Board was appointed by the Minister of Mines to administer the Act, with a nominally independent Miners' Phthisis Medical Bureau to examine suspected cases of silicosis.[12] 'Scheduled' mines (that is, mines which were officially recognised as producing silicotic dust) paid a lump sum to underground labourers who contracted silicosis. Calculations were based on the mine labourer's average monthly earnings and depended on the stage the disease had reached. By contrast, white miners were paid much higher settlements in the form of pensions through a Consolidated Revenue Fund. The state claimed it would be too difficult to pay pensions to Africans in remote areas, even though machinery for remitting wages was already in place.[13] The mineowners further argued that whites deserved better compensation as their permanent status on the mines made them much more susceptible to respiratory diseases. With the election of the Pact Government and its promise of a new deal for the white working class, the Act was revised in 1925, but the changes did not greatly affect blacks. According to the Miners' Phthisis Board, from 1919-29 Africans received average benefits of £37 for ante-primary silicosis, £55 for primary silicosis, £72 for secondary silicosis and £50 for simple tuberculosis.[14]

Major changes were instituted in the Miners' Phthisis Act of 1925, the Silicosis Act of 1946, the WC Acts of 1934 and 1941 and the amendment to the WC Act in 1945. In each case, separate sections were drawn up for Africans suffering from injuries and respiratory diseases.[15] Discrimination against black workers was further extended in the 1934 WC Act, which enshrined lower rates of compensation in the actual statute, rather than merely in the regulations. Administrative segregation was retained by allowing the DNL to function as an intermediary between the

Miners' Phthisis Board or WC Commissioner and the African worker.

These laws did not evolve without problems. From about 1927, officials in the Native Affairs and Labour Departments became heavily involved in attempts to develop a new system of compensation. Ultimately, the politicians determined the extent of changes in the legislation when they reviewed the bills in the four Select Committees of 1931 to 1932 and 1934, but the civil servants played an important part in drafting bills and giving evidence to parliamentary committees.[16]

The GNLB's heightened interest in compensation was originally triggered by fears of African protests. From 1926-30, NAD officials were worried about the rapid growth of Clements Kadalie's Industrial and Commercial Workers' Union and the possible effects this would have on black worker militancy. As Cooke wrote to the SNA JF Herbst, in 1927, the department must be seen to take the initiative 'before it is made a plank in the policy of the Industrial and Commercial Workers' Union or other organisation concerned with native welfare'.[17] The DNL was particularly worried about discrepancies between compensation offered under the NLR and WC Acts. He wanted to introduce revised scales under a bill for compensation for African workmen, including £90 (instead of £10) if a labourer died. The Chamber of Mines accepted Cooke's figures without much argument.[18] They also agreed that no payment should be offered for temporary incapacity if the injured man were housed, fed and treated at the employer's expense.[19]

This meeting of minds between the GNLB and the Chamber of Mines in the early 1930s arose partly out of a conjunction of interests between them. The mineowners saw Cooke's scheme as less costly than assessing all African labourers under the WC Act which, the mines claimed, would more than double their liabilities for injuries from £33 000 to £80 to £90 000 per annum. As in other areas, the mines preferred segregated administration by the NAD, as this contributed to maintaining divisions between white and black workers.

In his dealings with the mineowners, the DNL may have felt constrained by the enormous political influence wielded by the Chamber of Mines. At the same time, as his later reaction to the Department of Labour's draft bill would suggest, he was concerned to maintain his power in this area, not only because it represented an important part of his duties, but also for the public relations value it offered. Among the black population being seen to hand out benefits to sick and needy families helped to balance some of the sub-department's more repressive functions. As Herbst wrote to his minister, EG Jansen, in 1932, there was no point in the NAD being involved in compensation payments if its officials could not reap the credit for them.[20] Within the state, the DNL was also anxious to preserve his department's status as the experts on black labour questions.

In defending his authority, the DNL found himself at odds with the Labour Department, which wanted to bring all workers not subject to the NLR Act under the same authority. In 1930, a Technical Committee (headed by the departmental Chief Clerk and later Wage Board Chairman, Frank McGregor, but excluding representatives from the NAD) produced a draft bill which incorporated African labourers in a special chapter.[21] A Workmen's Compensation Commissioner and Board were to be established under the auspices of the Labour Department. Employers were to be obliged to insure all workers against injury. The bill provided for higher rates of compensation for blacks than those under the NLR Act. The insurance scheme it proposed meant that Africans were much more likely to receive their benefits than they were under the 1914 Act.[22] Temporary total disability was to be compensated at the rate of sixty per cent of monthly earnings for six months; the permanently disabled were to receive lump sums beginning at £75, depending on the degree of disability and monthly earnings.[23] A parliamentary Select Committee reviewed the draft bill in 1931 and again three years later, but it was passed in substantially the same form in 1934.[24]

The DNL attacked the bill on the grounds that its provisions were much too complicated for African workers. Unscrupulous

lawyers would be encouraged to intervene on their behalf and
workers would lose their common law rights and the 'protection'
of the GNLB.[25] Faced with a possible loss of power, Cooke
retreated from his earlier proposal of a redrafted WC Bill for
Africans and recommended an amendment to the NLR Act.
However, the GNLB's qualms now counted for little: the Labour
Department's only concession was to offer the DNL the job of
assessor for Africans in labour districts. In May 1934, Herbst,
never one to resist government directives, ordered Cooke to drop
his opposition, ostensibly for the sake of securing the benefits
that the Act offered African workers.[26] The GNLB settled down
to its new duties, though the DNL and the Workmen's Compensation Commissioner argued over the interpretation of the
statute for years to come.[27]

The GNLB was not only motivated by personal interests. In
fact, the DNL fought a number of battles to turn the administration to the better advantage of the African labourer. For example,
on the question of medical examinations under the 1925 Miners'
Phthisis Act, Cooke criticised the experts from the Medical
Bureau and the Mine Medical Officers' Association.[28] He argued
that the system of weeding out tuberculosis sufferers by weighing miners fully clad as they came off shift, was inadequate.
Instead, Cooke persuaded the mines to introduce periodic stetho-
scopic examinations. The Mines continued to resist X-rays, the
only sure way of detecting early lung disease. In 1929, when the
government's law advisers ruled that African miners should be
compensated on the basis of accommodation and rations as well
as cash wages, Cooke tried to persuade the Chamber of Mines to
increase its assessment of wages per shift by 1s 4d.[29] The TCM
made an undignified about-turn. Whereas the mineowners had
previously stressed the value of incidental services to migrants,
they now said that they were not worth much at all. The mines
argued, to more effect, that the original intention of the Act was to
base compensation on cash wages alone.[30] The SNA and the Secretary for Mines and Industries overruled the DNL's efforts and
the matter was held over until it could be settled by legislation.[31]

Cooke made several other attempts to turn regulations (and legislation) to the benefit of black workers. In 1931, he told the Select Committee on the WC Bill that farm labourers should be brought under the Act and that a start should be made in paying pensions to Africans.[32] His more enlightened initiatives were generally condemned by higher authority. It was all very well for the GNLB to retain a role in administering the Acts, but the politicians and big employers would not allow a branch of the bureaucracy to hold too much power in matters of such enormous financial import. In this, they were helped by the way the laws operated: rates of compensation were drawn up in advance and placed in the statute books. The government did not allow the DNL as much autonomy over compensation as it did in other areas of labour regulation.

In the later 1930s and 1940s, several factors operated to improve Miners' Phthisis and Workmen's Compensation payments for all races. The Purified National Party, founded in 1934, mobilised poor Afrikaners on these issues and raised public awareness of the declining health standards of white workers.[33] One must add to this the pressure from white liberal interests which, from about 1936, highlighted the maltreatment of African workers under existing legislation. The Native Representative Council and the MPs elected by Africans were also involved in this effort.[34] By the 1940s, boom conditions in primary and secondary industry made employers more willing to shoulder their most obvious responsibilities to the workforce. The simultaneous expansion of trade unionism among black and white workers and, from 1939, the government's desire to avoid major confrontations during the war, encouraged the state and employers to agree to improved conditions. Within the state, proponents of increased compensation could count on the support of key figures in the civil service, including the Secretary for Labour, Ivan Walker, Public Health Department officials such as Peter Allan (who conducted the first survey of the spread of TB in rural areas in the 1920s), Harry Gear and George Gale, and the SNA Douglas Smit.[35]

Under the 1941 WC Act, temporary total disablement was assessed at 66.7 per cent of earnings (instead of 60 per cent) and lump sums for the permanently disabled were raised by similar proportions. The Silicosis Act of 1946 extended the list of diseases and established new compensation rates for African mineworkers.[36] The government anticipated that this would increase the scheduled mines' liability from £125 000 to £275 000 per annum as well as raising their net outstanding liability for blacks by £2m. The largest benefit was for silicosis, which entitled a labourer to thirty-six times his monthly earnings or £180, whichever was the greater.[37] Both Acts improved benefits to injured and sick black workers.

Even so, the new legislation was not as ground-breaking as the Smuts government liked to imply. Disability payments under the WC Act were assessed as fractions of workers' wages. As these were in the main notoriously low, compensation payments left the labourer and his family well below the poverty line. The lack of pensions under either law allowed employers to wash their hands of black workers after paying out the initial lump sum. In the case of the Silicosis Act, this meant sufferers from respiratory diseases could not apply for more support as their condition deteriorated. As a White Paper of 1945 explained, their only recourse outside the Act was to the DNL's special silicosis fund, consisting of 'unexpended balances'.[38] This provided minimal relief for disease-racked former mineworkers who had used up their lump sums.

By 1948, the state had expanded the system of compensation introduced in the first decade after Union. The civil service played a significant part in this process but did not equal its importance in certain other spheres. Successive governments limited the autonomy of their civil servants and used the separate administration for black workers to apply discriminatory compensation laws. The reservations of at least one DNL were ignored and compensation for injured and sick African labourers and their families was kept well below that of white workers.

'Outdoor Relief' for the Urban African Proletariat

In the 1930s and 1940s, South Africa took the first faltering steps towards the establishment of a 'welfare state'. Some of the reasons for this were the same as those for increases in compensation and included advances in the organisation and economic muscle of white and black workers; political pressure from the National and Labour Parties and protests from white liberal groups, liberal MPs and black political organisations, such as the ANC. More specifically, heightened public awareness of the 'poor white' problem in the 1930s, fuelled in part by meetings of the Afrikaner nationalist Volkskongres, the Report of the Carnegie Commission and the 1936 National Conference on Social Work, encouraged the government in the direction of social welfare.[39] In 1935, the Labour Department was renamed the Department of Labour and Social Welfare, and two years later a separate Department of Social Welfare was established.

A second major factor behind the beginnings of state-sponsored relief for the underprivileged arose from white perceptions of African living conditions in and around white urban areas. ' "Horrible" Native Townships', the *Rand Daily Mail* proclaimed in 1935: 'Hovels and mangy dogs: Plague spots that must be cleared up'.[40] The emphasis here was on the plague aspect. Besides being an outrage to the conscience, the spread of slum conditions, malnutrition and disease among black people was a 'positive danger to the community' and required remedial action by the state. While health services were recognised as a necessity in both the rural and urban contexts, the forms of 'outdoor relief' discussed in this section, namely pensions, unemployment benefits and subsidised housing, were primarily aimed at the urban-dwelling, proletarianised population. All branches of the state agreed that mine employees were well enough cared for under existing provisions, whereas white farmers were considered too poor to contribute to such schemes for their workers. The government took action where opposition nationalists most demanded it. It treated the symptoms where they impinged on white sensitivities and quality of life.[41]

Neither of these factors would have shifted the state towards social planning if it had not been for events overseas. In America, President FD Roosevelt introduced the Social Security Act in 1935. In doing so, he was consciously following legislation in Germany, Denmark and Austria.[42] Even more important for South Africa was wartime planning in Britain, especially by the Beveridge Commission on Social Services, which reported in 1942. In the words of the British social scientist, Victor George:

> There is no doubt that the promised improvements in social services were seen by the government as part of the strategy of winning the war; it was felt that such improvements, in the words of Galbraith referring to the American situation, 'would reassure those who were fighting as to their eventual utility as citizens'. Plans for the re-organization of the education, the employment, the social security and other services were prepared and widely discussed during the war years.[43]

The wartime Smuts government was just as eager to reassure its citizens that they were fighting for a better future. Following the British example, it appointed wartime commissions to formulate health and welfare schemes. These were supposed to ensure a better quality of life for all. No matter that the state could not immediately effect the plans – the important thing was to keep people's minds focused on the post-war era, when a much expanded economy and welfare-minded state would deliver all things to all men. The government naturally enlisted the assistance and expertise of its civil servants. Officials in the Labour, Public Health, Social Welfare and Native Affairs Departments helped to formulate schemes in all the aforementioned areas.

From the start, the departments were anxious to portray their efforts as a meaningful contribution to living standards. The Departments of Public Health and Labour, which administered housing and unemployment benefit legislation respectively, were themselves products of a 'changing pattern of society'. Their purported function was to 'improve economic and social conditions'. Like the Social Welfare Department, they claimed to promote these ends on a colour-blind basis. The NAD could hardly make similar boasts. Its officials manipulated (and, to a certain extent, were manipulated by) a different legitimating ethos, based on trusteeship and protection. The degree to which officials in each department stuck to these lofty principles was displayed in the evolution of social welfare laws and in their application.

The influenza epidemic of 1918 underlined the fact that disease knows no colour and was one of the original impulses behind the Public Health Act (1919). However, the Public Health Department had limited powers and financial resources. Its chief purpose was to give advice to other departments and to private employers. Moreover, although the Act made no specific reference to race in any of its nine chapters, the fact that the bulk of health provisions were to be applied by local and provincial authorities rather than by the central state department meant that the department could not enforce equal treatment for all the races in health care. In any case, as a memorandum penned in 1921 suggests, Public Health officials were not thinking in terms of equality. White 'equity and justice towards the natives themselves' were factors requiring consideration, but the real reason for taking action on such issues as housing for blacks was to protect the white population against 'native discontent ... and the carriage of disease from natives to whites'.[44]

This view was expressed by P Targett Adams, Assistant Health Officer, in his 1921 report on Native Locations. The Secretary for Public Health, JA Mitchell, was himself unusually well acquainted with the miserable social conditions prevailing in Cape Town's African locations.[45] Yet despite this awareness, neither the will nor the money was available for the Public Health Department to launch large scale housing schemes for Africans or to enforce decent standards of planning, construction, hygiene and sanitation. The Housing Act of 1920 established a Central Housing Board (CHB) under the department's aegis to provide government loans for approved schemes. But it was left to local authorities to decide whether to take up the offer, and the money was loaned at market rates. By the end of 1930, only 7 609 dwellings had been built for Africans and coloureds with loans provided under the Act. A large proportion of these were single rooms in barracks, while many of the actual houses had only two rooms.[46] From 1930, the government approved sub-economic loans for housing for the 'poorer classes' but excluded Africans from this category until 1934. From that year, munici-palities could build location housing using state funds at two per cent interest (in 1936, the interest was reduced to three-quarters of a per cent). The initiative was still left with local authorities. Central state bureaucrats were well aware that municipalities were not taking advantage of the scheme. For example, Mitchell's successor as Secretary for Public Health, Sir Edward Thornton, sat on the 1935 commission which found that Johan-nesburg had been clearing slums under the 1934 Slums Act with-out building sufficient new housing in the locations.[47] Even so, the Department of Public Health preferred not to interfere. As Thornton informed the Cape Eastern Public Bodies in 1936:

> In addition, large sums of money at low rates of interest have been lent to local authorities for native housing, and further sums are available. It is not considered possible for the department to obtain parliamentary sanction for the making of further grants to local authorities.[48]

By 1939, the state had approved £3 750 823 in sub-economic loans 'to assist low-paid workers in receipt of wages too small to permit of their participating' under the economic housing scheme. Again, this figure was an aggregate for black and coloured people. A total of £5 445 100 had been lent from the sub-economic fund, which was set at £13m. Nearly 13 000 dwellings had been built for 'non-Europeans' under the sub-economic scheme and 10 000 constructed under the economic scheme.[49]

It was not until World War II that the state began to take the shortage of affordable housing seriously. By this time, the situation was acute. Whereas the 1920 Housing Committee estimated a shortfall of 10 000 houses, the 1936 Public Health Department Report put the figure at 16 000 in the eight largest cities alone; by 1942, accelerated urbanisation had made things even worse (see Appendix 3). The Smit Committee found 'large numbers' of Africans living in makeshift dwellings. The shacks were insanitary, overcrowded, had no foundations or protection against damp and were overrun by vermin.[50] Even when housing was provided by local authorities, there was overcrowding in 'most, if not all' dwellings, because high rents forced tenants to take in lodgers and relatives. Overcrowding was a prime factor in the spread of infectious diseases, such as tuberculosis. The problem was compounded by the lack of washing facilities, latrines and refuse disposal services.[51]

Both the Thornton Committee on Peri-Urban Areas (1938-9) and the Smit Committee (1942) gave officials the opportunity to voice their dissatisfaction.[52] The Smit Report called for the accelerated development of housing schemes and suggested municipalities should make up the losses from their General Revenues, and not solely from their Native Revenue Accounts. A further spur for the government came from squatting movements which mushroomed around Johannesburg from 1944. In that year, the Housing Amendment Act abolished the CHB and set up the National Housing and Planning Commission (NHPC), the Natal Housing Board and an advisory body called the National Housing Council. The Housing (Emergency Powers) Act of 1945 allowed the central state to take the initiative by undertaking housing schemes and recouping the costs from local authorities.[53] In the process, the state came to see low-cost housing not just as an aspect of public health or as a means to control the urban proletariat, but also as part of the wider task of social welfare provision. It was no longer simply a question of providing the minimum safety net. The government was now supposed to be thinking on a grand scale, planning for after the war when workers of all races would not accept the poor lot they had put up with for so long. As a 1944 House of Assembly resolution read by Labour MP for Krugersdorp, MJ van den Berg, stated:

> This House requests the Government to consider the advisability of introducing a comprehensive programme of legislation and administrative measures embracing the subjects of the provision of employment, social security, housing and public health, nutrition and education, such programme to constitute the people's charter as the outcome of the war.[54]

One indication of this, in administrative terms, was the increased involvement of the Social Welfare Department in housing provision. For example, it was the Minister of Social Welfare, rather than the Public Health Minister, who was given the powers to expropriate land and limit contractors' and suppliers' profits under the 1945 Act.

The NHPC speeded up the rate of building at sub-economic rates. In 1947, the Commission financed 10 355 'assisted' dwellings at a cost of £4 667 531. Yet there was still a marked difference between the size of the problem and the attitudes which prevailed in the various departments as well as the extent of the state's commitment. The Smit Report asserted the traditional NAD position when it argued that the government would not engender 'gratitude and appreciation' by waiting until progressive measures were inevitable.[55] In effect, the Committee (which also included senior members of the Public Health and Social Welfare Departments) saw welfare work primarily in terms of limiting unrest. The Public Health Department's own reports for 1946 to 1948 show that officials still preferred to pass the buck to the municipalities, despite the state's new powers.[56] The government itself soon showed signs of flinching at the size of the crisis. It imposed limits on losses under assisted schemes, while the

Treasury left the NHPC doubting whether it would be granted the necessary funding. There were signs that the Treasury would make further funds available in the last few months of the Smuts era, but the outgoing government bequeathed a huge and escalating problem to the National Party.[57]

Africans also accrued increased pensions and unemployment payments as a result of government-sponsored investigations into post-war social welfare provision. The impetus came in part from the Social and Economic Planning Council (SEPC), set up in 1942 as a semi-official body reporting to the Prime Minister on social and economic conditions and policies. The SEPC embraced social security as one of its basic 'guiding principles' and sought to advance schemes which were within the 'productive capacity' of the country.[58] The Council secured the appointment of the Social Security Committee in 1943, which included several senior civil servants: P Allan, Secretary for Public Health, GAC Kuschke, Secretary for Social Welfare, WJG Mears, Under Secretary for Native Affairs and IL Walker, Secretary for Labour. When it reported the following year, the Social Security Committee advocated a full programme of pensions, and health and unemployment insurance.[59] This was to be the 'welfare state' providing minimum subsistence standards for all contributors, plus a system of smaller benefits for Africans in the reserves.

Having already accepted the need for social security, the government could not dismiss this report out of hand. Instead, Smuts shifted SF Waterson from Commerce and Industry to the new position of Minister of Economic Development.[60] As Chairman of both the Inter-departmental Committee on Social Security and the Select Committee on Social Security, Waterson whittled down the rates set by the 1943 Social Security Committee. The government's White Paper on Social Security carried this a step further in 1945, proposing to restrict state expenditure on pensions, contributory schemes and other allowances.[61]

The laws passed in the war years were even smaller in scope. The Pensions Laws Amendment Act of 1944, which brought Africans under pension legislation for the first time, established three levels of £21, £9 and £6 per annum, depending on whether the recipient lived in a city, town or rural area.[62] Prospective pensioners were subject to means tests of £18, £13 10s and £9 respectively. By the end of 1946, Native Commissioners operating on behalf of the Pensions Commissioner were giving out 140 000 pensions. The NAD estimated the eventual number of participants at 367 000, with an anticipated annual expenditure of £2 336 000.[63] Blind people were provided for at the same rates. Grants for invalids were issued at the SNA's discretion at an anticipated expenditure of £781 000. Poor relief grants could be made in exceptional cases. This might involve local relief of famine, drought and epidemics, with feeding schemes for pre-school children and short-term work projects for the semifit.[64] The Act fell far short of the minimum subsistence envisioned by the SEPC, but it put a considerable strain on local NAD officials. Once again, the government's policy of 'doing it on the cheap' meant woefully inadequate payments for people without any other means of subsistence, coupled with much extra work for the NAD, whose role in welfare administration for blacks expanded through the 1940s.

The Unemployment Insurance Act of 1946 was a direct product of the 1944 Social Security Committee Report and the 1945 White Paper on Social Security.[65] The original law of 1937 permitted the establishment of unemployment benefit funds by employers and unions in certain scheduled industries. The number of Africans affected was kept to a minimum through the exclusion of labourers regulated by the NLR Act as well as those earning less than £78 per annum.[66] The government claimed the new Act would cover about 700 000 workers under a central Unemployment Insurance Fund. The lowest paid were to contribute 3d a week, while the state and employer put in 9d each. The smallest benefits would be about £5 per month which the government accurately predicted, 'should not be so high as to affect the stimulus to work'.[67] The Act was to be administered by the Department of Labour, with local work performed by Magistrates.[68]

The 1945 White Paper deliberately left vague the issue of which classes of employee would be brought under the Act. From late 1945 until the Unemployment Insurance Act was passed in 1946, this became a focus of conflict between the Departments of Labour, Mines and Native Affairs as well as the NAC, Natives Representative Council and the Chamber of Mines. The confrontation began when the TCM realised the government's proposals would include South African miners and others not subject to compulsory repatriation. The thought of paying ninepence a week for some 200 000 labourers from the Union and the High Commission territories horrified the mine-owners, who used every argument they could think of to excuse themselves.[69] The TCM claimed in March 1946 that workers would resent the statutory deductions; their fixed contracts would mean they would never benefit from the scheme; the Social Security Committee had only supported contributions for urban dwellers; the plan would encourage black former miners to swell the ranks of the urban unemployed; and any such levy on the mines would have nasty repercussions on working costs and therefore on the national economy.[70]

The Chamber enjoyed the full support of the Department of Mines, then under the ministerial guidance of Colonel Stallard.[71] The SNA, WJG Mears, provided further backing, arguing that the scheme would be impossible to administer because of impersonations and the difficulty of making migrants from remote areas appear before claims officers. Mears argued that mineworkers who stayed on in the towns and found other employment would be brought under the Act anyway. Although he couched his language in administrative terms, his underlying concern may well have been to preserve the system of migrant labour which his department oversaw. The entire system would have been seriously undermined if ex-miners were given the means to remain in the towns and look for more lucrative jobs. The scheme would also interfere with the government's commitment to influx control, reasserted in the 1945 Natives (Urban Areas) Consolidation Act.[72] The SNA eventually accepted a compromise offered by the Labour Advisory Board and the NAC, that the mines should be spared from paying contributions for workers whose return fares were provided by the employer. This forced a real monetary concession from the mines, while also bolstering the long term future of the migrant labour system and discouraging the drift to the towns with all its contingent social problems.[73]

The mines' chief opponent (other than the ineffectual Native Representative Council) was the Secretary for Labour, FLA Buchanan. Like the Chamber and the NAD, he put his case in practical and economic terms. On the first count, Buchanan saw no reason to exclude a large and wealthy group of employers like the mines, who would be hit no harder than any other business. For administrators it was very hard to distinguish between 'tribal' and 'urban' Africans, as many migrants already drifted between the towns, mines and rural areas. The scheme would provide real coverage for the unemployed and it could not be made economical unless the 'good risk paid for the bad'. The Labour Department also pointed to a possibly adverse international reaction: the ILO would not ratify the Act unless it included the mining sector. If the TCM was really worried about the mineworkers' negative reactions to contributing towards the scheme, Buchanan added slyly, they could always pay the employees' share themselves.[74]

The Department of Labour needed the mining industry's support to make the new law work. Labour officials were unlikely to worry if it later transpired that African miners could not get a return on their threepence a day. However, the government came down heavily on the side of the mining industry. The 1946 Act specifically excluded African gold and coal workers who were provided with accommodation and food, along with farm labourers, domestics, Africans employed in rural areas (but not in factories) and casual labourers.[75]

The government thus reduced the potential threat from African unemployment in the towns, where the problem would be most visible and where workers were better organised. It also dealt with it at a time when business was booming, before any peacetime slump could swell the ranks of the jobless. Given the government's waning support among whites in the mid- to late 1940s, its attempts to provide a social safety net for Africans may have been politically foolish. Its measures were not sufficient to satisfy critics on the left, but were more than sufficient to provide ammunition for the Malanite nationalist opposition. In taking the steps it did, the state was responding more to long-term planners in South Africa and to the example of developments overseas. It envisaged a social welfare programme fit for a fully developed, industrial economy, on American or British lines.

On the other hand, the government effectively rejected the SEPC's call for 'minimum protection against want'. Instead it paid heed to the needs of the most important sector in terms of revenue and to political fears of alienating white voters by raising taxation or demanding contributions from farmers. So, the debate over unemployment benefits for the post-war era ended, as did that over pensions and housing, in something less than half a loaf for the African population.

The SEPC saw the debate as the direct result of the war. It 'broadened the social conscience' and 'showed what could be achieved by deliberate organisation'.[76] To SEPC members, this meant planning by experts, including scientific management of resources by people without political bias – academics, administrators, representatives of business and capital and groups involved in social work of various kinds. This followed developments in Britain, where Beveridge's Interdepartmental Committee on Social Insurance and Allied Services was already writing the blueprint for Britain's welfare state.[77] Locally, the social welfare debate increased in stridency during the 1930s, at a time when rapid industrialisation and townward migration were causing unprecedented social problems.

Faced with the peculiar demands of the wartime situation, the Smuts government adopted the language of the international social reform movement and gave the impression that much thought was being put into creating a better world for all. Founding such bodies as the NHPC, the SEPC and the National Health

Council allowed the government to appear committed, while in fact it held back to weigh the political and financial costs. State civil servants generally welcomed these initiatives. The occasional repudiation of their proposals by a semi-governmental organisation, as in the conflict between the Labour Department and the NAC and Labour Advisory Board over unemployment insurance, was still irritating, but the freedom permitted to the bureaucrats as they sat on committees of experts, planning for the future without the usual restraints of budget votes and anxious political masters, could not have been inimical to their sense of prestige.

Nevertheless, the government had no intention of taking more from all the proposals and counter-proposals than it felt was politically necessary or financially expedient. The Smuts regime in its last years was not a reforming government set on implementing a new deal for all its citizens. Rather, it was a hard-pressed coalition, torn by pressures arising from the Opposition's growing popularity among Afrikaners. Black working class poverty and unrest were taken seriously in the later 1940s; but in the eyes of the government, it was easier to contain them with repression and half measures than to risk a white backlash to the introduction of an expensive 'welfare state'.

'Mother Wit' versus National Medical Health Services

The development of a mining economy from the 1860s onwards had an enormous impact on public health. Overcrowding, landlessness, very low wages and poor conditions affected the bulk of the working population. With the mineral revolution, agricultural transformation and industrial growth, came malnutrition and infectious diseases. No part of the country was safe. Migrant mineworkers continued to carry tuberculosis back to the rural areas (though there was a sharp decline in the incidence of TB on the mines from the 1920s and again after the introduction in the 1940s of X-rays for all mineworkers). As the Native Economic Commission observed in 1932, Africans in the rural areas faced a bleak future: 'a desolate picture of denudation and erosion' in parts of the Ciskei; the spread of weeds, overstocking and erosion in the Transkei; low yields and no irrigation in the Free State; 'general congestion' of people and cattle in the Transvaal; and sleeping sickness and malaria in Natal (the latter was alleviated in the 1930s by local malaria committees and the NAD under the guidance of the Public Health Department).[78] Malnutrition was common in various parts of the country; it caused deficiency diseases (such as scurvy) and lowered resistance to infections.[79]

Conditions in the towns were no better. Municipalities were slow to apply basic regulations on sanitation and garbage disposal. Councils insisted on self-balancing Native Revenue Accounts. Some diverted revenue from Africans for other purposes instead of making money available to improve locations.[80] Infectious diseases spread rapidly in the cramped and overcrowded conditions of town life.[81] In 1940, there were 2 000 doctors in the country for a total population of over 10 000 000.[82] Existing health services, in the towns and in rural areas, did not come close to meeting the needs of the people. To quote from the National Health Services Commission appointed by Smuts in 1942 and headed by Dr Henry Gluckman, who was to become Minister of Health:

> Poverty denies many of the resources of modern medicine to large sections of the population, who under existing conditions can only attain medical help through the charity of individuals or voluntary organisations quite unable to provide the full range of modern therapeutic measures; or through the inadequate facilities afforded them by the district surgeoncy system and free beds in public hospitals.[83]

Two of the problems identified by the Gluckman Commission were the 'limited conception of public health which obtained in 1919' (when the Act was passed) and the complex division of powers between local, provincial and central authorities.[84]

Although parliament had the power to override provincial authorities, the provinces administered general hospitals and had overall control of local authorities and pauper relief. Local authorities handled non-personal matters such as sanitation, water, hygiene and outbreaks of infectious diseases.

Under the 1919 Act, the Union government took charge of district surgeons (who, as part-time servants of the state, were supposed to provide for indigent patients) and leper and mental hospitals. As the Gluckman Report put it, this still left considerable work for 'mother wit' in the training of personnel. From the 1920s, though, the Public Health Department found itself building hospitals for other communicable diseases, including venereal diseases and tuberculosis. Local authorities were expected to contribute to maintenance. By an amendment of 1935, the department began to support district nursing services. Two years later, following the Report of the Inter-Departmental Committee on Poor Relief and Charitable Institutions, poor relief services (except in Natal) were transferred to the Department of Social Welfare.[85]

Two other laws referred more specifically to African workers. The Native Labour Regulation Act allowed the government to issue regulations on medical examinations and vaccinations of labourers and their families, the care of the sick or injured, and measures to prevent communicable diseases.[86] The Public Health Department played a role in enforcing these regulations. It encouraged large employers to build their own hospitals, laid down minimum conditions and, on occasion, assisted the DNL in investigating allegations of maltreatment.[87] The department also supervised medical examinations of African males at Pass Offices in the larger urban centres, under the 1923 Urban Areas Act.[88] On the negative side, the examinations were perfunctory, partly because doctors believed they were inadequately remunerated for their services. In the 1920s and 1930s, the department repeatedly refused to include women or to introduce further periodic tests.[89] The purpose of the examinations was more to reassure the white public that their towns were not awash with disease carriers than to protect the health of African workers.

The fact that health care was divided between so many different authorities and under several laws made it at once easier to ignore the lack of provision for Africans and harder to do anything about it. The department published annually the upward trend in the number of hospital beds available to 'non-Europeans', showing a steady rise from 12 520 in 1932, to 23 593 in 1946.[90] But these were total figures, including mine and factory hospitals, mission hospitals, private nursing homes and provincial and general hospitals. The number of beds in the department's own infectious diseases institutions rose from 1 081 to 2 340 in the same period.

In the later 1930s, Hertzog's government resisted pressure from both the Purified National Party and the Labour Party to create a national health insurance scheme for whites. However, in 1942, as part of the ongoing planning for the post-war era, the National Health Services Commission was appointed.[91] Marks shows the role of the Native Affairs and Public Health Departments in this process. The NAD was calling for a rural health scheme from the late 1930s. The Chamber of Mines had considered (though not provided) financial aid to improve the health of migrant labourers at source.[92] The Smit Committee of 1942, which included prominent members of the Native Affairs and Public Health Departments, recommended increasing the subsidy for health visitors and district nurses, and introducing compulsory child welfare and maternity schemes.[93]

As Public Health files on hospitals and medical services show, officials in that department were divided on their commitment to a comprehensive health care system.[94] George Gale's appointment in 1938 added an important voice to those calling internally for preventive care clinics.[95] On the other hand, the department had long been concerned about the cost of such a scheme and did not open the first clinic (at Polela in Natal) until the provincial authorities threatened to close their African hospitals for lack of funds. The department feared for its own position in the early 1940s in the face of calls from the medical profession for a national health service. Finally, senior officials dropped their opposition and George Gale guided Gluckman in drawing up the report which was published in 1944. But the Smuts government rejected the national health scheme outlined in the report as too expensive.[96] The one positive outcome, the establishment of another fifty health centres in the next five years, withered away in the 1950s as the National Party government sought alternative solutions for improving Afrikaner health.

Even without the extra administrative difficulties involved in this area, neither the Public Health Department nor the central state as a whole possessed the will to develop a basic health care system for Africans. When the need had become too obvious to disguise in the later 1930s, officials had maintained the polite fiction that the change was due to the increased African regard for western medicine rather than to widespread poverty and disease.[97] It was only in the 1940s with the publication of the Smit Committee Report, the SEPC Reports, the Van Eck Commission and, most importantly, the Gluckman Report, that the state was forced to admit the need for change. Senior personnel in the Public Health Department had long supported the government in its unwillingness to press local authorities beyond the barest minimum requirements; in its attitude that public health was about preventing white people catching diseases from blacks; and in its fear of heavy demands on the public purse, or adverse effects on the medical profession. At the same time, officials such as Park Ross (at Durban), Allan, Gear and Gale had tried hard to improve public health within the limits of their powers and resources. The degree of autonomy they were allowed by the government, the lack of consensus within the department and the effects of severe financial constraints and white public opinion in general, are reflected in the half measures they had achieved by 1948.

Conclusion

The manner in which successive governments organised compensation, subsidised housing, 'outdoor relief', and medical services, speaks volumes about what they regarded as the state's basic priorities. The underlying structure for compensation, housing and health care already existed by the early 1920s. Yet, it was only with the pressures of the 1930s and 1940s, coupled with shifts in the public debate about what the role of the state should be, that they were expanded beyond the bare minimum. Even then, the Smuts government used the apparatus of committees and commissions to appear more enthusiastic about health and welfare than it actually was. In the meantime, the government remained committed to winning the war before implementing any full scale revisions.

It remains to be explained why the state was so unwilling to accept responsibility for health and welfare. The chief factor here was cost. White voters were afraid of disease among Africans, but they would not have welcomed substantial tax increases for black social services. As the TCM showed in its protests against unemployment insurance, the mines were strongly opposed to social policies which interfered with low wage migrant labour, or with profits. In parliament, the Nationalists attacked the government for wasting taxpayers' money on Africans and thereby encouraging the black influx to the towns.[98] More specifically, Dr K Bremer, a leading National Party spokesman on health, argued that South Africa could not afford public health for the entire African population until Africans 'contributed to the national economy'.[99] Once the need for wartime propaganda passed and both political parties began to focus their attention on the first peacetime general election, the government judged the time unpropitious for heavy spending on the disenfranchised majority.

The SEPC, Social Security and National Health Services Commissions had done their planning without detailed attention to cost constraints. The SEPC, for example, recommended increasing social security and health spending by over 200 per cent by 1948 (from £17.5m to £52m). The Select Committee endorsed the spirit of the SEPC Report but called for drastic cuts to the original plan, amounting to £32.5m.[100] The Gluckman Report put the cost of a national health scheme (for the central government) at £12m, with further expenditure by provincial and local authorities.[101] In parliament, the government accepted the Gluckman Report in principle, but stressed that it could not be implemented overnight. It made Gluckman Minister of Health, created an advisory committee and a co-ordinating council and built relatively inexpensive health centres. The government did not envisage expenditure on the scale proposed in the Gluckman Report. Provincial administrations, which controlled general hospitals, also strongly opposed a rapid, costly expansion in their facilities and the government rejected coercion.[102] As a result, legislation passed between 1945 and 1948 on unemployment insurance, pensions, housing and health care, did not approach the heady expectations of wartime planners.

As in its regulation of working conditions, the state's participation in health and welfare further serves to illustrate its use of propaganda to buttress its power. The fact that some of this propaganda originated overseas and was promoted by specific branches of the state, which thereby found themselves at odds with other branches, did not necessarily work to the government's disadvantage. The former merely helped to show that the Union was in step with the rest of the world, and must be seen within the context of its efforts to maintain close ties with other western nations, and to prevent the isolation of South Africa in the post-war era. The latter allowed the government to appear to be providing a forum for the expression of different views while in fact coming down heavily in favour of a narrow vision of the 'welfare state'. Nonetheless, the line purveyed in speeches, press releases and official publications always emphasised the state's commitment to developing better welfare provisions. That there were limits to the extent to which civil servants could oppose or reject this position is shown in George Gale's chapter in the 1949 *Handbook of Race Relations*. As Secretary for Public Health, Gale was forced to temper his long-standing contempt for the state's inactivity and to toe the official line about ongoing improvements in health services.[103]

The study of health and welfare provides us with valuable

evidence of how the central state interacted with other authorities at the provincial and local levels as well as in the business world, and how it operated within its own entanglement of laws and departments. The complexity of state apparatuses allowed officials to 'pass the buck'. They deflected criticisms onto other authorities and salved their consciences with the comforting thought that it was not their duty to interfere. This was critical in health care, with its overlapping jurisdictions. It was also important in such areas as workmen's compensation and unemployment insurance, where the NAD's function in administering to Africans gave it a right to comment on amendments, but where the primary responsibility for drafting legislation lay with another department.

By 1948, the state was alive to the need for social stability and to the possibilities of legitimating itself in the eyes of diverse groups by extending its participation in health and welfare provision.[104] This had to be balanced against the danger of going too far – of demanding too much from the white taxpayer and of leaving itself open to the charge of negating the 'work ethic', by which workers were assumed to have a fundamental duty to provide for themselves and their families. The state bureaucracy played an important role in resolving these two components. Sometimes it acted in the interests of Africans and ahead of white public opinion; at other times, it created a public appearance of government action while in reality little significant change was taking place. Civil servants in the Native Affairs, Labour, Public Health and Social Welfare Departments both influenced and were constrained by the political process. They perceived the long-term benefits of developing health and social security, but operated under governments tied to more immediate, short term political interests.

4

CONTROL OVER MOVEMENT

Introduction

Along with the welfare functions for African workers the South African state developed an extensive apparatus of repression based primarily on control over movement. This chapter deals with the elements of that apparatus – passes, urban areas legislation and the administration of recruiting – as three distinct components. In a sense, this is an artificial division: both urban areas laws and recruiting regulations involved passes, and laws that gave effect to these forms of control constantly overlapped. Nevertheless, the distinction is necessary to allow for clearer analysis because the officials who enforced the regulations saw them as serving several different purposes. The pass is defined as a document required for movement in, out of, or within a specific area. It had to be produced on demand from a designated official.[1] 'Passes' included standardised government documents as well as certificates such as 'trek-passes', written by employers and issued at the conclusion of a labour contract. The 'pass question' was seen as involving control over movement across the country as a whole. Urban areas laws were more narrowly concerned with limiting access to the towns, enforcing residential segregation and providing employers with the sorts of criminal sanction normally associated with masters and servants legislation.

The reasons for control over movement involve a combination
of economic, political and social impulses. By the 1930s, there
was a general assumption in state circles that there would eventually be free labour markets and full African mobility. In the
meantime, however, passes and influx control were seen as
necessary because of the uneven nature of economic development. Farmers demanded a secure labour supply while officials
believed passes for blacks were essential as long as the workforce
remained only partially proletarianised. In addition, social
motives, including fears of crime and vagrancy and of Africans
swamping residential areas, persisted right through the period.
The state's interference in recruiting was originally aimed at
ensuring a regular flow of migrant labour to the gold mines,
limiting competition between employers for labour and preventing the worst abuses of labour agents. In the process, the state
protected labour supplies for less successful and under-
capitalised farmers. For example, the entire Orange Free State
was virtually closed to mines' recruiters by 1924.

While there were broad historical patterns in state regulation
of movement there were significant constraints on state apportionment of black labour between employers, which certain more
recent commentators have inappropriately presented as a grand
strategy. The first controls appeared in the slave economy of the
Cape Colony, to prevent fugitive slaves escaping. The second
half of the nineteenth century saw major developments as Boer
farmers, anxious to compete on the growing market for agricultural produce, sought to secure adequate black labour through
pass laws. Other pressures arose in Kimberley from 1867, and on
the Witwatersrand from 1886. By 1910, the state had accepted an
active role in canalising the flow of labour between competing
sectors. The NAD's Government Native Labour Bureau had its
origins in a more sustained effort to control labour on the mines
from 1907 to 1908. Twenty years later, in the debate over Hertzog's 'Native Bills', one can see the beginnings of strategic planning.

However, the state's ability to implement such plans was

limited. The various forms of control developed over time and in response to changes in society and the political economy. They were then made to work in practice through regulations, applied mostly by the Native Affairs Department, whose officials had their own ideas about the proper functioning of controls over movement. The problems encountered by officials and the attitudes they brought to bear on their work, impacted on both the effects of those regulations on the African population and the content of subsequent legislation.

Pass laws

For a hundred years administrators and politicians alike regarded passes as necessary for controlling the African population.[2] Passes allowed the ruling classes to keep African workers in a permanent state of subordination. They helped to provide each set of capitalist interests with the type of labour it needed – cheap, easily exploitable labour on the farms; migrant labour on the mines; and a small complement of more fully proletarianised, urbanised labour for commerce and industry in the towns. In the inter-war years, successive governments accepted the reality of a permanent African presence in the urban areas. At the same time, the state was concerned to prevent the undercutting of workers in the towns by even lower paid migrant labour. Lastly, the state was flexible enough to relax the pass laws at critical times. This was most notable in the early 1940s when the fear of African unrest was at its height and industrial employers were crying out for labour to serve the booming, wartime economy.

In considering the deployment of passes, we must be careful not to treat the state in a monolithic manner.[3] The state was not a thinking being capable of perceiving the needs of employers in different sectors and providing for them accordingly. It did not automatically introduce modifications to the system when changes in the economic structure demanded them. The South African state did not, and indeed could not, operate in this fashion. It was too inefficient and divided within itself to solve major economic and social contradictions by simply applying repressive, regulatory machinery. Its approach was *ad hoc*, slow-moving and split between a number of semi-independent authorities. In fact, the most striking feature of the pass 'system' in this period was the *lack* of effective action by the state, rather than the development and refinement of pass controls.

Another consideration is that the state, at the administrative and political levels, could not serve employers' interests to the exclusion of all other pressures. For example, NAD officials showed considerable sensitivity to the African population's opposition to passes. This was the case from the Godley Report in 1920 to the Fagan Commission of 1946 to 1948. Similarly, administrators feared white opposition to the pass system. This opposition assumed several forms. Some liberal and left wing whites, including trade union leaders, rejected passes on principle. Some business leaders, especially in urban areas, favoured a free market in labour supply. Many farmers who supported passes were unwilling to fulfil their side of the bargain by keeping records so that absconders could be traced. Although there was a very wide consensus among whites that passes for Africans were necessary, trade union leaders, farmers, liberals, *verkrampte* nationalists and progressive-minded industrialists all had different ideas on the issue.[4] In seeking to mediate between these groups, the government was also anxious to avoid protests over the pass system with its many ramifications. Thus the state had to resolve not only the tensions within the ruling classes, but those between different social groups. Furthermore, it had to consider its own reputation or legitimacy as well as that of the ministers holding power at a particular time.

Finally, permanent officials in the Departments of Native Affairs and Justice and in the police were concerned about the very real difficulties of operating a system comprising so many discrete local and provincial laws. These laws involved half a dozen pieces of paper and discriminated between Africans according to age, sex, nationality, social position, wealth and region of origin. As the clerk of court at Umgeni, Natal, noted in

1918, it took two hours, looking through years of registers, to renew just six identification passes which had come in by post.[5] Africans often had several aliases, he protested and employers frequently failed to send in full particulars. The only comment from the Justice Department official who read his complaint was that 'these renewal passes must presumably serve some useful purpose, but I must confess to being unable to see it'.[6]

The correspondence was passed to the NAD for possible action, but the relevant section of the statute was not repealed until 1932.[7] Not surprisingly, much of the energy put into reorganising the pass system involved administrative efforts to overcome inefficiencies and inconsistencies, as they appeared in practice. With the introduction of the Native Taxation and Development Act of 1925, passes were linked to the compulsory carrying of tax receipts. However, subsequent efforts to apply a fingerprint system swamped NCs' offices with the immense regulatory effort required by the growing weight of legislation.

Before tracing the chronological development of the pass system from 1918, it is worth outlining the attitudes of the major economic interests which impacted on state policy. As one might expect, the lowest-paying, most exploitative group of employers – the white farmers – were the most ardent supporters of rigid controls.[8] Led by the Transvaal Agricultural Union, farmers contended that Africans must be prevented from swelling the ranks of unemployed in the towns, where they represented a menace to white society. The farmers were especially incensed by the 'desertion' of tenants' children, who, they insisted, were legally party to whatever verbal 'contract' the farmer arranged with the child's parent, guardian or kraal head. By the 1930s, male juveniles were leaving the farms in droves, but because they were not subject to taxes it was difficult to trace them. Of course, the farmer could retaliate by expelling the whole family, though this meant losing even more labour. The NAD was prepared to extend the NLR Act to large scale farmers such as the Zululand planters. The latter rejected the proposal on the grounds that the Act would entail an expensive registration system as well as offi-

cial supervision of their labour. The only direct relief the state
granted to farmers as a whole was the ineffectual Native Service
Contract Act of 1932. The lack of means of identifying a passless
African as belonging to a particular farm was never really overcome. As O'Meara has suggested, Transvaal farmers turned their
backs on the United Party in 1948, partly in the hope of receiving
better treatment under a Malanite government.[9]

The Chamber of Mines generally avoided expressing an
opinion publicly on passes, except to reject blame for the labour
shortage on farms. The NAD sent an advanced copy of the
Godley Report of 1920 to the TCM to canvass the views of that
influential body. HO Buckle replied on behalf of the mineowners
that they supported a relaxation of restrictions in other provinces
until they were the same as those in the Cape.[10] Buckle accepted
that special restrictions on entry to industrial areas were still
necessary, though whether he felt they were essential to shore up
the integrity of reserve labour pools (from which migrant miners
were drawn) or for more general, social reasons, is unclear. For
the most part, the gold mines were not directly affected by passes
as migrant mineworkers were registered and their contracts
attested separately. The Native Labour Regulation Act of 1911
had largely done away with the mines' interest in the pass issue
by drawing the control and recruitment of mine labour into a
distinct, coherent system.

Industrial employers had even less reason to support a rigid
pass system. A *Rand Daily Mail* editorial in 1923 suggested that
freedom of action following the abolition of passes could lead to
strikes which would paralyse the industrial world, but there is
little evidence that most industrial interests shared these fears.[11]
Passes restricted industrial employers' access to labour. The pass
laws further interfered with normal employer-employee relations when they caused the arrest of workers who were found
without one or other identification document. The Industrial and
Agricultural Requirements Commission recognised this when it
called for a relaxation of 'operative restrictions on the industrial
employment of native labour'. This was also a popular argument

among white liberals, taken up most notably in the House of Assembly by Donald Molteno in 1944.[12] Molteno argued that the pass system restricted economic growth by forcing Africans to remain permanently domiciled in rural areas. He was backed by GK Hemming who highlighted the disruption caused by the arrest in the preceding three years of 317 000 blacks for pass offences.[13]

The actual laws on which the pass system was based were already several decades old in 1918. The Transvaal Republic's Law 22 of 1895 was still on the statute book, as were the Free State's Act 4 of the same year, Natal's Law 48 of 1884 and Acts 49 of 1901 and 3 of 1904.[14] The original Natal Act obliged Africans travelling to and from the province to obtain a pass. The Transvaal legislation required every servant to carry a pass from his master when moving from one district to another. Following African unrest after World War I, the government appointed an Inter-Departmental Committee under the Chairmanship of the Acting Under Secretary for Native Affairs, GA Godley.[15] The committee was given apparently contradictory orders. It was simultaneously to remove alleged grievances, simplify the pass laws, and make them more effective. Significantly, the Native Labour Regulation Act was to be left out of the picture as far as possible. The government's attention in relation to passes was now focused on farms and urban areas rather than on the mines workforce.

The NAD dominated the Godley Committee and the solutions it suggested were typically administrative. It recommended the repeal of all previous legislation and the substitution of a Native Registration and Protection Bill. Adult, male natives were to be issued with lifelong registration certificates, to be carried outside their home districts. Only Justices of the Peace, Registering Officers and white police officers of the rank of sergeant and above could request to see the form. A central bureau would be established to record the movement of Africans. In urban areas and proclaimed labour districts, contracts would be recorded at the pass office. In rural areas, employers would furnish particulars of contracts to Registering Officers. Curfew hours would be changed to between 11 pm and 4 am. The government paid heed to opposition from WT Welsh, Chief Magistrate for the Transkei, to the introduction of passes in the Cape (other than for Africans entering or leaving the Transkei and British Bechuanaland).[16]

The Smuts government actually introduced a bill to this effect in 1923, but withdrew it before the 1924 election. Instead, some of the recommendations were incorporated into the Natives (Urban Areas) Act of 1923 (see next section). The actual pass laws were retained. Far from simplifying matters, the Pact government complicated them further in the Native Taxation and Development Act of 1925. Africans were now obliged to carry annual tax receipts, travelling passes, contracts of service and whatever municipal documents were required locally under the Urban Areas Act. The government had no intention of consolidating the pass laws by act of parliament.[17] Instead, it drew the issue out of the political arena by empowering the cabinet to repeal all pass laws and to substitute new regulations under the Native Administration Act of 1927.

Although it was passed during the same period, the Native Service Contract Act of 1932 was not a complement to the tightening of influx controls in the towns.[18] In fact, the Act was the result of action by Pirow and his Justice Department officials, and was informed by a general concern especially among platteland MPs to keep blacks on the land and out of towns. It was not supported by the NAD or the municipalities and it proved very difficult to administer. If the government had intended to consolidate the pass regulations, it would surely have paid more heed to the Native Economic Commission Report of the same year. That report repeated the findings of the Godley Committee in favour of a comprehensive registration system. It argued that the pass system did not assist white farmers and that their best protection was to use written contracts. The financial cost of administering pass controls was enormous. Moreover, passes were deeply resented by Africans and they diminished the deterrent effect of penal sentences.[19] The government, fearing to offend farmers, daunted by the huge task of overhauling the system and doubting the political gains to be made from acting on passes, responded with customary evasiveness. The only major innovation was Proclamation 150 of 1934, which consolidated travelling passes and made them compulsory in the Transvaal and Orange Free State. The number of convictions rose dramatically through the 1930s. Transvaal saw a total of 98 971 in 1940, compared to 47 000 ten years earlier. From 1939 to 1941, there were a staggering 318 858 convictions for pass related offences.[20]

The 1932 Native Economic Commission Report presented a balance of reasons for preserving some form of identification system. The registration of contracts in urban areas, though a significant part of the pass control system since registration certificates had to be produced on demand, was only one side of the issue. Likewise, although the report referred to the need to prevent labourers from absconding, it acknowledged that passes were little help in this regard. The more cogent reasons presented for preserving the system were that passes limited the influx of Africans into towns, they were essential for identification and they reduced crime. NAD officials raised these points repeatedly in Young's report to the Native Affairs Commission in 1939-40, in the Smit Report of 1942, and in the Fagan Report of 1948.[21] On the Smit Committee's advice, the police eased up on pass-related prosecutions, but the laws were more forcefully applied again from 1945. What came out particularly clearly in the 1940s was that the state lacked an articulate, rational defence of pass controls. In the 1944 House of Assembly debate on passes, the Minister for Native Affairs struggled to answer Molteno's cogent criticisms of the system. Four years later, the Native Laws (Fagan) Commission's hearings exposed the lack of consensus about the value of passes. During the Commission's hearings, AS Welsh had to use the Native Economic Commission Report to remind himself and the witnesses why passes existed at all. His arguments were dismissed by the Anti-Pass Committee, represented by ENC Duna and CX Tshume. The former DNL, EW Lowe, contended that passes aroused hostility among Africans and were totally ineffective and unnecessary in regulating labour. In response, another former DNL, AL Barrett, vaguely suggested that Africans 'would rush around doing things they should not do' if passes were abolished.[22] The Fagan Report clung to the idea that passes were necessary for identification purposes, and to facilitate measures against 'idlers'.

The state was not only concerned about controlling the flow of labour and preventing desertions from farms. Politicians, officials and the white public alike were seriously preoccupied with preventing urban areas from being 'swamped' by African refugees from the white farms and impoverished reserves. The urban African population rose from 657 620 in 1921, to 2 328 342 in 1951, or from 14 per cent of the total African population in 1921, to 27.2 per cent in 1951 (see Appendices 2 and 3). This, together with the belief that crime would run rife if blacks could not be easily identified, had an enormous psychological impact on the white population. On both counts, the actual situation was not nearly as threatening as the perceived danger, but the *swart gevaar* could not be dispelled by a few statistics. These ideas were reinforced from within the state by the police, who insisted that passes were an essential element in crime prevention. If anything, the police would have been happier with more passes.

The Deputy Commissioner for the Free State argued in 1920 that a stock removal pass should be introduced to counter cattle rustling, while his opposite number in the Transvaal opined that travelling passes could not be effectively replaced by a central bureau.[23] In the 1930s and 1940s, officials gradually appreciated the economic cost of maintaining the pass system. But at a time of unprecedented urbanisation, with the National Party howling for further measures of control, farmers complaining daily about desertions, and the police warning of the imminent dangers of easing up on passes, it is not, perhaps, surprising that the Smuts government failed to take any decisive action. Its last contribution to influx legislation, the Natives (Urban Areas) Consolidation Act of 1945 provided for travelling passes, seek-work permits, local authorities' approval certificates for African women, badges for casual male labourers, tax receipts, night passes, lodgers' permits and visitors' permits.[24]

The one scheme which might have paved the way for the abolition of passes was the Department of Labour's Registration for Employment Act (1945). This was intended as a facilitating law for a general employment insurance plan. All work-seekers were to register with the new labour exchanges and employers were to inform these offices of all engagements and terminations.[25] If the Act had been applied, it would have obviated the need for at least some of the passes and certificates which Africans had to carry. Yet the Department of Labour was wary of poaching on the NAD's existing registration system, conducted through pass offices in urban areas. For its part, the NAD feared a further division of control among departments and between central and municipal authorities. The DNL claimed that the Act conflicted with existing laws and that the registration card would merely become another pass.[26] The Act was duly restricted to white workers and the plethora of passes, certificates and receipts was retained for Africans.

Urban Areas

The development of urban areas legislation after 1918 appears at first sight to be a logical and incremental process. Colonel CF Stallard's Transvaal Local Government Commission of 1922 argued that Africans should only be allowed in the towns while they were required by white employers.[27] The government followed this up with the Natives (Urban Areas) Act of 1923. As industry and commerce expanded and the mines labour system came under pressure from overcrowding in the reserves, the state revised the legislation in 1930 and 1937. The Native Laws Amendment Act of that year is often seen as the triumph of the view that Africans were temporary sojourners in the urban areas.

However, the main contention in this section is that the state never really worked out a comprehensive, effective strategy for dealing with Africans in the towns.[28] The ongoing political battle over the extent to which urban Africans should be treated as a permanent feature was by no means decided by 1937. In any case, the influx question was tied to the provision of land in the countryside, to which 'surplus' urban Africans and squatters on white farm land would be displaced. Neither the Smuts nor the Hertzog governments (nor, for that matter, the NAD) enunciated a clear policy on this. The issues continued to be debated, right up to 1948 and beyond.

It is necessary to consider why the laws were introduced at all. The chief reason was quite simply to prevent residential mixing of whites and blacks at a time when people of both races were flocking to the towns in search of work. Straightforward, crude racism played a more important role here than the desire to regulate the labour market.

On the other hand, one cannot wholly discount the labour issue. After the African labour unrest following the Great War, and in the wake of the 1922 Rand Revolt by white workers, the state feared the emergence of a racially-mixed, militant working class. Such a class would no longer fulfil the variety of functions required by the diversified South African labour market. Employers with a broad spectrum of interests feared that prospective racial unity among the working class would undermine the employment of low-wage, migrant labourers on the gold mines.[29] In a broader sense, this would pose a serious political and economic threat to the state, the ruling classes and the prevailing social order as a whole.

Perhaps the most publicised and politicised strand of the state's response to this threatened racial unity was the post-1924 Pact government's 'civilised labour' policy. There was a genuine desire within the political and administrative communities (in particular, in the Labour Party and the Labour Department) to protect the white working class against what they saw as unfair competition from Africans. The fact that the state sought to counter this by placing restrictions on the employment of blacks, was only partly related to fears of a united working class. By the same token, the 'civilised labour policy' cannot be explained merely as an attempt to offset opposition from white working class voters. More fundamentally, it was a response to deep-seated, racially-inspired fears of seeing fellow whites 'over-whelmed' by blacks, whom even intelligent, supposedly enlightened whites still tended to stigmatise as 'uncivilised' and potentially dangerous. In this sense, one may regard the urban areas laws as protection for the 'poor whites', whose prospects of obtaining employment in supervisory or semi-skilled positions were correspondingly enhanced.[30]

Influx controls and restrictions on residential rights were hardly in the interests of the industrial and commercial sectors. An open labour market, with workers going to the highest bidder and with ready access to affordable accommodation, would have suited them better. But the state compensated urban employers through registration of contracts of service (carried out by the NAD in the Transvaal and by the municipalities in the other provinces), the breach of which was a criminal offence. To some extent, this acted as a quid pro quo for the extra time and effort employers now had to expend in ensuring that their workers fulfilled all the regulations. Meanwhile, the government was loath to shoulder the burden of 'providing family housing and services'. The state accepted responsibility gradually and reluctantly, and only after it became clear that employers could not be coerced into adopting the sort of high wage policy which would have made government intervention unnecessary.[31]

As with pass controls generally, the administrative dimensions of urban areas legislation were vitally important. Two schools of thought emerged within the bureaucracy.[32] The first believed the legislation was too cumbersome to be applied effectively. The second claimed that there had never been any concerted attempt to give effect to its premises at all. Right from the start, there was a more or less constant battle between local authorities and the NAD over the content and control of urban areas legislation. As the Young-Barrett Report and subsequent conflicts in the 1940s show, officials in the NAD were often at odds with the govern-

ment on aspects of urban areas policy.[33] Given the fact that regulations under the Acts were very extensive and that local officers
of both the NAD and municipalities were given a wide degree of
latitude in their application, the result was that policy implementation on the ground had little resemblance to the legislators'
original intentions.

In the original Natives (Urban Areas) Act of 1923, the government sought to place primary responsibility for urban segregation on local authorities. The Act allowed municipalities to set up
locations and provide accommodation for Africans.[34] The local
authority could force non-exempted Africans (all those who had
to carry passes) to move to the location once there was sufficient
accommodation. It was up to the municipality whether or not it
took advantage of this legislation. Other important clauses dealt
with the creation of Native Revenue Accounts (funded by location residents but administered by the town council), Location
Advisory Boards and the control of 'kaffir' beer. Whites were not
allowed to own property in the location; landowners could not
permit Africans to reside within three miles of the town; and
employers were supposed to accommodate workers who did not
live in the location.

Sections 12 to 15 covered the registration of service contracts.
All African males had to carry 'seek-work' permits, which were
renewable after six days, or registered contracts of service, for
which employers paid a monthly fee. The municipality could
insist that females left the area after six days. Juveniles could
only enter if accompanied by an adult. The registering officer
had to approve the form of employment held by a juvenile.
Africans from outside South Africa and the British Protectorates
received documents entitling them to stay for one month. Regulations issued under the Act specified that an employee was
guilty of an offence if he failed to fulfil his contract in any way.
This included 'using abusive language against a person in
authority, and damaging property'.[35] If an employee fell ill, the
employer was bound to provide full wages for one month and
then half wages for the second month. Thereafter, the employer

could rescind the contract. The employer was also released from his obligations if the worker caught tuberculosis or syphilis. Daily labourers had to apply for contracts of service themselves and were responsible for the fee. The registering officer could order them to find regular employment.

As Godley noted, these regulations were an extension of existing restrictions enforced under the Transvaal Labour Districts and Urban Areas Regulations.[36] Other local authorities, including those in the previously pass-free Cape Province, could now apply to have them enforced if they wished. Nonetheless, the municipalities did not welcome all the new rules. The Pretoria Town Clerk immediately protested that, if the city was to incur heavy expenditure, it should have the power to control African 'servants'.[37] The NAD insisted that it should run the registration process in the Transvaal. This procedure was only changed in 1945. Local authorities spent the intervening decades trying to secure for themselves the revenue accrued from pass fees. In the meantime, most municipalities simply neglected to apply the Act. By 1931, there were only fifty-five proclaimed areas in the whole country in which Africans were not allowed to reside.[38] The department was thus caught in a double bind. Although local authorities might well pander to their white constituents by calling for extra-tight controls on their black populations, they balked at actually footing the bill for these measures.

In 1930, the government introduced an amending Act. This was intended to extend the restrictions on Africans' freedom of movement and association in the towns. There were tighter restrictions on women and on movement from a proclaimed to an unproclaimed area. The Act extended the categories which could be removed from the town and gave local authorities wider regulatory powers. The Natal Municipal Association welcomed the amendment, but the equivalent organisation in the Transvaal was still not satisfied.[39] Transvaal local authorities wanted much more stringent controls over the entry of Africans. They set themselves against the interests of industrial employers by arguing that firms with labour complements of more than fifty should be forced to compound their workers. The state, with the NAD's full support, refused to take influx control any further at that stage. The government was concerned that if municipalities were granted wider discretionary powers, they would restrict the employment practices of urban employers beyond what was good for business. The NAD further feared that its trusteeship role would be undermined by excessively officious local authorities. Meanwhile, the African population continued to grow.[40] Most municipalities registered their African locations with the NAD, but they did not consistently prevent Africans from entering the urban areas.[41]

As the industrial economy expanded in the 1930s and 1940s, the state was increasingly divided on the whole issue of influx control for Africans. Forward planners, such as the Secretary for Finance, JE Holloway, who chaired the Native Economic Commission in 1930 to 1932, argued that it was inefficient to limit the flow of 'tribal' Africans to the urban labour market.[42] Yet the NEC Report accepted that passes were necessary, while restrictions on Africans in urban areas were essential to protect white labour.[43]

In later years, the problem of white unemployment receded, and other reports put the case more strongly for allowing a freer flow of labour to the towns. The Young-Barrett Report (1937) rejected the view that Africans could be considered temporary sojourners in the towns, though it agreed that influx controls should operate in situations of high unemployment.[44] This was hardly a liberal viewpoint in the classic sense, but it was more enlightened than Hertzog's Native Laws Amendment Act which was finally passed in 1937. Under this Act, the local authority could now, with the government's permission, prevent the entry of Africans. The Minister of Native Affairs (at that time, HA Fagan) could require the municipality to provide lists of 'redundant' Africans who would be removed to land made available under the Trust and Land Act. Blacks could no longer acquire land in the towns and employers were made liable for up to twenty-five per cent of an employee's rent in the locations. The new law was especially hard on foreign Africans, whose employment in the cities was prohibited. Municipalities would conduct biennial censuses to establish who was necessary and who was not. Fagan told parliament the Act established once and for all that Africans could only remain in the cities if required by the white population.[45]

There are two important points to note here. Firstly, local authorities were still not satisfied. Durban wanted employers to provide all accommodation and called for town councils to be consulted on entry restrictions. There was no point in the government insisting that all contracts be registered if the local authority decided the system was too inhibiting, cumbersome or expensive, they would not apply it. Johannesburg favoured tighter controls over compounds while Cape Town was more concerned that location-dwellers be excluded from voting.

For its part, the NAD had no intention of allowing the town councils the powers they coveted, nor of implementing the Act in the draconian manner envisaged by the Hertzogites. By the late 1930s, there was consensus in the department, fed as much by practical experience as by liberal sentiment, that Africans were in the towns to stay and that something would have to be done urgently to improve their living conditions. For example, when PG Caudwell of the NAD's Urban Areas Branch reported on Africans in Cape Town in 1941, he blamed miserable conditions not on dissoluteness or unemployment, but on low wages. The local authorities could not even remove the more recent arrivals, as they were 'entrenched in the economic life of the community'.[46] Africans predominated in quarrying, brick-making, carrying heavy loads, certain types of factory work and in dairies (because according to Caudwell, coloureds were averse to rising early). He and the SNA argued that local authorities had a duty to make use of government subsidies to provide stable and adequate accommodation within a reasonable distance of the workplace.[47]

The belief that African urbanisation was inevitable and that the state had a duty to provide low cost housing, transport and, if possible, health and education facilities, won limited support

from the Prime Minister. Smuts grudgingly accepted the findings
of the Van Eck Commission of 1941 that the flow to the towns
should not be restricted to the detriment of industrial enterprise.[48] Instead of enforcing the Native Laws Amendment Act, he
appointed the Secretary for Native Affairs, DL Smit, to find
ways, short of simply raising wages, to ease the lot of the urban
African worker. In the event, the wartime government was not
prepared to allocate enough funds to make a significant impact
on urban African conditions.[49] But the state made little effort to
turn back the townward tide of black workers. As Hellmann
notes, the African population of Johannesburg rose from 113 000
in 1936, to 163 000 in 1944.[50]

The Natives (Urban Areas) Consolidation Act of 1945, the last
major piece of legislation on this subject before the 1948 election,
reinforced the main points in previous laws. The Minister of
Native Affairs from 1943, Piet van der Byl, regarded the bill as
his responsibility. Van der Byl later commented on his department's uncertainty about whether to apply segregationist legislation or not, following a much-publicised speech by Smuts that
segregation as a policy had failed.[51] For Van der Byl, though, the
issue was straightforward. He felt that labour migrancy should
be restricted to the mines, but that regulation of the permanent,
urban-dwelling African population was still necessary.[52] As soon
as he could get Smuts to agree that blacks could not be 'crowded
onto the reserves', he introduced a law to simplify, rather than to
change, the rules.[53]

From the time Deneys Reitz became Minister of Native Affairs
in 1939, officials in the NAD exercised considerable influence
over their ministers. Reitz spoke out firmly against passes, just
when his senior official was calling on the government to ease up
on them.[54] Smit was also responsible for persuading the next
Minister, Van der Byl, that Africans should be regarded as permanent residents in the towns, thus modifying the Stallardist
doctrine on which the 1937 Native Laws Amendment had been
based. In so far as a policy on influx control existed by 1948, it
was based on the NAD's belief in the orderly regulation of

urbanisation, a process which, the department claimed, stood to benefit Africans as well as employers and white residents.

The Native Laws Commission of 1946 to 1948, led by the former Minister of Native Affairs, HA Fagan, expressed admiration for the NAD's work.[55] The Fagan Report underscored the NAD's general practice of allowing a regulated flow of labour into the towns. By contrast, the incoming National Party rejected the basis of this policy. Elected on a platform of eventually relocating the entire African population to the reserves, DF Malan's government soon began purging the NAD's staff in the period after 1948.

Recruiting

Under the Native Labour Regulation Act of 1911, the state consolidated its control over the recruitment of African labour.[56] The main executive officer was the Director of Native Labour. In addition to regulating compounds, contracts and compensations, he was responsible for issuing licences to labour agents and recruiters, as well as to employers of recruited labour.[57] Licences were renewable annually and could be cancelled summarily at the Minister of Native Affairs's discretion. The DNL was also in charge of attesting the prospective migrant labourers' contracts. The attesting officer (usually the Native Commissioner or Magistrate in the worker's home area) was supposed to ensure that the migrant understood the contract. When he reached the place of work, the migrant could not begin until he had passed a medical examination.

The NLR Act defined a 'native labourer' as 'a Native employed upon any mine or works or recruited under this Act or a prior law for labour upon any mine or works'. The terms 'mines' and 'works', were defined in the Mines and Works Act of 1911. A further Act, passed in 1921, permitted the government to limit wage advances offered by labour agents to recruits.[58] These were duly restricted to £2 and £3, depending on whether the contract was valid for less or more than nine months.[59] Howard Rogers of the NAD claimed the GNLB ensured

the general adoption of clean methods of recruiting,
fair and careful consideration of the legitimate
grievances of Natives, [and] greater attention to the
efficiency and conservation of labour.[60]

In reality, the GNLB could not have functioned effectively had it
not been for the monopsony of migrant labour which the gold
mines had achieved by about 1920. On the other hand, the GNLB
could at least claim to have played a part in the development of
the migrant labour systems.

The NAD's report for 1913 to 1918 states that the NLR Act was
also used to 'secure as far as possible a more equal division [of
labour] between conflicting industrial, mining and agricultural
interests in the different parts of the Union'.[61] This could be
effected in two ways, by restricting the number of licences issued
to recruiters or by closing certain districts, either wholly or partially, to recruiters and their 'runners'.[62] It also implied a crucial
role for the NAD in operating these regulations. The department
was not merely concerned with holding some sort of balance of
interests between white employers and black workers, it also
sought to allot the labour as the state (or, rather, as those administering the regulations) saw fit.

Over the years, though, the NAD failed to hold the balance in
either case. In terms of protecting Africans, there were certain
aspects of the regulations which benefited workers. The attesta-
tion of contracts and limitation on wage advances probably prevented unscrupulous labour agents from exploiting gullible
'first-timers'. Anti-usury laws curbed the credit system by which
trader-recruiters could trap debt-ridden Africans into signing up
for the mines. Medical examinations, cursory as they usually
were (especially in the early years), weeded out the least healthy
recruits and thus did not add to the already high mortality
figures on the mines. However, while benefiting workers, these
three aspects were either of equal benefit to employers' long term
interests or would have been achieved in other ways. The registration of contracts helped to prevent the recurrence of com-

petition among gold mining companies which had plagued the industry in the late nineteenth and early twentieth centuries.[63] It also hindered agents from creating unreasonable expectations in the minds of migrants. NAD officials were well aware of the existence of informal networks by which migrants passed information on the reality of working conditions back to their home areas. If a labour tout lied to the locals to achieve his quota, Africans might be discouraged from coming forward in the longer term.

Similarly, restrictions on advances helped to prevent the dislocation of reserve economies through excessive lending. In the Cape Province, the gold mines' Native Recruiting Corporation made extensive use of white traders as labour agents. Their stores would often serve as central meeting points for a district, and they were in touch, through their ordinary business, with large numbers of people. But there was a danger of allowing them too strong a grip on the African population. If poverty-stricken rural families put themselves at the traders' mercy through large advances, and mine work meant nothing more than paying off a debt to a trader, then once again, labour migrancy could lose its attractions and the mines workforce could be diminished. This specific problem shrank in the mid-1920s, when the TCM introduced its assisted voluntary scheme. This allowed the mines to provide small advances for voluntary migrants, who then went directly to the mine of their choice. Throughout the 1920s, worsening rural impoverishment forced more and more Africans out to work and further lessened the mines' dependence on trader-recruiters. This dependence reappeared in times of labour shortage, as in the later 1940s.

Lastly, the attestations did not, as Rogers claims, ensure that only adults were taken on. The vast majority of recruits had no documents proving age, so the minimum age of eighteen was either guesswork or was taken on trust. On the farms, children under sixteen years of age could be apprenticed by their parents under masters and servants laws. Juveniles aged between sixteen and seventeen could be recruited with their parents' consent.

While these factors were important, they pale into insignificance beside the NLR Act's broader role in legitimating the migrant labour system to the general public. The gold mines established a fairly efficient recruiting network between 1890 and 1920, both inside South Africa and in Portuguese East Africa and the High Commission Territories.[64] The mines' monopsony of the migrant labour force was hard won, but by the start of our period, it was unlikely that any other group of employers would be able to challenge it. Nevertheless, labour migrancy came under sustained ideological and political attack. The first challengers were the would-be champions of white workers in the Labour Party who claimed that, as the basis of a cheap labour policy, migrancy undermined employment opportunities for 'civilised' labour. Liberals – both white and black – argued that migrancy broke up family life, used the reserves to subsidise the reproduction of the mines' labour force, and ultimately turned them into dumping grounds for superannuated miners. Finally, those with South Africa's long-term economic interests at heart, such as Van Eck of the Industrial and Agricultural Requirements Commission, believed that the low wages paid to migrant labour restricted the potential growth of South Africa's domestic market. His commission's report painted the future in terms of a large, fully-proletarianised, internal African market for home-produced goods, the development of which would go hand in hand with further industrialisation and urbanisation.

The gold mining industry was well able to defend itself and devoted considerable resources to propagandising. The propaganda was partly based on the claim that its recruiting methods enjoyed the full support and approval of that branch of the state entrusted with the task of protecting the African population. Although difficult to prove, it could be argued that NAD officials had vested interests in endorsing the gold mines' assertions. The department's refusal to countenance a major shift in the labour process on the mines may have been the result not only of the state's need to maintain a highly profitable mining sector for taxation, but of the fact that the NAD's structural position within the state demanded it.

The NAD upheld the migrant labour system as almost legendary proof of its ability to administer to the needs of white employers and black workers at the same time and as evidence that these needs were not incompatible and of the efficacy of expert administration by well-trained, caring officers. For the department to have turned around in the later 1930s and agreed with its most ardent critics that migrancy was evil and destructive, would have been to accept its utter inability to perform its duties. NAD officials had no intention of doing any such thing. Even the most liberal statements from senior departmental officials, such as the Smit Report of 1942, maintained the line that the migrant worker was well cared for in comparison with the hard-pressed urban African. The chief problem identified by the NAD in the 1940s was thus not the rural-based migrant, whose poverty was at least hidden from the public eye, but the more visible, less easily-controllable town-dweller, whom, for the various reasons discussed above, the pre-1948 state bureaucracy found it much more difficult to administer.

The retrenchment of white labour on the gold mines after the Rand Revolt, coupled with the mining industry's insistence that it needed maximum access to African labour to keep the low grade mines (those with the lowest ratio of gold to ore mined) profitable, led to a renewal of the long-running debate on state control over recruiting. The mineowners' main opposition came from ex-mine manager and Labour Party MP, Colonel FHP Creswell. He had been campaigning in favour of white unskilled labour on the mines since the turn of the century. His star waned after he led a successful attack on 'tropical' labour (the use of labourers from north of latitude 22° south) from 1909-1913, but Creswell gained a new lease of life under the Pact government of 1924 to 1929, under which he held several cabinet offices. His basic argument was that...

> ...any addition to our human labour force required
> to develop the resources of our country in excess of
> the present native labour force here must come from

civilised lands and that the objection would be
found insurmountable to making the Union a sort of
sink into which would be attracted all the cheap
native labour to be drained from the rest of Africa.[65]

Creswell reluctantly acknowledged that the government could
not prevent the employment of black South Africans on the
mines. On the other hand, he was incensed by the importation of
cheap labour, mostly from Portuguese East Africa, under the
convention of 1909.[66] In this, he had the support of the Mine
Workers Union, though not of the breakaway Transvaal White
Miners Association which bought the mineowners' argument
that foreign migrant labour permitted the maximum expansion
of the industry, thereby protecting white supervisors' jobs.[67]
Creswell had his own alternative solutions. He wanted to use a
larger proportion of white labour, especially on the shallow, relatively healthy, Transvaal coalfields and for surface work on the
gold mines.[68] Underground, he favoured limiting the allottable
supervision of the white ganger to two drilling machines and
twenty-six labourers.[69] The low grade mines would be reorganised so they could be operated by white labour. According to
Creswell, this was preferable to turning the whole country into a
'big compound where you have a large number of natives living
under unnatural conditions away from their wives and families,
away from their homes.'[70] If this failed, he believed the government should control the distribution of imported labour to
ensure that low grade mines had their full complement of workers. This, for Creswell, was a last resort, to prevent the mineowners using the labour shortage as an excuse for closing their
less profitable concerns.

The mining companies backed their search for the cheapest,
most reliable labour supplies with a mixture of threats and
promises. According to Arthur French, president of the Gold
Producers' Committee in 1927, the mines faced increased competition from the expansion of industrial and agricultural activity
since 1922. In order to extend the shaft-sinking programme and

to mine at increasing depths and with narrower stoping widths, the mines claimed they had to have labour from Portuguese East Africa.[71] Otherwise, the companies warned ominously, they would have to close mines, laying off white labour; or they would compete for African labour with farmers, to the latter's detriment.

The state's response, even when Labour Party members found their way into ministerial office, was generally to support the gold mines. As early as 1921, a meeting of chief civil servants agreed that recruitment of Portuguese migrants had to continue.[72] The SNA, Edward Barrett, insisted that the agreement with Portugal was 'a good thing' from the African's point of view. His Under Secretary, ER Garthorne, argued that the supply from Mozambique must continue lest the farm labour force be affected. He received full support from Du Toit, the Secretary for Agriculture. This was basically the line adhered to in later years by the NAD, though in the early 1920s, the Smuts government imposed a temporary quota on Mozambican labour to put pressure on the Portuguese. In 1927, the DNL, Herbert Cooke, suggested that limits might be placed on the Portuguese complement to allow for the maximum employment of South Africans at times of crisis such as drought, but he was not prepared to recommend this formally.[73] In the 1928 convention, the Portuguese introduced their own quota, which brought the official number of Mozambican migrants down to 80 000 a year by the early 1930s. With the onset of the Depression, the NAD pressed the mines for a South Africa-preference policy to relieve distress in the countryside.

In other ways, too, the department passively and actively supported the TCM. In 1925, white labour associations alleged that the introduction on the mines of nine-month contracts for recruited migrants as a way of reducing the labour supply from South Africa and persuading the government to relax restrictions on Mozambican workers. The DNL categorically denied this. He argued that the new contracts, introduced in 1924, would merely increase the number of voluntary labourers who went directly to the mines of their choice.[74] He concurred with William Gemmill, general manager of the Native Recruiting Corporation, that the supply varied according to the economic position in the reserves. He denied that it was affected by longer contracts.[75] The NAD further assisted the mineowners the next year when ER Garthorne joined forces with the GME to see off Creswell's plan for government-controlled distribution of recruited labour. Much better, Garthorne argued, to leave it in the hands of the TCM's own Complements Committee. If steps were to be taken, it would be easier to use informal agreements with the mine-owners rather than legislation. In any case, the state could hardly control the supply from British South Africa: 'It does not seem clear that the Government could logically assert any particularist restriction where it can confer no countervailing privilege', wrote Garthorne.[76] There was a degree of self-interested fear of political embarrassment in this position. Departmental officials were worried about taking on responsibility in a highly sensitive area where they could attract a hail of recriminations from all sides.

The NAD was even more useful to the gold mines in the 1930s, when it and the Department of Public Health endorsed the reintroduction of so-called 'tropical' labourers. The government had prohibited this since 1913 because of the very high mortality rates among northern labourers unused to the rigorous working conditions and colder climate on the Rand. The Low Grade Mines Commission of 1920 and the Low Grade Ore Commission of 1932 both recommended recruitment of 'tropical' labour.[77] The new recruiting strategy was all the more necessary following the reduction of the Mozambican contingent under the renegotiated convention of 1929. This had been the culmination of years of debate with the Portuguese, in which the Pact government had taken a more conciliatory line than the pre-1924 Smuts administration. Fearing a shortfall in labour, the mines then lobbied harder for access to 'tropical' labour. On the advice of the Secretary for Public Health, Sir Edward Thornton, and the DNL, an experimental contingent was brought to the gold mines in the early 1930s. The mines claimed that immunisation against pneumonia and more hygienic living conditions would reduce death rates. In 1935 the government allowed the TCM to increase the contingent from 2 000 to 5 000, though mortality figures remained more than double the average among migrants. By 1945 there were 31 791 'tropicals' on the gold mines, compared with 80 332 from Mozambique.[78]

Generally speaking, the NAD accepted the opinions of the leaders of the NRC and WNLA, and co-operated with them to ensure an adequate labour supply. This was made easier by the sheer size and resources of these organisations, coupled with the energy and abilities of such managers as William Gemmill.[79] NAD officials treated them as equals, aware that they served different masters but regarding them as professionals akin to themselves, doing a professional job. In their attitudes to the Natal coal mineowners and the farmers, however, the civil servants were far less respectful. The Natal Coal Owners' Society first protested to the government in 1928, when they demanded the same recruiting privileges as the gold mines. Their request was thrown out by the GME who argued that if the coal owners guaranteed a certain number of shifts a month and recruited in a 'businesslike' manner, they would easily fulfil their labour needs.[80] Ten years later a private recruiting organisation, TA Theron and Co, requested the DNL's permission to recruit Bechuana labour for the Natal coal mines.[81] The local Inspector of Native Labourers and the DNL supported the application. But Douglas Smit, acting on the recommendation of the Herbst (Farm Labour) Committee, turned them down again. Smit informed Theron that it was against policy to encourage clandestine immigrants to find jobs on the mines, and that the coal mines could afford higher wages to induce Union Africans to take up employment.[82] He might have added that the WNLA was now actively recruiting in Bechuanaland. The opposition of governments in neighbouring territories, the TCM's greater political muscle and the NAD's preference for the way the NRC and WNLA did business, were surely important factors in the refusal to oblige the Natal mines.

The NAD may also have rejected the request because of poor living and working conditions on the coal mines, which were markedly worse than anything to be found on the Witwatersrand goldfields. Despite the department's concern to facilitate labour recruiting and its unwillingness to drive down profitability, its officials insisted on enforcing minimum standards in labour districts. Whether these were enforced for reasons of trusteeship, to satisfy foreign authorities like the British High Commissioner and Portuguese Curator or to safeguard the labour supply in the longer term, is not immediately clear. It is unlikely that even the officials themselves would have been able to give only one reason. But in 1943, when the needs of the wartime economy forced the Minister of Native Affairs to relax his restrictions on recruiting for the Natal coal mines, the department still would not allow work to begin until its inspectors were satisfied.[83] In this way, they were at least able and willing to effect some improvements in conditions by manipulating recruiting regulations.

The NAD likewise considered the farmers to be second rate employers because of their inability to organise large scale, efficient recruiting and because of the appalling working conditions which prevailed on farms in certain districts. For example, the NAD argued in the 1918 Departmental Report on the Alleged Shortage of Native Labour in Natal, that employers should improve conditions and band together to recruit labour.[84] In the farmers' case, though, the state was prepared to assist. Large areas were marked off, from which mines recruiting was forbidden. Under the NLR Act, neither the farmer nor his servants needed a licence to engage Africans for farm work.[85] Later, when farmers were hard pressed by competition for labour from other sectors, a twenty mile zone south of the Limpopo was demarcated, in which farmers were given sole rights to recruit clandestine immigrants.[86] Sugar planters were also given preferential access to Mozambican clandestine labour from 1935.

In the 1940s, the NAD established reception depots to hold labourers – a scheme which turned out to be a dismal failure.

Farmers in the eastern, northern and western Transvaal, some of whom had already been recruiting for forty years, created new organisations to take advantage of these privileges.[87] Their work was co-ordinated and encouraged by special conferences between the South African Agricultural Union and the NAD. Yet departmental officials, used to setting forms of procedure and spoilt by the well-oiled organisation of the NRC and WNLA, appear never to have fully accepted the farm labour recruiters. As notes of a meeting in 1948 show, their tolerance was sapped by repeated allegations of kidnapping and selling of recruits by labour touts, which corroborated claims of 'near slavery' on farms in the Bethal area in the eastern Transvaal.[88] The problems faced by commercial farmers could not, ultimately, be solved in this way as there were too many holes in the recruiters' nets to prevent labour from seeping away to other areas.

Conclusion

Although the scope of recruiting changed in the decades between 1911 and 1948, the principles under which it was allowed to operate, and by which the state assisted the major organisations in securing their labour complements, were basically the same. In the course of the 1950s and 1960s, the government gradually armed itself with powers which further restricted freedom of movement and divided the African workforce more rigidly between industrial, agricultural and mining employers.[89] The National Party to some extent built on legislation it had inherited from the Smuts and Hertzog governments. In the 1950s, the state extended its armoury of repressive controls well beyond what would have been politically and administratively possible in the pre-apartheid era. Even if the pre-1948 state had possessed the political will to orchestrate the labour force more stringently, it would not have had the means to enforce this will. The economic situation was changing too rapidly and unevenly for the bureaucracy to keep up, as the growth of squatters camps and shanty towns around Durban, Johannesburg and

Cape Town showed. This was especially so in the 1940s, a time when the NAD was short-staffed because of war service.

In any case, it seems doubtful that the NAD in its pre-1948 form would have implemented the sort of regulations introduced under the Natives (Abolition and Co-ordination of Documents) Act of 1952, and subsequent laws. The NAD exercised considerably more power in the administration of the state's repressive apparatus than it did in its welfare functions. Whereas in the latter sphere, the government could limit the civil service's autonomy by controlling the budget, the state had to allow the NAD much more discretion in applying repressive controls. This is not to say that the NAD operated a different policy from the government's but, that there were times when the traditions of paternalism and trusteeship, deeply embedded in the department, acted as a brake on the dominant ideology of segregation and control. Further evidence of this emerges in the hotly contested area of farm labour policy, discussed in the following chapter.

5

FARM LABOUR

Introduction

The plight of the African in rural South Africa has attracted much attention from historians in recent years. The work of Colin Bundy, William Beinart, Peter Delius, Tim Keegan, and others has helped to explain the impact of state domination and dispossession on blacks in various parts of the country.[1] This has emphasised the disparate conditions and responses which prevailed among and within different black communities, and the tenacity with which some black peasants clung to their position as producers for the market. Their work also underlines the unevenness of agricultural change in South Africa. As late as the 1960s, the state struggled to promote a prosperous white commercial farming sector and to ensure the return of farm labourers to complete their contractual obligations to white farmers.

Despite this, one finds oneself returning again and again to the crucial role of the state in rural transformation, enforcing an unequal division of land, creating a biased access to markets and capital loans, and developing its powers of control over black farm labourers. It is this last aspect of the state's functions which forms the chief subject of this chapter. In the nineteenth and early twentieth centuries, it appeared most notably in the masters and servants laws which operated in all four future provinces. After Union, it found expression in amendments to those laws and in the Native Service Contract Act of 1932 and the Native Trust and Land Act of 1936. In many ways, this legislation is closely linked to the forms of control over movement analysed in Chapter 4. As the NAD increased its authority in farm labour policy-making and implementation, and partly shifted the state's attention away from coercive measures, it also attempted welfare-oriented interventions analogous to those described in Chapters 2 and 3.

*   *   *   *

Just as change in the countryside was slow-moving and fraught with contradictions, so the development of state policy was anomalous and uneven. In part, this resulted from changes in government. For example, elements in the National Party (founded by Hertzog, 1914), which came to power in 1924, regarded themselves as the representatives of white farmers and were anxious to appear to be doing more for that constituency than had their predecessors. The lack of consistency in state policy also owed much to competition between different sectors in the economy, with mineowners, industrialists and farmers competing for cheap labour and trying to influence the state for their own ends. The third reason, highlighted in this chapter, concerned the internal dynamics of various branches of the state, in particular, the Departments of Agriculture, Justice and Native Affairs. Their differing positions on farm labour arose partly from their respective roles within the state, with the Agriculture Department representing white farmers, the Justice Department constituting part of the more overtly repressive arm of the state, and the NAD protecting the interests of the African population. Several other factors also have to be considered, including the role played by individual ministers and administrators (in all three branches), pressure by white farmers on the Justice Department, and the NAD's regulation of recruiting for the gold mines. The significance of these elements and their impact on the state's handling of farm labour merit careful examination.

Throughout the period, white farmers regarded themselves as

a hard-pressed, hard-done-by group who received little assistance from the state in taming a harsh and inhospitable environment. The road to profitable white agriculture was not an easy one. Land speculation, beginning with the diamond and gold mining boom of the later nineteenth century, created grossly inflated prices for land.[2] In the 1920s, the cost of land was still rising much more quickly than its productive value. This, plus government allotments of state-owned land for 'poor white' settlement in the 1920s, resulted in widespread sub-division of farms. The majority of farms were heavily mortgaged and farmers could not afford to mechanise because of debts to bond-holders and local traders, very high local prices for machinery, recurring natural disasters and, from 1926, falling prices for agricultural produce.[3] With the exception of the Cape, the bulk of their workforce consisted of African labour tenants. They were supplemented by significant numbers of sharecroppers and rent-paying tenants who continued to farm 'white' land, especially on farms owned by small, struggling white agriculturalists, and large-scale absentee landowners or speculative land companies.

Already in the 1920s, a minority of successful, capitalising farmers were maximising their profits from the land. They tended to be located in the plantation areas of Natal, in the Highveld 'maize triangle', in the south-western Cape and in parts of the eastern Cape. They were the first to move away from sharecropping and labour tenancy towards the system of full-time wage labour which the Native Affairs Department came to favour. The success of such farmers and their 'progressive' tendencies (in terms of supporting the proletarianisation of farm labour) meant that the state was dealing with divided interests within the farming community. This was true despite the illusion of unity created by the wealthier farmers' pre-eminence in provincial and national agricultural unions. Gradually, the state subordinated the interests of the wealthy to those of smaller farmers, through loans from the Land Bank, the creation of marketing schemes, the extension of a transport infrastructure, assistance to co-operative societies and technical assistance.

From 1929 to 1934, the Depression, together with a series of natural calamities and South Africa's retention of the gold standard (until 1932), threatened many farmers' livelihoods. The prices of some export products did not reach their 1928 levels again until World War II. However, between 1931 and 1935, parliament passed a series of Acts designed to service white farmers' debts and save white agriculture from collapse. As a result, farmers were able to continue investing in improvements in land, seed, stock and machinery.[4] One index of the increasing capitalisation of farming can be seen in the increase in the number of tractors, which rose from 231 in 1918, to 1 302 in 1926, to 20 292 in 1946.[5] The expansion of state aid and the improvement in agricultural produce markets in the 1930s allowed white farmers to realise the value of their land by farming more intensively. This directly affected the conditions of service for African farm workers. In some cases, sharecroppers were compelled to hand over two-thirds, rather than half of their produce; squatters faced increasing restrictions on livestock, which in turn affected their milk and meat diet, fostering malnutrition; and many labour tenants received no cash wage at all for their period of service.[6] The growing pressure on Africans on white farms further stimulated the flow of labour, both temporary and permanent, to the towns and exacerbated the labour shortage in the countryside.

The root of the problem, as white farmers saw it, was that young African farm workers were drifting to the towns in ever increasing numbers, depriving farmers of their most productive labour. In the past they had been able to keep Africans on the farms by granting land, grazing rights and a paltry wage in cash or kind to families of squatters in return for labour. The growth of secondary industry, especially during the Great War and again after South Africa came off the Gold Standard in 1932, made this more difficult. Across the country, farmers responded by bonding together in local, regional and provincial associations and by bombarding the government with requests for state assistance.

In the 1920s, senior bureaucrats in the Department of Agriculture approached the problem from the standpoint of the overall production costs of white farmers. Agriculture officials argued that the state had a duty to assist farmers in securing labour.[7] In doing so, they agreed with the majority of white farmers that they could not stem the seepage of labour from rural areas on their own, and that the interests of white agriculture were those of the country as a whole. This view was shared by the Minister of Agriculture from 1924-35, General J Kemp.[8]

In the Department of Justice, policy in the later 1920s and early 1930s was dictated more by the ministers than by their senior civil servants, for whom farm labour was not a central concern. Ministers Tielman Roos and Oswald Pirow both contributed to the extensive range of powers which could be used to control African farm workers. They steered through parliament the Transvaal Masters and Servants Amendment Act (1926) and the Native Service Contract Act (1932). The draconian nature of the latter law produced a storm of protest, not least from the Native Affairs Department. African organisations and newspapers made common cause with liberals in the Joint Councils, the SAIRR, several Churches and the left wing of the South African Party, complaining that the NAD should have been responsible for drafting and introducing the bill.[9]

From 1929, the NAD was removed from the portfolio of the Prime Minister and given its own Minister in the person of EG Jansen. Jansen did not exert any great influence on his department's policies, and the opinions of its chief bureaucrats continued to prevail. In the rural areas, Native Commissioners faced more immediate pressure from irate farmers who demanded action against absconding labourers. At least some district officers sympathised with the farmers' plight.[10] However, at NAD headquarters in Pretoria, senior officials generally rejected the view that white farmers deserved further state intervention to provide them with labour. The farmers themselves, they argued, should attract workers through better remuneration and enhanced living and working conditions.[11] The NAD's position was based on three considerations. First, there was the belief, widely held among Native Commissioners and Magistrates from the 1920s to the 1940s, that farmers would never have sufficient labour until they raised cash wages and improved amenities. Connected with this was the fear that assistance in the form of government-run recruiting schemes would interfere with the supply of labour to the gold mines. Finally, many officials regarded the maltreatment of farm labourers by their employers as morally offensive. This is a particularly difficult factor to pin down, as administrators, no less than politicians, were prone to claiming the 'moral high ground' when in fact they were moved more by the need to improve the labour supply or by pressure from the ICU. Nonetheless, a measure of genuine outrage at the appalling living conditions endured by large numbers of black farm workers is evident in the minutes of some NAD and Public Health officials. Characterised as it was by mutual back-slapping and heavy paternalistic rhetoric, the moral dimension was nevertheless significant in the evolution of farm labour policy.

This theme is illustrated in the following section, which deals with the debate between the NAD and the Department of Agriculture over farm labour conditions and related topics, between 1924 and 1939. Section (iii) re-examines the same period, focusing on relations between Justice and the NAD during and after the passing of the Transvaal Masters and Servants Amendment Act and the Native Service Contract Act. By 1935, the Justice Department had given up trying to regulate farm labour and the policies of the NAD had gained wider credence within the state. The government underlined this by appointing the former Secretary for Native Affairs, JF Herbst, to head a committee on the farm labour shortage in 1937. With the onset of World War II, the state made some effort to pull together to aid white agriculture, exhorting blacks to remain on the farms, supplying farmers with prisoners of war and experimenting with state-run labour gangs. The causes, nature and extent of this apparent unity within the state are considered in the section on farm labour after 1939.

The NAD and the Department of Agriculture

> Mr Menge said that he felt inclined to take up the
> cudgels on the part of the farmer. There were hun-
> dreds and thousands of Natives who would not
> work at all no matter how attractive were the condi-
> tions offered to them – surely the Government could
> do something about these Natives. Could they not
> be put into organised Government camps and sent
> out to work wherever they were needed. If the idea
> was to have an orderly state then it was not sensible
> to allow the Natives to do just what they liked.[12]

As these remarks by the Additional Native Commissioner at
Bushbuckridge suggest, the differing positions adopted by the
NAD and the Department of Agriculture were not entirely clear
cut. While the Agriculture Department was normally more sympathetic to white farmers' interests, there were always a few
Native Affairs officials ready to 'take up the cudgels' for Mr
Menge. Magistrates, in any case, did not owe allegiance to only
one department, as they received directives from the Ministers of
Agriculture and Justice as well as from the NAD. Despite this, in
the period from 1924 to the late 1930s, senior administrators in
the Agriculture and Native Affairs Departments clashed on
questions of policy towards African farm workers. On the whole,
Agriculture Department officials placed the onus to provide
farmers with labour on the state and accused African labourers
of sloth, ignorance and greed. By contrast, the NAD blamed
white farmers for turning labour away with bad conditions and
low wages.

One obvious point of conflict arose over the Department of
Agriculture's Veterinary Laboratory at Onderstepoort near Pretoria where 180 Africans were employed on research-oriented
agricultural work.[13] Protests from the ICU in 1928 caused an
investigation by the local Additional Native Commissioner who
found a range of inadequacies in the laboratory's care for its

workers.[14] The SNA was incensed by this report. If the state could not set suitable standards, he argued, how could the Native Affairs and Public Health Departments persuade farmers to change their treatment of African employees? On the basis of the NAD's role as trustee, the department's officers claimed they were obliged to intervene:

> This Department... feels that it is its duty, in the interest of that section of the population committed to its charge, to urge that conformity on the part of State Departments with more modern ideas regarding the treatment of labour is at the present day eminently desirable.[15]

The Department of Agriculture approached the problem from a completely different angle. As the debate developed, the underlying reluctance of Agriculture officials to make any meaningful reforms at the laboratory came to light. With the support of General Kemp, the department contended that they already paid their workers more than neighbouring farmers, who had protested about the difficulties of finding labour for this reason. They implied that any further increases would be deeply resented by the farming community and that the department was not prepared to cloud its relationship with the farmers for the sake of a few labourers.[16] The department's contempt for African workers emerged in some of their other arguments: the labourers would not know what to do with the fresh vegetables the Native Commissioner had advised; and the whole point of employing blacks was to keep costs down. If a wage increase was introduced, it would be as well to sack the entire staff and take on whites.[17]

The controversy over Onderstepoort passed into history along with the disintegration of the ICU's rural protest, but farm labour remained on the agenda of the Native Affairs and Agriculture Departments. Three major reports addressed the issue, each one considering how to provide farmers with adequate supplies of labour, given the general shortage and the impecuniosity of many farmers. The first two reports, the 1930 Labour Resources Committee and the 1932 Native Economic Commission, produced few solutions. The 1930 committee gently supported the amelioration of working conditions, but accepted squatting as a necessary part of the economic system for the time being. The Native Economic Commission paid heed to farmers' evidence that labour tenants were well fed, treated and remunerated, but recommended experiments with written contracts and cash wages. It was not until the 1939 report of the Farm Labour Committee, a body chaired by the former SNA and manned by prominent and successful farmers, that a blueprint for state policy towards farm labour was drawn up.

In the meantime, the NAD and the Department of Agriculture continued to pull in different directions. Although often critical of farmers' labour practices, the NAD sympathised with their difficulties. In 1928, the SNA went so far as to outline a scheme for recruiting black South Africans for the farms.[18] Thereafter, the department encouraged Native Commissioners and Magistrates to do what they could to put employers and prospective farm labourers in touch on an informal basis. For example, in Louis Trichardt, a depot was opened in 1928 to distribute to local farmers hapless clandestine immigrants from the north.[19] When two copper mines closed at Springbok in 1930, the word was passed to the Secretary for Agriculture that farmers should contact the local magistrate if they needed labour.[20] Periodic attempts were also made to tighten up on travel passes and urban service contracts, and to prevent labour tenants from overstaying their leave in the towns.

In general, though, the NAD had grave reservations about introducing further coercive measures against blacks for the sake of white farmers. There were several reasons for this. In the case of blacks who moved from white farms to the reserve areas, the NAD regarded restrictions as contrary to the segregation policy expounded by Hertzog's government in the mid-1920s. Hertzog's goal was to extend territorial segregation. Only Africans who were economically necessary as employees would remain in white areas, while the rest would eventually be accommodated in enlarged reserve areas. The department was prepared to discourage labourers from leaving for the reserves, but Native Commissioners would not refuse passes.[21]

On another tack, the NAD insisted on the right of Africans to sell their labour in the dearest market. The NAD's position on passes was always equivocal. The usual line was that the irresponsibility and lack of stability of the Africans made passes necessary and that passes helped to stem an influx of so-called 'raw natives' to the towns. But Native Affairs officials were aware that enforcing the pass laws outside the Cape tarnished their reputation amongst blacks. Some officials also considered passes unnecessary since the Urban Areas Act of 1923 allowed municipalities to control their own African populations. In any case, the mass of unemployed, idle, urban Africans, which many farmers believed was behind their labour problems, simply did not exist for most of this period.[22]

With regard to recruiting, NAD officials again felt their reputation was at stake. Could the department be both protector and recruiter, asked Herbst, when he mooted his experimental scheme in 1928. His colleagues shared his reservations and the plan was dropped until the war. An attempt to aid white farmers on a national scale would also have aroused the ire of employers in other sectors of the economy. The Native Labour Bureau, as a sub-department of the NAD, was charged with regulating the mines' Witwatersrand Native Labour Association and the Native Recruiting Corporation. These organisations had taken years to develop their monopsony over the supply of migrant workers, and it would have been extremely difficult for the NAD to enter into competition with them at this stage. In fact, far from challenging the status quo, the department supported the activities of the WNLA and the NRC. In 1934, Herbst unsuccessfully opposed negotiations with the Portuguese to allow permits for Mozambican farm labourers, even though he agreed that Mozambicans were cheaper and 'more amenable to discipline' than local workers.[23] Eleven years later, his successor as SNA turned down a request to close the district of Eshowe to the NRC, on the grounds that only a few mine labourers were recruited there.[24]

Rather than supplying farm labour, the NAD sought to help farmers keep workers by ameliorating conditions. NAD officials argued (ineffectively, for the most part) that farmers had to provide cash wages, proper housing, schools, medical care and a balanced diet.[25] The department viewed the labour tenant system as disastrously wasteful of land and labour. On occasion, the NAD made a direct attempt to change things. In 1928, the SNA proposed the introduction of inspectors of farms similar to those in proclaimed labour areas under the Native Labour Regulation Act of 1911. Of course, this would not have produced a well-cared-for and contented labour force overnight, since the NAD was not about to destroy the livelihood of white farmers and risk the enormous political backlash that this would have involved. But it might at least have limited the worst excesses of maltreatment by agricultural employers.

The SNA hoped farmers would accept inspectors as a means of combating the current wave of ICU activity, but the Department of Agriculture rejected the idea.[26] In 1937, the NAD was compelled to turn to the Department of Public Health to deal with a shocking wave of maltreatment in the eastern Transvaal district of Bethal.[27] On the whole, NAD officials lacked the resources and power to enforce changes in farm labour conditions by themselves. It would have required a major government initiative extending the NAD's ambit beyond labour in mining and industry. During the period 1924 to 1939, Hertzog's government was not prepared to alienate an important constituency by expanding the regulation of African labour in this way. In the meantime, local officers were ordered to use their influence to improve conditions. It was up to the farmers to decide whether or not they listened to them.[28]

The Department of Agriculture took a more direct approach to solving the farm labour problem. Unlike the NAD, Agriculture officials adopted a lenient attitude towards the labour tenant system.[29] They conceded that it was to the advantage of the farmer to pay cash but argued it was impossible for him to keep his labour without providing land and grazing. For years, the Secretary for Agriculture pleaded with other departments to help alleviate the white farmers' position. A stream of letters was dispatched to persuade provincial and national roads departments and the Railways and Harbours authorities not to strip the agricultural sector of its labour,[30] which was a perennial complaint of farmers. As one platteland MP pointed out in 1937, labourers could earn up to 2s a day in cash on the roads, while most farmers paid much less.[31] Yet the department rejected any suggestion that the state should enforce uniform standards on farms. After the initial failure to persuade their colleagues to concede direct assistance to farmers in the late 1920s and early 1930s, Agriculture Department officials preferred to eschew responsibility for farm labour. In the later 1930s, its officials appear to have been less active on the issue, passing correspondence to the NAD and quoting the SNA in replies to farmers' associations.[32] Instead, they concentrated on other forms of state aid, such as subsidies, protection and price stabilisation.

However, when the Native Farm Labour Committee (the Herbst Committee) met, SJ de Swardt provided a clear statement on labour policy for the Department of Agriculture. He agreed that farmers should try to improve conditions for labourers in the long term, but his emphasis was on the practical steps the state could take to help farmers.[33] These included importing indentured labour from the north during acute shortages and establishing labour exchanges to eliminate 'waste' in urban areas. De Swardt stressed that farmers could not afford to raise cash wages within the cost restraints which existed at the time. This was very much in tune with the provincial agricultural unions, who would also have endorsed his condemnation of those who 'preached' to farmers, and with his argument that the remuneration received by farm labourers was as good as that obtaining in the towns. De Swardt advocated propaganda work among farm labourers to emphasise the value of a wage in kind and the importance of sharing a cash wage among the whole family. Significantly, he favoured measures which would be carried out by the NAD rather than the Department of Agriculture. In this way, he reaffirmed certain aspects of his department's old policy of direct state action to improve the lot of white farmers.

The Herbst Report of 1939 saw the ascendancy of the NAD's attitude towards farm labour.[34] A few of the recommendations did in fact suggest a role for central government: the state should help the gold mines to secure 'tropical natives' from the north to ease the position in the Union; an agency should be created to find suitable employment for foreign Africans; and chapter IV of the Native Trust and Land Act of 1936, aimed at eradicating rent tenancy and regulating the number of labour tenants on each farm, should be implemented. As against De Swardt's recommendations, though, the weight of the report was behind steps which the farmers and the municipalities could take at the local level. Further coercive controls of Africans on the farms by the NAD were pointless, the report argued, and the time was not ripe for written contracts for all. Farmers must improve conditions and bring an end to labour tenancy. The towns must strictly enforce the Urban Areas Act against the influx of casual black workers. The farmers must establish their own labour organisations which could be regulated under the Native Labour Regulation Act. The role of Magistrates and Native Commissioners would be restricted to giving farmers advice on new Local Advisory Boards. Shortly after the report was published, the outbreak of World War II disrupted the government's careful evaluation of the Herbst Committee Report. It is impossible to guess how far the government would have been prepared to go had it not been for the war. Most likely, the structures later implemented, such as Advisory Boards and Inspectors of Farm Labourers, might have been introduced earlier and more extensively. After September 1939, the report was not forgotten, but the chances of realising its more far-reaching proposals – in favour of improved conditions and against squatting – were at once diminished.

The Native Service Contract Act and the Ascendancy of the NAD

Through the 1920s and 1930s, the NAD advocated improved farm labour conditions and rejected the extension of punitive legislation against farm workers. This was in harmony with the State's broad objective of stabilising a pool of farm workers by promoting wage labour and controlling the drift to the towns. However, the state's approach to the farm labour 'question' was uncertain and contradictory. The period saw major conflicts within the state over the extension of existing mechanisms of control. At the same time, between 1925 and 1937, the government passed laws aimed at achieving administrative and territorial segregation. These laws were not designed to have a direct impact on labour in commercial agriculture. The contradictions can be partly explained by a closer examination of the state.[35]

The first piece of legislation which directly affected farm labour was the Masters and Servants (Transvaal and Natal) Amendment Act of 1926. This Act was an attempt to patch up the holes in the masters and servants laws created by a series of Supreme Court decisions in the early 1920s.[36] In the nineteenth century, masters and servants laws in all four future provinces made breaches of contract between employers and employees criminal offences. The Rissik Act of 1909 was intended to remove all doubt that squatters, defined as Africans living on white land other than as full-time wage employees, should come under these laws.[37] The Act was overturned in the 1921 case of Maynard versus Chasana, in which it was ruled that squatting agreements created different relationships from those described in masters and servants laws.[38] The squatter or labour tenant could now only be charged once he was already in service. Two years later the situation was complicated by the case of Rex versus Gelbooi, which laid down that contracts to perform service for ninety days did not fall under the masters and servants legislation as they did not stipulate a time for the commencement of service.[39] Employers continued to protest that many labour tenants who left to work off the farm for part of the year did not return to complete their period of service. This extended beyond the heads of families who entered into contracts. Their dependents, who were usually party to the agreements, often resented being bound in this way and absconded to earn money for themselves.

The nationalists were not the only ones who felt this had to be remedied. Faced with widespread protests from farmers, the Smuts government had drawn up a Native Registration and Protection Bill (1923), only to be swept from power before it was introduced.[40] The cause was taken up by a private member, Colonel Collins, whose bill sought simply to bring all labour tenants' contracts in the Transvaal under the masters and servants laws. Amendments at the Select Committee stage failed to produce a bill of sufficient intricacy, so the government stepped in to settle the matter.[41] The impulse behind the state's Amendment Act came from the Minister of Justice, Tielman Roos.[42] Roos earnestly desired to help farmers by introducing repressive legislation, but the 1926 Act did not meet the more extreme (and legally unenforceable) demands of the provincial agricultural unions. The unions demanded that the word of a farmer should be enough for the arrest of a labourer and that chairmen of farmers' associations should be allowed to try labour tenants.[43]

The Act of 1926 resulted from memoranda drafted by a former Native Commissioner in Pietersburg, JM Young and the long-serving Secretary for Justice, WE Bok.[44] It covered both the Transvaal and Natal and brought oral and written contracts between farmers and labour tenants under the masters and servants laws. Under the Act, farmers were not obliged to stipulate when service should begin. This merely restored the position to what it had been before 1921 and was therefore acceptable to the NAD.

Departmental officials generally disliked the draconian nature of the masters and servants laws but felt they were still necessary, given the lack of stability in the rural labour market. The fact that the Department of Justice had introduced the bill helped to shield the NAD from criticism by Africans and liberal white sympathisers. The SNA thanked Bok for taking on this 'thorny subject' and politely spurned the Secretary for Justice's attempt to hand responsibility for the Bill to the NAD.[45]

Ceaseless complaints from farmers about the difficulties of securing and controlling farm workers soon provoked Roos to hatch new amending legislation which emerged as the Native Service Contract Act of 1932.[46] The Joint Councils, Churches and the remnants of the ICU in the Orange Free State strongly opposed the Act. In parliament, South African Party MPs complained that the Act would not work, as, for example, the state could not compel Africans currently squatting on company-owned farms to distribute themselves evenly round other farms.[47] The Act would also cause widespread opposition among Africans; and as JH Hofmeyr pointed out, it would be seen overseas as a measure facilitating forced labour.[48] In offering these arguments, Smuts and his supporters appeared much more concerned about African and international opinion than did the ruling National Party.[49]

The Native Service Contract Act was introduced at a time when the government was anxious to find ways to assist white farmers through the depths of the Depression. It represented a partial attempt to shift the burden of low agricultural prices and the effects of a series of natural disasters from the white farmer to his hapless labourers. Its champion was Roos's successor as Minister of Justice, Oswald Pirow. Pirow had campaigned, while still on the back benches, for more stringent controls over farm labourers.[50] As Minister of Justice, he had the full support of the Departmental Secretary, Hans van Rensburg, who later gained notoriety as the head of the pro-Nazi Ossewa Brandwag.[51] Van Rensburg was a highly qualified jurist in his own right and was not afraid to take executive action when he felt it necessary. He was later to write:

> Our Department of Justice would be betraying its trust if it did not do everything in its power to keep Communistic agitation and activities in the Union taped. It must take action where the law demands it!

And where the existing law is not demanding
enough it would be suicidal not to change the law in
order to meet the growing requirements of the situation. That is how I saw it as head of the department,
and I have no doubt that in this view I was not
alone.[52]

Out of this stable came a bill of unsurpassed repressive qualities
which caused a huge stir both inside and outside the bureaucracy. The chief clauses strengthened the power of African
parents to enter binding contracts on behalf of their children;
allowed the farmer to evict the whole family if one member
failed to render service; prevented labour tenants from acquiring
'seek-work' passes for the towns without written permission
from the farmer; gave the government the power to tax owners
of land worked by sharecropping or rent-paying tenants; and
introduced whipping for contraventions of the masters and servants laws. The Cape Province was excluded from the Act, while
the Free State was only affected by a few minor clauses.[53]

In parliament, the Minister of Native Affairs, EG Jansen, kept
a low profile during the debates on the bill. This was partly due
to his own conservative leanings. It was also due to his structural
position as head of the NAD. The African Press and the conference, summoned (as representative of informed black opinion)
under the Native Administration Act of 1927 to discuss the bill,
harangued Jansen for failing to fulfil his duties as 'Father of the
Natives' and condemned the 'whipping clause' (Section 11) as
barbaric and medieval.[54] RR Dhlomo referred with horror to
Jansen's defence that 'Cuts could only be inflicted by order of a
Magistrate'. Other papers, such as *Umteteli wa Bantu*, reported
widespread opposition to the bill from predominantly white
Churches and liberal organisations.[55] The Johannesburg Joint
Council argued that the bill was 'so ill considered and so badly
drawn up that it is impossible for anyone who carefully examines its provisions to contemplate that there is any possibility
whatsoever of its becoming law'. The Council added that it

would have 'a disquieting and unsettling effect… on the native mind'.[56]

Senior NAD officials were deeply disconcerted by this barrage of protest and refused to follow their Minister in defending the bill publicly. Under-Secretary Howard Rogers, in his account of *Native Administration in the Union of South Africa*, published in 1933, simply describes the bill as it stands in the statute book. Privately, he joined other officials in pointing up the bill's weaknesses, and calling for its postponement.[57] The main concern for the NAD was that its officers would be left to enforce the provisions. It was all very well for Pirow to take the credit from farmers, but it was the NAD that faced the anger of urban employers and Africans affected by the new regulations. The NAD's reputation as the organisation which kept the peace between the races took a severe hammering because of this bill, and members of the department felt the blow keenly.[58]

Equally irritating for NAD officials was the fact that the Native Service Contract Act was a nightmare to administer. Before the Act was promulgated, Rogers and his colleague, AL Barrett, had already identified a range of obstacles which would be encountered by native commissioners and pass officers.[59] In 1933 and 1934, a flood of other problems arose as officials battled to make sense of the Act's seven schedules. The central difficulty concerned the co-ordination of the many different forms of pass which now existed. The 1932 Act sought to combine all these into one official document, but its effect was to create yet another piece of paper which had to be produced on demand. If a juvenile appeared at the Native Commissioner's office without permission to seek work, he now had to be sent home (regardless of the distance) to retrieve it. Employers were prevented from paying their workers' taxes all at once as the new law required that a man's fingerprints be taken prior to the issue of a new tax receipt. And the old tax receipt could no longer be used as an identification document because the Act insisted on the issue of a new one.[60]

Herbst dealt with complaints about the Act's administration by sending them off in batches to the Secretary for Justice. This was not the end of the matter though, for within months, farmers' organisations were again complaining that the law failed to ensure the return of labour tenants for their contracted period of service.[61] The NAD was divided internally as to how far the department could be expected to assist farmers who had not drawn up written labour contracts. The DNL argued that his overworked staff should not take responsibility for contacting urban employers when the leave period of farm labour tenants came to an end. Such a move would, in any event, have had little effect, as Africans could simply destroy their existing passes and apply for new ones, or move from one district to another. A lucrative trade in forged farmers' 'leave-notes' developed, about which the pass office could do little.[62] Other problems, too, rendered the Act less and less workable. It was discovered, for example, that 'extra-Union Natives' could not be bound by its provisions as they were not required to carry the specified form of identification. More damaging still, the case of Rex versus Mnyeza brought back the old problem that contracts had to state an actual time when the labour tenant should commence work.[63] Yet another Act would be necessary to allow farmers more latitude.

In 1934, the Department of Justice, now with the steadying hand of General Smuts at the helm, quietly passed the administration of the Native Service Contract Act to the NAD.[64] By coincidence, the same year saw the transfer of DL. Smit, formerly Under Secretary in the Justice Department, to the job of Secretary for Native Affairs. In the past, Smit had deflected the NAD's complaints by countering that they, and not Justice, were in charge of 'Native Administration'. Now, by contrast, he immersed himself in the attitudes of his new department, rejecting a scheme to tighten up the Act with the comment: 'We have gone as far as we can in the way of assisting farmers'.[65]

The NAD made periodic attempts to appease farmers by ordering closer liaison between town and country offices on the movements of labour tenants. In 1938, officers in urban areas were ordered to mark service contracts of labour tenants with the words 'Not to be employed after...'.[66] At no point, though, did the NAD agree to the farmers' request to contact urban employers when labour tenants were due to return to the farms. This would have required the co-operation of urban employers, which was often not forthcoming.

Equally problematic was the fact that the urban-based NAD officer's writ only extended to the town limits. African workers who had been expelled from the town could find clandestine employment in peri-urban areas. In general, the problems encountered over the Native Service Contract Act appear to have convinced NAD officials that additional coercive measures were pointless. Responding to a resolution by the Transvaal Agricultural Union, JS Allison wrote to the Secretary for Justice that 'the department... is at present inclined to the view that an improvement in the native labour position would not necessarily follow from the provision of wider powers of punishment'.[67] Like their colleagues in the Department of Agriculture, Justice officials no longer argued with the NAD line. Protests from farmers' organisations were referred to the SNA, and the Justice Department was not represented on the Herbst Committee.

Why did the NAD, which was supposedly committed to improving conditions for farm labourers, support these laws? There are two answers to this. The first involves the NAD's perception of what Hertzog's government was trying to do. In 1942, after several years of administering the Hertzog Acts, Smit claimed that the state was moving towards 'the adoption of a policy of modified segregation and trusteeship, under which, while the native would be allowed to play his role in the development of and to obtain employment in the industries of the country, there would be residential and political separation between and parallel development of the two races.'[68] In other words, Smit regarded these Acts as providing for separate administration, coupled with distinct residential areas for Africans. He did not see them as a scheme to guarantee cheap, coerced labour for various sectors of the economy.

The second point concerns the actual content of the bills. The new legislation could not have assisted in solving the farm labour 'problem'. The 1925 Native Taxation and Development Act did away with the old farmer's certificate in the Transvaal, by which labour tenants were taxed at a lower rate as long as they worked for a farmer for ninety days. Farmers complained bitterly about the removal of this device.[69] Moreover, the whole question of desertions arose partly because farmers did not give high enough wages to allow agricultural labourers to pay their taxes. The 1925 Act did not drive rural-based Africans to work for farmers. Rather, it forced them to abandon their homes and look for work in the towns.

Likewise, with the Urban Areas Amendment Act of 1930 and the Native Laws Amendment Act of 1937. If the government had really intended to help farmers keep their labour, it would surely not have increased the rights of municipal authorities over location residents. By doing so, the state gave away the very powers it would have needed to assist farmers in trapping African labourers on the farms. Urban authorities felt no duty to help farmers by keeping labourers out of the towns. They used the new laws to serve their own local requirements as and when they saw fit.[70] The one group the NAD did try to keep out of the towns in order to reserve their labour for farmers, was clandestine immigrants from central Africa; but this initiative was only sporadically effective. While the government thus raised the barriers between separate pools of mining, industrial and agricultural labour, the barriers themselves became increasingly porous, both because of structural changes in the economy and because the barriers were designed to permit this.

The only other piece of legislation which might have had a significant impact on the rural labour market was the 1936 Native Trust and Land Act. Here again, the Act pulled in different directions. Anti-sharecropping clauses established incremental fines for landowners with 'unemployed' squatters. This strengthened the state's long-running opposition to sharecropping, though in the short term, it was no more effective in curtailing it than the 1913 Act had been. The Act also lengthened the period of service for labour tenants in the Transvaal to six months (in that an employee could only be registered as a labour tenant if he contracted for 180 days) and created mechanisms for a more even distribution of labour tenants to prevent some farmers monopolising the supply.[71] Only the six months' clause stood to benefit farmers generally, the others would merely have helped one section of the farming population in preference to another. At any rate, the gains would have been offset by the apportionment of millions of morgen of land for Africans to further the spatial separation of the races. With the exception of a brief effort in the eastern Transvaal district of Lydenburg, the relevant chapter of the Act was not implemented until after World War II, partly because of the lack of unanimity among farmers.[72]

Clearly, there were cogent reasons why NAD officials were able to applaud Hertzog's segregation laws while remaining opposed to further coercive measures against farm labourers. The very fact that the government felt the need for a Farm Labour Committee in 1937 would suggest that it had not created a successful 'coercive labour system' in the previous twelve years. On the contrary, the later 1930s saw the ascendancy of a less repressive, more constructive policy towards farm workers, which had its roots within a department of the state's central bureaucracy.

Farm Labour after 1939

The 1941 Van Eck Commission initiated a policy which favoured the labour requirements of secondary industry and mining by encouraging Africans to leave their homes in the rural areas.[73] This was in keeping with the state's long term aim of promoting more efficient farming based on mechanisation and scientific methods, rather than cheap labour. These recommendations were not intended to deprive farmers of the labour they needed under wartime conditions. The Van Eck Report assumed that the transfer of population would take place only after the reform of agriculture. There was a further assumption that most of the manpower absorbed by industry would come from the reserves and not from white-owned farms.

From 1939, the concerns of all government departments turned towards finding short term ways of helping farmers to keep their labour and so sustain production levels for the war effort. As we have seen, disagreements over farm labour between the Justice, Agriculture and Native Affairs Departments were less marked from the late 1930s. During the war, there was even more incentive to pull together. The state came under increasing pressure from farmers to ensure an adequate labour supply through the later 1930s and into the war years. This pressure was brought into the political arena by the many MPs who represented rural constituencies, some of whom had personal experience of labour shortages.[74] The farmers' problems were exacerbated by the rapid expansion of war related activity, which further stimulated the flow of labour away from the countryside. Although a fair proportion of this outflow was temporary, successive government commissions had already recognised by 1939 a growing permanent, urban African constituency which had irrevocably cut ties with the rural areas.[75]

The NAD was in no way shielded from the pressure of such economic and political forces on the government. However, in most areas it chose means other than brute force in its efforts to improve the farm labour situation. This was due to several factors – the belief that influx controls would not be effective, the clamour of industrial and mining employers for more labour, the realisation that coercion would lead to unrest, the threat of opposition to repressive measures, and the feeling that restrictions without adequate official protection were morally indefensible. The department resorted to crude propaganda which, it hoped, would dissuade Africans from seeking higher wages away from the farms.[76] Officials were motivated not just by economic factors but by the thought that white women would be left running farms in the company of 'strange natives'.[77] Since the department had seen a third of its staff depart on active service, the issue of white women's safety was particularly close to home.[78]

At the inter-departmental level, a more determined effort was made to ensure an adequate farm labour supply. At the Food Controller's instigation a committee comprising the Native Affairs, Agriculture, Justice and Defence Departments and the Food Controller's representative reported on ways to remedy the situation. The committee made three recommendations all of which involved direct action by the state. The first – the appointment of a Controller of Unskilled Labour to ensure a 'fairer' distribution of labour – was never taken up, largely because of the DNL's strenuous opposition to further coercive measures. The other two – the extension of a scheme to send Italian prisoners of war to work in the fields and to prevent the indiscriminate enlistment of farmers – were accepted by the government.[79]

In August 1944, the NAD embarked on yet another farm labour initiative, and held meetings with the Minister of Native Affairs and the Transvaal and South African Agricultural Unions in quick succession.[80] At both meetings, Van der Byl pushed the line that the state could not intervene on behalf of one industry while there was a shortage of labour in all sectors. He also repeated the argument that Africans had to be allowed to take up employment with the highest bidder. One by one he and the SNA rejected the local farmers' associations' more radical proposals. They argued that the NAD could not clear surplus labour from the urban areas without providing alternative accommodation as required under the 1936 Trust and Land Act. The only surplus labour available in the towns was of the criminal type, which would be useless on the farms. Africans in urban areas already had to carry up to five passes at once and the introduction of another identification document would be seen as retrogressive. Moreover, the department could not comply with the Agricultural Union's demand that farm labourers be compelled to work all year, because farmers were divided over whether or not they favoured a purely cash wage system.

The sort of government intervention the Minister was prepared to applaud had more of a welfare orientation. The Secretary for Social Welfare, GAC Kuschke, was invited along to speak. He expressed his department's support, in a general sort of way, for better housing, medical and school facilities. Smit emphasised that the NAD could make money available for farm schools for African children in which the education would have an agricultural bias. The Minister proposed inspections of farms by NAD officers, if and when the local farmers' associations felt ready for them. In an internal memorandum, the SNA also supported sub-economic housing loans for farmers on the same basis as for municipalities. All these points involved the extension of state assistance for the farming sector, but in a fashion which was more in keeping with the Herbst Report of 1939.

Various branches of the state came to the help of farmers in more direct ways as well. Smuts himself sanctioned the extension of a scheme to distribute illegal immigrants to the farms from depots in Johannesburg and Louis Trichardt.[81] Between 1939 and 1942, the NAD tried unsuccessfully to convince the Portuguese Curator to allow Mozambicans rejected, on medical grounds, by the gold mines' recruiting depot in Zoekmakaar, to be sent to the farms.[82] The sub-department of Native Labour relaxed its controls over recruiting by unlicensed farmers' organisations near the Mozambican and Rhodesian borders.[83] Meanwhile, the Department of Agriculture lobbied the Director of Prisons to supply white farmers with convict labour on demand.[84]

Following the 1944 meetings with the TAU and SAAU, the NAD faced increased pressure for greater intervention on behalf of white farmers. At the instigation of the Minister of Native Affairs', the SAAU formed a Special Farm Labour Committee which subsequently met NAD officials for more intimate colloquies.[85] The committee made several recommendations, chief among which was the division of the African population into more rigid rural and urban groups. It also called for a harsher application of influx controls, government regulation of company farms, an end to the squatter system, standardised identification documents, farm labour apprenticeships and the regulation of youths leaving the farms for work. The SAAU favoured wage labour but was unwilling to dispense with repressive controls over farm labourers and their families. The recommendations further showed the extent to which farmers believed existing controls, under masters and servants laws, urban areas legislation and the Native Service Contract Act were not functioning.

The state's response to this pressure revealed its ambivalent attitude to white farmers. On the one hand, the NAD made a great show of tackling the committee's recommendations and keeping the SAAU informed about its progress.[86] Smit and Van der Byl also grew quite excited about the idea of varying Hertzog's segregation policy of 1936 to 1937, by acknowledging the creation of a permanent urban/industrial population. This would involve recognising the right of Africans to live in the towns, ending the wasteful migrant labour system (except to the mines, which would continue to draw labour from the reserves and other territories) and proletarianising the core of African farm labour as a permanent class of wage workers.

With the Prime Minister's permission, Van der Byl outlined the scheme to parliament and met with no opposition.[87] However, the government did not make any major interventions in farm labour, for reasons clearly demonstrated by the official files. Once again, both political and administrative considerations had to be taken into account. While the government as a whole was anxious to be seen to be helping farmers, Smuts was sensitive to divisions within the farming community.

The SAAU Committee members GJ Rossouw, T Wassenaar, HC Steyn, JH Botha and DT du P Viljoen represented progressive farmers who organised their agricultural operations on sound business principles and were committed to full-time wage labour. They were, as Smuts told Smit and Van der Byl, 'men like ourselves'.[88] On the other hand, there were still large numbers of smaller, less successful farmers who depended on labour tenants and who would strongly oppose the abolition of squatting. Smuts was not prepared to arouse that opposition. Instead, he drafted a statement that the government would proceed 'tentatively and provisionally' on the lines suggested. Van der Byl later proposed the long term policy of dividing the population between rural and urban areas and encouraging the employment of full time, agricultural labour.

The senior NAD officers, Smit, Alport (DNL) and Rodseth (at that time Chief NC for the Northern Areas, and later Under Secretary), had other problems with the SAAU's recommendations. Most importantly, squatting could not be abolished unless the Native Trust found land for those removed from the farms. Investigations showed there were few surplus Africans in the urban areas. In any case, as Van der Byl had said, the lumpenproletariat of the big cities would not be suitable for farm work. Officials repeated their argument that new identification documents would cause 'great resentment' if applied, as the SAAU envisaged, only to Africans.[89] As for moving labour off company farms and ensuring a more equal distribution, the farmers should tackle that by themselves through their local associations. There was no point in the NAD inviting criticism from business interests by becoming involved.

Three schemes started in the mid- to late-1940s suggested that the government was, as Smit said, 'anxious to help farmers'. The first, started in 1945, involved creating reception depots at Louis Trichardt and on the Rand, at which clandestine immigrants from the north could be attested and hired out to farmers.[90] The depots were established (in the face of opposition from the labour recruiters, who feared losing business), but as Smit's successor, WJG Mears, admitted in 1948, they were a miserable failure. The department could not compete with recruiters working on behalf of farmers in the twenty mile zone, who used every possible means to press-gang Africans as they crossed the border.[91]

The farmers were more enthusiastic about the initiative of one PJ de Beer, a staff member at the Native Commissioner's office in Johannesburg. In 1947, he formulated a plan to offer petty pass law offenders work on white farms, instead of prison terms.[92] The DNL, at that time JM Brink, was not overly concerned about the illegality of the venture. By 1950, the Department of Justice had decided that once someone was arrested they had to stand trial. In practical terms, the venture was open to much abuse, and eventually PJ de Beer was transferred to other work. In the meantime, the Native Commissioner's office had provided a total of 4 722 labourers to farms in the eastern Transvaal by the end of 1948.[93]

The third NAD initiative, the appointment of an inspector of farm labourers under the DNL, was less appealing to farmers. It was in keeping with the NAD's traditional solution of improving living and working conditions and so enticing Africans into farm labour. The appointment arose out of the scandal which erupted in the Bethal district. In 1947, the Rev Michael Scott exposed the appalling conditions under which Africans, many of them captured by labour recruiters as they crossed the border into South Africa, lived and worked in that area.[94] It was normal to work labourers in gangs from before sunrise to sunset, locking them up at night to prevent desertions to the nearby Rand and housing them all together in ramshackle, flea-ridden compounds. As a further precaution, some farmers removed the new recruits' clothing and distributed sacking in its place. They provided only a minimum of food, beatings were common, and wages (as little as ten shillings a month) were retained until the end of a contract. To quote DM Mtonga, an aggrieved ex-serviceman from Malawi:

> What I am going to say further is that the system of work at this place is too hard. The owner of this place is doing too much damage to African boys making work hard, and the most bad thing is too much beating, and the ration scale is almost that of the pigs, the housing is very nasty too, where we get packed about fifty men in a room, with the guard standing at the door. We therefore have no chance of standing out alone, but with a sentry standing behind, which means to say that we purely taken to captivity for six months.

> Boys and men have gone out from here while having heavy scars over their bodies and our ears are now rather deaf. Weeping is made the daily food, and we always bleed blood. Could my mother Government think this over, please.[95]

The NAD had been aware of conditions in Bethal since at least the 1930s but had made no coherent attempt to change the situation until the outcry in 1947. The pass law offenders scheme was the brainchild of one minor official and its effects were regionally specific. Generally, farmers in the later 1940s continued to complain bitterly about the lack of NAD assistance with regard to labour. For their part, NAD officials' resources were severely stretched. They remained unwilling to supply labourers to the farms without compensating controls over wages and conditions.

Scott's revelations prompted the government to take several farmers to court.[96] Thereafter, JJ Smit, Inspector of Farm Labourers, produced report after report on conditions in the eastern Transvaal, describing what needed to be done on each farm to bring it up to a minimum standard. His investigations were sometimes prompted by complaints, like that from Mtonga, passed through the Nyasaland government representative in Johannesburg. Smit's visits were occasionally followed up by the Public Health Department. The two authorities then tried to persuade the farmer to provide adequate housing, cooking facilities, sanitation, diet, clothing and proper contracts. Their efforts were partly frustrated by the lack of personnel (only one IFL was appointed) and by the intransigence of farmers, who often argued that their lease would soon be up, or that they could not afford the necessary improvements. Faced with mounting political pressure from the right, the Smuts government did not provide the NAD with the power necessary to overcome such problems.

As Mears admitted in 1948, the NAD still had a very long way to go in regulating farm labour by the time the Smuts government was defeated. The National Party, which took over in 1948, had no intention of extending state supervision of wages and conditions. The introduction of an IFL in the eastern Transvaal had clearly become an irritant for white farmers in that area, but given his lack of powers of enforcement, he could not have much impact on the overall plight of farm labourers. When the SAAU Farm Labour Committee met the new Nationalist Minister of Native Affairs, EG Jansen, in 1948, the Transvaal representative protested about surprise visits and claimed the IFL had not been tactful in his method of approach. The SNA was quick to assure the SAAU that this would change.[97]

Conclusion

The regulation of farm labour between 1918 and 1948 was a complex process. On the one hand there was more or less constant pressure from farmers for state assistance, with governments especially after 1924, at least making an appearance of trying to alleviate the farm labour shortage. This political pressure was particularly important in the later 1920s and early 1930s, and again during and after World War II. In the latter period, though, Smuts's government was much more cautious than had been Kemp and Pirow, whose hands-on approach to solving the farm labour shortage had provoked considerable opposition without really helping farmers.

At the same time, one has to consider the debate on farm labour at the administrative level. In the Departments of Agriculture and Justice, the initiative came both from the ministers and from the bureaucrats who advised them. The solutions they favoured involved direct state intervention, usually of a repressive nature and often involving extra duties for the NAD. In that department, the officials themselves were responsible for devising an alternative policy based on extending the system of regulations already existing for mines and industry.[98] They came out more strongly in favour of the complete proletarianisation of farm labour but realised this was impossible unless the Native Trust could provide land for surplus squatters.

The period from about 1933 to the Herbst Committee Report of 1939 saw the ascendancy of the NAD's policy, with both Agriculture and Justice allowing Native Affairs to take the lead in dealing with the farm labour 'problem'. In the 1940s, the war and political pressure from the farmers' lobby prevented any major changes in policy. Instead, the various departments were compelled to pool their resources to help farmers locate labour through a number of different schemes. Yet these initiatives did not go nearly as far as the SAAU wished in terms of coercing Africans. Smuts was cautious about any rapid or radical change in policy, both because he still sought votes in white rural areas and because of divisions within the farming community. NAD officials still felt that farmers themselves could do more to improve the situation, and were wary of African opposition and resentment. As with influx controls in urban areas, the department helped to limit the application of repressive controls in the countryside. This was so even when legislation providing for such measures was already on the statute books. The period ended with farmers, especially in the Transvaal and Orange Free State, still pressing the government to assist in augmenting their labour supply.

6

WAGE REGULATION

Introduction

While the bureaucracy's role in regulating farm labourers remained restricted, by 1948 there had already been major developments in the mediation and arbitration of wages and terms of employment in industrial and commercial concerns. The Industrial Conciliation Act of 1924, the Wage Act of 1945 and all the subsequent amendments and refinements all increased the role of state officers. This was no automatic response to South African economic expansion, as wage regulation was heavily fought over and was highly contentious and ambiguous. The issue was contentious because unions, employers, and governments disagreed on the extent to which the state should be involved in determining wages and settling industrial disputes. In the 1920s, the government, its bureaucracy and the major political parties (with the exception of the Labour Party) tended to favour the minimum possible interference. By 1948, all sides accepted, and indeed demanded, a much wider role for the government. The same parties were at odds over which classes of worker and which sectors of the economy should be regulated, which groups required mediation and which arbitration, and whether the arbitrators should be swayed primarily by market forces or by some other vision of the 'national interest'. As in any political battle, the government claimed that its priorities were those of the 'national interest', but what that interest was, or for that matter, what the 'nation' was, provoked much debate.

Ambiguities arose for four reasons: because successive governments were caught between irreconcilable political demands; because opposing forces were driven by differing visions of national economic development; because administrators who implemented the laws were given a wide degree of latitude in their interpretation; and because legislation was confounded by complex procedural problems. As a result, civil servants enjoyed a significance far beyond what was originally envisaged when the laws were formulated.

The first tentative effort in the field of wage regulation was the Regulation of Wages (Apprentices and Improvers) Act of 1918.[1] This introduced boards to control remuneration in specific industries. The use of government-appointed boards was to become a lasting feature in state industrial legislation. However, the 1918 Act referred only to women and juveniles and was not applicable to Africans. In any case, the Act was used far too sparingly to have a significant impact. The 1918 Act also paved the way for the Apprentices Act of 1922, but this effectively excluded Africans by allowing skilled trade unions to restrict artisanal apprenticeships. In terms of African wages, the real drama did not begin for another two years, with the 1924 Industrial Conciliation Act and the Wage Act of 1925.[2]

Africans under the 'Civilised Labour' Policy, 1924-1930

From 1924, the state developed apparatuses to provide for the needs of employers and to ensure the political quiescence of white workers who represented a threat to social and economic stability.[3] This meant controlling wage levels in secondary industry to discourage employers from relying on a low wage policy based on cheap black labour. The plan benefited both white workers and employers. For the former, it constituted part of the government's plans to increase employment opportunities for whites. For the latter, the Acts drew white unions within the bureaucratic structures set up by the state and so helped to prevent labour unrest.

While the basic strategy was simple, the ways in which it operated became more and more complex. This was partly because the individuals and parties which collectively constituted the state tended to emphasise different aspects of the 1924 to 1925 legislation. The Prime Ministers from 1919 to 1948, Generals Smuts and Hertzog, were both, in their own ways, notoriously ill-disposed to the labour movement, whether it consisted of whites or blacks. Smuts personally led the suppression of the miners' strikes of 1913, 1922 and, in his old age, the 1946 black mineworkers' strike. Hertzog was little better. Though he opposed the Smuts government's harsh response to the Rand Revolt and formed an alliance with the Labour Party, he dismissed his Minister of Public Works, Posts and Telegraphs, Walter Madeley, when he dared meet with an ICU deputation in 1928.[4]

Both Smuts and Hertzog treated wage regulating machinery primarily as a political solution to the political problem of buying off white workers. Wage regulation would not be allowed to alter radical industrial employment practices, nor would it be used to bring about any large scale redistribution of the national income. The fact that the state adhered to these principles throughout the period indicates once again the ability of the men at the very top to give direction to state policy, as well as the capacity of employers from all sectors to make their voices heard at the most exalted levels of national politics.

Beneath the lofty heights of the Prime Minister's office, among the men who grappled with the intricacies of writing and applying the legislation, it was not so much the control aspect of the laws which was stressed as the upliftment of the white working classes. The Department of Labour, set up to administer the Acts, had vested professional and ideological interests in ensuring that white workers benefited from the new structures. The acts also created a further enclave of bureaucratic power in the Wage

Board itself, which developed its own partisan interests in wage regulation.

Two other factors were involved here. First, the employers rejected the Acts as unnecessary interference. The administrators faced a protracted struggle to justify their work to this constituency and to ensure that employers co-operated. To make matters worse for the bureaucrats, the two main acts did not fit together as neatly as the government's propaganda claimed. Department of Labour officials soon recognised that employers could evade industrial council agreements by replacing whites with blacks, as the latter were not covered by the Act.[5] As the first Wage Board Chairman, FAW Lucas explained, the IC Act tended to cause the displacement of whites by blacks.[6] The IC Act thus pushed employers in the opposite direction to that envisaged by the government. This happened in a number of cases, notably in the baking and furniture trades on the Rand.[7] Labour Inspectors saw this as a direct challenge to the 'civilised labour' policy, which sought to increase, not diminish, white employment opportunities. The department duly called for a widening of the statutory definition of 'employee' to include all Africans (regardless of whether they carried passes or not) except those who came under the direct jurisdiction of the NAD through the Native Labour Regulation Act. This would put the Labour Department 'in a position to exert control over the wages and conditions of employment of natives engaged in most industries', but would maintain the exclusion of Africans from wage regulating procedures. E Muller, for the Secretary for Labour, dressed this up as establishing minimum wages 'irrespective of colour', but it was to be used only where white workers' jobs were perceived to be threatened. The Wage Act, despite its apparent absence of discriminatory clauses, could operate in the other direction, in other words, the displacement of blacks by whites. The problem of handling black and white workers, of dealing with their diverging roles in the industrial labour market and their disparate rights before the law, was a major concern for the Labour and Native Affairs Departments and their subsidiary bodies.

The Industrial Conciliation Act of 1924 was originally introduced under the Smuts government. It provided for collective
bargaining by employers and unions in industrial and commercial enterprises.[8] Industrial councils were the most important
means of settling disputes under the act. One employers' organisation and one union were registered for each industry with the
state's Registrar, as was the industrial council itself. The council
consisted of equal numbers of employers and employees. Councils passed agreements on wages and working conditions to the
Minister of Labour, who could make the terms binding on
employers and employees, including those not directly represented on the industrial council. If a dispute arose in an industry
with no industrial council, the Minister of Labour could set up a
conciliation board consisting of employees and employers and
appoint a mediator. If a council or board failed to reach a settlement, it could request the Minister to appoint an arbitrator. The
Act made arbitration compulsory for deadlocked disputes in
essential public services. Virtually all Africans belonged to
classes excluded from the Act, namely those subject to the pass
laws or the Native Labour Regulation Act, farm labourers and
government employees.

The Wage Act was supposed to cover enterprises in which
either the employers or the workers were not members of regis-
trable organisations.[9] Any employer or worker could request an
investigation. The chief innovation was the Wage Board, comprising three permanent members plus representatives of the
parties in a specific dispute. The Board heard evidence from
interested parties and then reported to the Minister of Labour,
making recommendations on wages and conditions. The Minister would not promulgate the recommendations if the employers
could show that the new terms would drive companies out of
business. Although there was no explicit race bar in the Wage
Act, Section 3(3) precluded the Board from making a recommendation of wages on which workers would not be 'able to support
themselves in accordance with civilised habits of life', unless so
directed by the Minister. This effectively excluded the Board

from tackling wage issues affecting African workers, except where blacks had intruded into trades in which other races predominated. The Act also excluded farm and domestic labour.

Although officially, the Wage Board could address conditions in the mining industry, the new legislation affected the gold mines only once, in a Conciliation Board report in 1925. Unlike the IC Act, the Wage Board issued determinations for specific trades or groups of trades rather than for entire industries. To prevent the two Acts overlapping, the Minister could cancel any wage determination if he thought employers' and employees' associations were sufficiently representative to utilise the IC Act. Finally, both acts prohibited the victimisation of workers who had been involved in councils, boards or wage determinations.[10]

The plan drew the wrath of the Native Affairs Commission and the NAD on the grounds that it would cause the displacement of black workers. There was a degree of racism in this assessment.[11] The NAC believed employers would automatically prefer white workers because of what officials saw as their superior intelligence and abilities. If whites and blacks were put on the same wage levels, this would naturally work to the detriment of the latter. These arguments made little impact on the Labour Department – the real reason the scheme was initially defeated was that Hertzog himself, as Minister of Native Affairs, opposed it. He was motivated by the fear of increasing costs for employers and therefore consumers, and the possible effects this would have on white and black employment.[12] Given his firm views, there was little the NAD could do. In any case, at this stage it was unclear whether blacks would benefit more in the long term from coming under the IC Act or from remaining outside it. In the meantime, NAD officials avoided direct confrontation with the labour department, preferring to quote the NAC and the Prime Minister's opinions, rather than tackling the department head on.

The NAD took a firmer stand on the issue of building work in African locations. In 1925 the National Industrial Council for the building trade reached an agreement on wages and conditions for the whole country.[13] NAD officials, in conjunction with the Public Health Department and the Central Housing Board, sought to have construction of houses in the locations by and for unskilled African and coloured labourers, excluded from the agreement. According to GA Godley of the NAD, this was the only way the Department could hope to make a success of segregation in urban areas.[14] Black rent payers could not afford the higher cost of white labour; it was only right that Africans should construct simpler dwellings for themselves under the guidance of white supervisors. As the cost would be met, in part, by the white ratepayer, there was also a valid political reason for demanding an exemption. The price of white labour provided an obvious grievance for town-dwelling Africans, who were hit by high rents. The Labour Department, however, was primarily concerned with the white worker. It supported the Industrial Council, which agreed to exemptions to the Industrial Council's agreement on an individual basis only.[15]

A much larger problem was also unfolding over the operation of the Wage Act. The Economic and Wage (Mills) Commission of 1925, appointed to address the problem of white unemployment, proposed a gradual increase in wages for unskilled workers, with a view to making this level of work more attractive to whites.[16] The government would effect this with due attention to the impact on farmers and the ability of an industry to pay. The Mills Report presented this as a solution to the lack of opportunities for white youths: improved remuneration would encourage whites to compete with blacks for unskilled jobs. This could have a negative effect on black employment levels, but it was preferable to outright job reservation and would benefit African workers who were not replaced by whites.

The Mills Commission saw the Wage Board as the main vehicle for implementing this policy. The Board should be more independent of the Minister of Labour, whom the Mills Report criticised for having too much power. The Board would act as the main co-ordinating authority for both Acts and would take the lead in raising the wages of the lowest paid. The Commission also endorsed the Board's own propaganda, that wage determinations would encourage efficiency on the part of employers by forcing them to make optimum use of their labour.

Some employers called for a gradual improvement in black wages as a means of increasing the internal market for South African manufactured goods and thus promoting long term economic expansion.[17] This line of thinking did not dominate state policy until after the Industrial Legislation (Van Reenen) Commission of 1935.[18] One might have expected the Labour Department and the NAD to support this argument – the former to open up unskilled employment for whites and the latter to improve black workers' standard of living. Instead, the two departments helped in different ways to entrench the exclusivist wage policy which had prevailed through the 1920s and which was refined at the height of the Depression in 1930.

In the later 1920s, the Wage Board under Lucas concentrated on developing a middle tier of wages, between the relatively high rates enjoyed by the skilled, artisan class and the very low remuneration of unskilled labourers. To an extent, this fitted with the expansion of manufacturing, which was taking on more semi-skilled labour for mechanised factories. As Lucas frankly admitted, wage determinations were intended to provide avenues of employment for whites. They left the African with 'a virtual monopoly of unskilled work, [but] offered him very little scope for improving his lot'.[19] The government also directed the Board to supplement certain Industrial Council agreements with wage determinations, to prevent employers undercutting whites by hiring cheaper black labour.[20]

Lucas was never entirely happy with his original brief. He envisaged a much grander role for the Wage Board, in line with the Mills Report's recommendations. In 1927, the ICU's popularity prompted officials in several departments to consider changes in aspects of labour regulation before they were forced on them by black workers. Lucas fully agreed:

The wage conditions of many natives are so bad that they must inevitably be improved some time. The choice before the country lies between the use of the machinery of the Wage Board or some form of compulsion by the natives themselves. The former would be a victory for constitutional means; the latter would savour of force, and would establish the dangerous belief among the natives that they can get only what they can take.[21]

Lucas remained Chairman of the Wage Board until 1935, and was a member of the Native Economic Commission (1930-2). He was known as a political maverick who nurtured his own peculiar brand of socialism. An able and forceful advocate, he may well have believed in his own ability to run a sort of benevolently despotic wage regulating system which would benefit all classes of labour, while improving efficiency.

Neither the Labour nor the Native Affairs Departments shared his faith. The Secretary for Labour, CW Cousins, was deeply antagonistic to the Mill's Commission's recommendation of more power and authority for the Wage Board.[22] He argued that, in contrast to the Wage Board, the IC Act, which Cousins himself had drafted, was the 'law of fundamental importance in the Industrial Code of the Union'. He opposed the Wage Board's 'wrongly conceived scope of operations in sapping the vitality of industrial organisation of the employees'. Department of Labour officials feared they had created a monster. While the Wage Board had been given extensive powers under the 1925 Act (to allow it to function as a credible arbitration service), the Labour Department was unwilling to see the Board develop its own policy of direct interference in work practices and wage rates.

Lucas's intended role for the Board was contrary to the department's aim of leaving trade unions to look after their own members, using the mechanisms created by the IC Act. Officers such as Ivan Walker genuinely believed they could promote the interests of white workers without damage to the economy, and did not see the IC Act as a mere ploy to wean whites from effective, radical action.[23] Moreover, the department did not initially accept Lucas's enthusiasm for bringing blacks to the centre of the picture. Only gradually, as Africans became more important in industry, did the Labour Department come to terms with the difficulties of administering to one group of workers while leaving the rest unprotected and uncontrolled.

The debate on industrial legislation came to a head at the conference of the Labour and Native Affairs Departments, the NAC and the Wage Board in October-November 1927.[24] The NAD now clarified its position. Like Cousins, NAD officers were worried about the impact the Wage Board might have on other policies. For the NAD, though, what was at stake was the extension of segregation under the Urban Areas Act and the Native Administration Act. Throughout the 1920s and 1930s, the state was under heavy political pressure to ease labour pressures on white farmers by preventing Africans from drifting to urban areas. As Herbst suggested two years later, wage increases for black industrial workers would encourage a further influx to the towns.[25] At the 1927 conference, he and Cooke affected a concern that the Wage Board would somehow lower wages for Africans by forcing employers to compensate for higher white wages. They did not explore the possibility of the Wage Board being used to prevent employers from doing this. Behind the NAD's arguments lay a broader anxiety that the segregated administration of African workers (which, along with control of the reserves and the mines' workforce, formed the bread and butter work of the department) would be undermined. The DNL called for an NAD official to be appointed to all Wage Boards dealing with unskilled wages, to allow the Department to exercise some control over wage regulation.

Despite a detailed survey of the options, the 1927 conference did not settle the matter. Labour Department officials felt they had done a good job preventing the exclusion of Africans from the IC Act once and for all.[26] The departments, the Wage Board and the NAC continued to disagree on the definition of policy, with the debate becoming further confused over attitudes towards African and mixed trade unions.[27] The government appeared to accept the force of Lucas's arguments in 1928 when it sanctioned a determination of wages for African labourers in Bloemfontein, but the Bloemfontein award arose out of special circumstances and was not intended as a precedent for the rest of the country.[28]

The Wage Board still insisted that its primary duty was to the 'bottom dogs'. Lucas's objective was to raise the lowest wages and so widen job opportunities for whites, increase Africans' capacity as consumers of the country's produce, encourage training and efficiency in business enterprises, and raise unskilled workers above the poverty line. Lucas and his fellow Board members, AT Roberts and JF Malherbe, repeated these assertions in subsequent reports in the early 1930s.[29] On re-election in 1929, however, the Hertzog government ignored calls from the Wage Board, black trade unions, white liberals and even some NAD officials, to deal with the problem of African poverty in the towns. Instead, it followed the Labour Department's advice and amended the IC Act (1930) to allow organised employers and unions on industrial councils to set rates for unrepresented workers. Regulations published under the Wage Act Amendment of the same year complemented this by making all applicants for a determination sign the form, thus preventing large groups of illiterate labourers from using the Board. The Minister of Labour instructed the Wage Board not to make recommendations on unskilled wages, at least until the publication of the Native Economic Commission. Such a solution was acceptable to the constituencies that mattered most – the Federated Chamber of Industries and the white voters.[30] Faced with the onset of an economic depression, the government was not about to embark on an ambitious, high wage policy for the easily-replaceable black labourer.

The Legislation Amended, 1930-1937

The government reinforced its policy of excluding African workers from potential benefits under the Wage Act by a direct instruction to the Board. As Lucas stressed in his report for 1929-31:

> The Board was asked by the Minister to refrain from making provisions for wages for employees doing unskilled work, which work is generally performed by natives, pending the receipt of the report of the Native Economic Commission.[31]

Lucas was unhappy about this, yet had little choice but to comply. If the Minister of Labour and his officials did not like the Board's recommendations, they could require changes.[32] There was still a chance at this stage that the Native Economic Commission would come out in favour of generally increased wages for unskilled workers. However, JE Holloway, at that time Secretary for Finance, one of the top civil servants in the country, believed that employers who were forced to pay higher wages would reduce their labour complements. He could see no merit in increasing the purchasing power of the mass of industrial workers, as argued by his fellow commissioners.[33] According to Holloway, this would lead to a diminution in employment opportunities. In the meantime, a minimum wage was politically risky as it would affect the labour supply to the mines and farms, where, as Holloway put it, 'the margin of productive enterprise is determined largely by the productiveness of natural resources'.[34] Furthermore, the NAD supplied evidence that the influx to the towns would be exacerbated by general wage increases. This would throw the government's segregation policies off balance and interfere with the existing distribution of labour.[35]

Three of the seven commissioners, RW Anderson, AW Roberts (of the NAC) and Lucas himself, disagreed with the majority report. They rejected the perpetuation of low wages in industry and commerce as a means of preventing the drift to the towns.[36] African workers could not take industrial action for themselves, they argued, as strikes were prohibited under the masters and servants laws and the NLR Act. On the other hand, present wages were too low to allow for a decent standard of living and had to be improved. Anderson, Roberts and Lucas repeated several arguments from the Mills Report and later Wage Board Reports: wage increases should be implemented slowly to avoid dislocating mining and agriculture; the government should take account of the capacity of an industry to pay before enforcing a wage determination; increases would have a positive effect on industrial efficiency, leading to improved productivity; higher wages would increase the market for industrial products; and poorer whites would benefit, as they would now be able to live on unskilled wages.[37]

It took another five years for the government to accept these points fully. In the meantime, the Wage Board was lenient on employers, who were still recovering from the Depression. While the ministerial directive represents the political reason for the Board's failure to have a significant impact on wages from 1930-1937, the Depression may be seen as the economic reason. There was also a third explanation, which arose out of administrative procedure. The Wage Act was so loosely drawn up and so complex in its regulations, that individual determinations were struck down in a string of court cases in the late 1920s. The Wage Determinations Validation Act of 1930, designed to address the invalidity ruling in the case of Rex versus Lewin of that year, in fact solved only one aspect of the problem.[38] The Wage Board Report for 1932 to 1933 shows in detail how the different divisions of the Supreme Court continued to declare many provisions in determinations *ultra vires*.[39] In other cases, employers could evade Wage Board determinations by dragging their feet in applying them.

This was made even easier by of the lack of a proper regulatory agency to enforce the Act. Workers under wage determinations were, by definition, not organised into trade unions, and if the courts found it hard to interpret the Act, it was inevitable that workers would have problems assessing their rightful dues. The Department of Labour's inspectors, on their infrequent visits to factories, did not enquire into rates of pay. Businesses which had introduced better rates of pay were anxious to ensure uniformity in their industry, but in the absence of national employers' associations, they lacked the means to regulate themselves. Despite a further Wage Determinations Validations Act (1935), it was only after the IC Act was widened in 1937 to include the vast majority of white workers, and following the rise of effective black trade unions in the later 1930s, that unscrupulous employers found it increasingly difficult to evade the Board's awards.[40]

The NAD slowly came round to supporting government intervention to raise unskilled wages. Already in 1925, the Mills Commission had put the case for the Wage Board to take positive action on black wages. Two years later, the DNL, Herbert Cooke, while expressing qualms about the possible effects of unfettered freedom for Lucas's Board, approved in principle the use of determinations to standardise wages and 'encourage the provision of good food and housing'.[41]

Opinion in the upper echelons of the NAD was uncertain and divided. JF Herbst, the SNA until 1934, was cautious and pragmatic, fearing that the department's commitment to influx control would be undermined by higher wages in the towns. This was also the view of the Chief Magistrate in the Transkeian Territories.[42] He argued that the existing population in the urban areas (in 1929) was adequate, and that it was therefore wrong to 'entice' more Africans away from farms and the reserves. But Norton, the Chief NC in Natal, felt it was time to grasp the nettle:

> If the Native were able to earn a sufficient wage to permit him to live decently and indulge in a reasonable amount of recreation under favourable conditions, I fully believe that most of our trouble with the town Native would disappear. His real

> grievance, though perhaps he would not express it
> in this form, is that he is exploited by the European
> employer who in turn provides him with no ameni-
> ties to lead a self-respecting life. To ensure this a rise
> in wages is essential.[43]

Norton appreciated that wage increases would augment the influx, but held that this should not be allowed to deter the department. He was influenced partly by principled opposition to sweated labour and 'scandalous' conditions, and partly by the fact that expansion of industry and commerce, coupled with the rising importance of black labour to those sectors, pressurised the NAD to develop new powers of control. There had been no general increase in wages since the war. He might have added that what increases there were tended to favour white workers, whose bargaining power was less restricted under existing laws.[44] Action on behalf of blacks was now long overdue, he argued, and would have the spin-off effect of forcing changes in farm labour conditions. The 'running glut of floating labour' which might arise, could be drawn off through a 'judicious use of labour recruiting laws'.

By 1934, the newly-appointed DNL, AL Barrett, and the new SNA, Douglas Smit, were no longer debating whether black wages in industry should be improved, as much as how this could be done.[45] NAD officials were conscious of the need to protect urban Africans both from being driven out by white workers (through the setting of wages at so-called civilised rates), or by rural-based migrants, who might undercut them. Consequently, it would be nearly impossible to fix a standard minimum wage. The DNL upheld the common belief that Africans ought to be paid less than whites because of their lower standard of living. No one seems to have seen the irony in this. The idea that people somehow deserve their miserable lot has shown remarkable staying power throughout the history of race relations in South Africa. In this context, it was combined with the argument that blacks could not compete with whites if paid the same wage.

This was inconsistent with Barrett's point (made in the same meeting) that whites would be driven out of skilled work unless the same wage was fixed for both races. The contradictions did not go away, but in 1934, the NAD at least threw its weight behind the opinion that 'the country generally would gain by an increase in the wage of unskilled native labourers'.[46]

This position was endorsed by the Industrial Legislation (Van Reenen) Commission of 1935, which prepared the way for the IC and Wage Acts of 1937. The Van Reenen Report took a more positive view of the prospects for augmenting the national income. It rejected the concept of the national income as a fixed quantity which could only be divided up one way or another, or diminished through excessive wage increases.[47] The Report argued that increasing lower incomes should become the Wage Board's first priority. The Board should operate on the principle of equal pay for equal work, but avoid recommending the artificially high rates which, in the past, had caused the displacement of blacks by whites.

By the mid-1930s, the Labour Department was able to exert enough pressure to prevent the Wage Board from damaging the Department's commitment to self-regulation of industries through joint control by white unions and employers. Frank Lucas retired in 1935, disillusioned by the Board's ineffectiveness.[48] His colleagues resigned or retired at the same time, so the Minister of Labour was able to appoint an entirely new Wage Board. The new Chairman, Frank McGregor, was a senior Labour Department official who conformed to the common opinions of his branch of the civil service.

In 1937, JH Hofmeyr took over as Minister of Labour from the old Labour Party stalwart, Walter Madeley. Hofmeyr was more ready to accept the need for wage increases for unskilled workers, but he also embraced the working principles of his department, steering through an IC Act which endorsed and extended the concept of self-regulation in secondary industry. The Van Reenen Report, too, appeased the department by affirming the primacy of the industrial council system in wage regulation. The

Report was 'against subverting the principles of self-government and consultation unless absolutely necessary'.[49] Moreover, the Minister of Labour, rather than the Wage Board, would be responsible for harmonising wage rates. There would be no uniform minimum wage; rates would be fixed, as in the past, for specific trades and industries. In other cases, industrial councils would be required to establish rates for every class of worker in the industry concerned.[50] The Report also dismissed pleas from Malanite nationalists that quotas of whites to blacks should be guaranteed by the state.

The Gold Producers' Committee greeted the 1937 bills with apprehension, fearing they would be used to force the replacement of blacks by whites, thus raising production costs on the mines.[51] In the House of Assembly, Dr Malan and some members of the Labour Party denounced the Wage Bill.[52] However, there was never any doubt that the bills would become law.

In part, the government's augmented role in wage regulation may be related to the worldwide trend towards increased state intervention in the economy. Under the pressures of Depression and mass unemployment, the USA in the 1930s 'developed, for the first time, a 'sense of state'. Power gravitated to Washington as it long had to Paris and London, and financial authority moved from Wall Street to the national capital just as it did from Sao Paolo to Rio de Janeiro.'[53]

The British economist, Maynard Keynes, whom FD Roosevelt hired as an advisor, claimed the American President was 'trying new ways boldly and even gaily with no object but the welfare of his people'.[54] The 'New Deal', with its unemployment programmes, public housing schemes and recognition of the role of trade unions, echoed around the globe, borrowing from some governments (especially Britain and Sweden) and lending inspiration to others. South Africa could not remain completely immune to this process.

More narrowly, though, the passing of the revised Wage and IC Acts resulted from internal developments. Black workers were becoming increasingly important in secondary industry, while the quality of life in urban locations continued to deteriorate. Employers came to recognise the essential moderation of the Wage Board and slowly discarded their fears of being driven out of business. A growing optimism prevailed as South Africa put the Depression behind it and secondary industry grew year by year. At the same time, far-sighted industrialists such as HJ Laite propagandised on behalf of higher wages as a means of expanding the market for home-produced goods. For a combination of reasons, the government could thus mobilise support for revised industrial legislation which would also remove the judicial and administrative sticking points in previous laws.

Labour Department officials drew up the original drafts and submitted them to industrial councils, umbrella organisations representing chambers of commerce and industries, municipalities and white unions. Employers now saw the Acts as a way of curbing worker militancy, ensuring greater uniformity in wages and conditions, and affording a larger measure of predictability about the future.[55] The only criticism levelled by the 1936 Congress of the Association of Chambers of Commerce of South Africa was that the Industrial Conciliation Act should have been passed earlier. The Natal Chamber of Industries concurred, and called for stiffer penalties to deal with 'unscrupulous employers' who failed to implement industrial council agreements. The English language press rallied behind the United Party in support of the Wage Bill. One *Cape Times* correspondent called it 'a very necessary piece of social legislation', and went on to slam the Malanites' 'colour prejudice'.[56] The idea of wage regulation as a vehicle of social welfare had finally caught on outside the Joint Councils, the Institute of Race Relations and the minds of a few enlightened Native Affairs officials.

The extension of the industrial council system in the 1930s had already asserted the IC Act's primary importance in wage regulation. The revised Act of 1937 underlined this by allowing councils to recommend not only wages and hours for other workers in their industry (as under the 1930 amendment), but also working conditions and holidays.[57] An inspector (from the NAD) was to sit on councils in which African interests were discussed. For the first time urban workers in the Cape Province were excluded from direct participation under the IC Act. The Wage Act was redrafted to tackle the ever-growing problem of the gap between unskilled and other wages.[58] The 1930 restriction, that all applicants for a wage determination should sign their names, was dropped. So too was the prohibition on recommending a wage which would not permit a worker to live at a so-called civilised standard (though the civilised standard clause was not entirely abandoned).[59] The way was thus cleared for the Wage Board to begin raising the wages of the vast bulk of African workers. But the dangers of moving too quickly and thus damaging the lower-paying employers, together with the Department of Labour's preference for wage regulation through all-white industrial councils, made the prospect of rapid, effective relief through the Wage Board, highly unlikely.

Wage Boards and War Measures, 1938-1948

The Wage Board's already limited efforts to improve African wages after 1937 were hampered by employers. While industrial employers did not unite to form the sort of monopsonistic organisations developed by the mineowners, they did combine, on occasion, to pressure the Board into keeping wages low. In some areas they purposely avoided forming organisations in order to make the operation of wage regulation more difficult.[60] The Wage Board was obliged to investigate an industry's capacity to pay before making a recommendation, and it was the employers who provided the information as to their financial well-being. McGregor himself accepted as a general principle that 'raising wages made less work', as he told the Acting DNL in 1943.[61] The SATLC contended in 1948 that numerous manufacturers were making forty to fifty per cent profits on their employees' labour, a response which the Wage Board ignored in its reply.[62]

The government took the view that mobility in the African labour market helped to prevent workers' exploitation. In reality, this was far from the case, as workers were so desperate to flee miserable conditions on the farms that they would accept even the poverty wages offered in the towns. Opportunities for improving one's lot by moving from one job to another were severely restricted because wages were almost uniformly low and because of restrictions on movement under pass laws and influx controls. In any case, craft union control over apprenticeships and the lack of access to education made it almost impossible for an African to advance up the ladder of industrial employment.

On the other hand, the changes introduced in 1937 were not simply a means to make the civilised labour policy more effective.[63] Certainly the government was still concerned that the growing wage gap between skilled and unskilled would limit employment opportunities for the white working class. But by 1937, with the growth of black trade unions, the government believed it must either control black wage increases in an orderly, closely regulated fashion, or watch the unions take what they wanted for themselves. The Board thus saw the very low wages paid to Africans in industry and commerce as an important problem in its own right. It did not see low wages for Africans merely as an extension of the 'poor white problem', which by this time was beginning to yield to employment by the government and parastatals and to the opening up of new jobs for machinists and supervisory staff.

From 1937-47, the Wage Board prepared determinations for 303 064 workers and participated in numerous arbitrations under War Measures (WM) 9 and 145 of 1942. The War Measures were introduced largely to prevent strikes, but they were also intended as a way around cumbersome Wage Board procedures. The first War Measure allowed the Minister of Labour to apply compulsory arbitration in an industrial dispute which could affect the war effort. The second placed a blanket ban on strikes involving black workers, with, again, arbitration at the Minister's discretion. The measures held some attraction for the Board members, as they allowed them to tackle certain difficulties for which the Wage Act was ill-designed. For example, in 1945, the

Wage Board members acted as arbitrators under WM 9 in a dispute in the preserved food industry. The Food, Canning and Allied Workers Union had been dissatisfied with an earlier determination, and rather than revise the whole thing, the new award raised the wages of two specific classes, namely mechanics and those earning less than £2 per week.[64] Other adjustments were made to certain workers' leave periods.

In 1947, the Wage Board was again called in, this time under WM 145, when a dispute arose between the Johannesburg City Council and its 15 000 African employees, who were represented by the Transvaal Municipal African Workers' Union.[65] The conflict had reached crisis-point because of foot-dragging by the council, with the local authority claiming the union's demands took a long time to process, as six different municipal departments had to be canvassed for information and opinions. Behind this, some clever politicking was afoot. The council was attempting to improve its standing amongst local ratepayers by cutting costs on workers' rations; the union called for an end to rations altogether. The Board rejected the union's demands. Instead, it accepted the council's proposals of 29-30s per week for labourers, plus a 9s 3d cost of living allowance. This was a mere 2s a week improvement on the previous determination regulating Johannesburg municipal workers. On the positive side, it was higher than twenty-three of the thirty-three determinations then in force in the city, which the Board naturally looked to as a yardstick. The Board refused to consider raising wages to Cape Town levels, on the grounds that labourers there were coloured and therefore had a higher standard of living. The arbitrators took the union's demand for 10s per day as proof of its unreasonableness and contrasted this with the council's enlightened generosity.[66] The Board, operating under the War Measures, was able to complete its investigation in only three months. The War Measures thus served an administrative purpose over and above their usefulness in preventing strikes. For this reason, the Board was keen to retain the WMs at the end of the war.

Despite the War Measures' importance, the bulk of the work

continued to be done under the Wage Act or through the extension of industrial council agreements. Private wage agreements and awards were not totally supplanted, but the Board's activities continued to expand in the late 1930s and early 1940s. Changes introduced to the Act in 1937 also made it easier to overcome the recalcitrance of individual employers. The Wage Board ploughed its way through determination after determination, constantly chasing the rising cost of living, which forced it back to the same territory year after year. Even after two decades the Board's work remained a source of much contention on all sides. Unions, employers, farmers, and bureaucrats regarded their respective group interests as threatened or damaged by the Board's work, and treated that institution as a punch bag for the difficulties they faced.

Trade unions, both white and black, protested that the Board's determinations were too low and that they failed to take account of the poor conditions described in the Smit Committee Report of 1942. In 1940, the Wage Board had argued for the first time that the ability of an industry to pay should not necessarily be the most important factor in wage determinations for unskilled workers, and some marginal firms might have to be sacrificed in the drive to narrow the skilled/unskilled wage gap.[67] Nonetheless, in individual determinations such as the Johannesburg municipal workers' award of 1947, the Board continued to spell out increases in percentage terms, with no reference to the lowest possible living wage scales occasionally drawn up by such organisations as the SAIRR. By 1946, moreover, as white servicemen returned from the war and employment opportunities were becoming less plentiful, the Board was expressing caution on the question of raising unskilled wages.[68] In this, the new Chairman, Dr JH Botha, may also have been influenced by the Board's failure to abate widespread industrial unrest in the 1940s by applying wage determinations.

In its 1948 response to the SATLC, the Board explained how average rates had improved by 135.2 per cent in Johannesburg, 186.9 per cent in Pretoria, and so on.[69] The unions argued that the bulk of this was eaten up by inflation and that the awards did not compensate for the prohibitions on strikes. The extent to which these increases would have been granted anyway if free labour relations had been permitted, can only be guessed at. One may assume that wages would have risen during the war, when pressure on labour resources was growing. On the other hand, the weakness of African trade unions and the unstable nature of their membership, would probably have prevented them from making any really significant gains before 1948.

The fact that the Board sanctioned such low wages was by no means the only grievance raised by the trade union movement. In 1946 to 1947, the Food and Canning Workers Union, led by Ray Alexander, fought a running battle with the Board to force investigations into the wines and brandy manufacturing industry.[70] The Board fobbed her off by arguing that the union was insufficiently representative to request a determination, and that the Board was over-loaded with work. This was a common problem in the war years. In 1942, the Board had hoped to acquire professional investigators to carry out preliminary studies, but because of staff shortages and cost restraints, nothing came of this.[71] There was another familiar problem in the wine industry. Employers were using the old argument that their business was agricultural and therefore not subject to the Wage Act.[72] The Board finally agreed to investigate, but set wages for workers in towns outside Cape Town at levels lower than those originally offered by the employers. The Board apparently feared offending farmers in the wine areas, as MPs from farming constituencies across the country still protested frequently against high wages in the towns.[73] In this case, the Board took the path of least resistance by condemning labourers in Paarl, Stellenbosch, Wellington and Worcester to a wage of £1 10s per week. As the union pointed out, the Wage Board was guilty in this case of ignoring its supposed non-discriminatory principles and awarding wages according to the worker's race. In this way, the Board perpetuated the exploitation of 'cheap, non-European' labour and failed to close the gaps between un- and semi-skilled, and skilled workers.

The Trades and Labour Council, too, drew attention to these and other matters. Apart from everything else, its leaders complained, the Board's machinery was slow and cumbersome.[74] But the SATLC had its own interests to pursue, and these were not always the same as those of black workers. The white unions wanted collective bargaining, with machinery for settling industrial disputes, an industrial court and state co-operation with trade unions to reduce prices and control profits. This was essentially the same as the Labour Party platform, and it was thus unlikely to do much for the ordinary black worker. Evidence from industrial council agreements after 1937 does not suggest that the white unions were going out of their way to help those not represented at the table. In the Engineering Industrial Council's agreement of 1942, for example, black workers were dealt with in the usual summary fashion zero increase in Cape Town, 3s more per week in East London and Durban, and 6s more on the Rand. This compared with a twenty-five per cent increase for operatives and journeymen, which, for the latter, meant 3s 3d more per hour.[75] As mechanisation and mass production techniques advanced during the war, the white unions were concerned to protect themselves against what they saw as unfair competition, whether from blacks, apprentices or underpaid, female labour. There was little room in their struggle for narrowing the gap between semi- and unskilled workers, which would have involved a long and arduous battle against racial segregation and prevailing trends in national politics. In the 1930s and 1940s, there were few altruistic white trade unionists ready to put worker solidarity before immediate self-interest.[76]

The other major critics of the wage regulating system were the farmers. Farm labourers were specifically excluded from regulation under either the Wage or the IC Acts. On the other hand, farmers blamed government-sanctioned high wages in the towns for the labour shortages with which they were faced. The Low Veld (North-East) Farmers' Association was following a time-honoured farming tradition when it addressed the Minister of Labour in 1948 on crime in urban areas:

It may be argued that the solution to the problem would be in such measures as better control of Native movement, better policing of our towns and cities, very severe punishment on conviction, deportation to reserves of surplus urban Natives and the like. While all such measures may have value and may even be necessary, it is still maintained that the root cause of the evil can, and must, be blamed to [sic] the creation, chiefly by artificially high State-fixed minimum wages, *through present regulation and legislation*, of conditions enticing natives from the country to the towns in numbers far in excess of the demand for such labour.[77]

This widely-held sentiment was influential, as in the wine industry determination of 1946-7, in holding down regulated wages in rural areas to even lower levels than those in the towns.[78] The fact that this made major urban centres even more attractive to rural blacks was a great irritant to white farmers who, during the war, held the prospect of vastly expanded markets and rising commodity prices before them, but were unwilling to improve wages and conditions to counter the townward drift of labour.

These external criticisms and pressures on the wage regulating system were compounded by internal disagreements within the state and by the burdensome nature of administrative procedure entailed in the two Acts. Civil servants were not the only ones to complain about this last difficulty. In 1946, the FCI asked the Department of Labour to publish a guide book for confused employers, explaining their obligations to African employees.[79] But it was the Labour Department's Divisional Inspectors, the DNL and his staff, and the Wage Board members themselves, who protested loudest about the red tape. At their annual conference in 1944, Divisional Inspectors agreed that enforcement of wage determinations was almost impossible where more than one determination was applicable to a single firm and where wages, annual leave, hours of work and other clauses, varied considerably.[80] Another problem involved overlapping definitions of industries, where employees spent part of their time in one industry and the rest in another. The defensive manner in which the new Wage Board Chairman replied, suggests a lack of communication between the initiators of the awards and the officials who ensured their implementation. Elsewhere, the Board argued that its work would be simpler if it had professional investigators, if it could ignore the ability-to-pay factor on amended determinations, and if it did not have to take account of fluctuating cost of living allowances in short-term, repeated determinations.[81] These points were not related directly to the interests of one group or another, but to the needs of the Board itself, as it struggled to conquer the growing mountain of work, and the mass of wartime bureaucratic regulations.

By contrast, the Acting DNL, JH Tandy, was clearly supporting the gold and coal mines when he argued in 1943 that high wage determinations and related concessions were having 'repercussions on the main industry of the country'.[82] The NAD was wary of voicing too clearly the interests of miners over those of the industrial worker. Indeed, we can take the SNA, Douglas Smit, at his word when he said in 1943 that he was 'anxious that the clock should not be put back in so far as the rates paid to Native workers are concerned'.[83] However, just as the Department of Labour's first priority in labour regulation was to preserve the industrial council system, so the NAD was preoccupied with defending its role in the control of migrant, compounded workers on the mines, rather than with workers' interests. Wage determinations which were significantly higher than the 2s 2d per shift traditionally paid on the gold mines created three problems. They drew labour away from the mines (especially in the case of miners who came to work on six or nine month contracts and then refused to sign up for a further period in the hope of finding a better paid job in commerce or industry); they affected working costs on the mines by raising the price of materials and services; and they damaged the mines' public image as a 'good' employer (and thus tarnished the sub-department of Native

Labour's reputation as the inspecting agency). This was particularly worrying for the state and the mines in 1943, when
African mineworkers were rallying behind the union and the
government was trying to stave off a strike by establishing the
Lansdown Commission on mine labourers' wages. But the NAD
could not say so in so many words, even to the Labour Department. Rather, its officials focused on the value of compound
accommodation and rations, and the African's so-called inability
to understand these benefits.

The DNL also blamed the growing wage disparity between
different sectors on administrative problems. He claimed there
was a lack of communication between departments, when in
reality he meant the ability of other departments to dissuade the
Wage Board from making high awards. The extent to which a
real administrative difficulty existed in this case is open to question, but the fact that the then Chairman, F McGregor, explained
his work to the SNA in the most basic terms, suggests that there
was little co-operation in making awards.[84] At any rate, the
DNL's attack illustrates strikingly the pressures brought to bear
on the Board, even from branches of the civil service which were
supposed to be advancing urban African workers' interests. That
the Wage Act continued to be applied to black workers in the
mid- to late-1940s, was a testimony to both the Labour Department's failure to find a more acceptable mechanism for regulating Africans' wages and to the Board's commitment to
improving wages largely within the confines of existing cost
structures in industry and commerce.

Conclusion

By the use of the machinery of the Industrial Conciliation Act and the Wage Act it should be possible
for South Africa, without any upheaval, to bridge
the gap that exists between the wages of its white
skilled workers and its black unskilled workers by
means of a scale of wages having regular rungs from

the 10s a week man to the £6 a week man. This will open the way for the civilised non-European worker as well as the European to rise rung by rung and to become a more efficient worker and a more efficient citizen.[85]

The Johannesburg Joint Council published the above statement in 1927, at a time when wage regulation was still geared to controlling the unions and preserving jobs for white workers. Over the next twenty years, the system underwent three major changes. In 1929-30, the laws (and regulations) were amended to preserve their racially discriminatory character by effectively excluding unskilled black workers from the benefits of participation under either Act. Then, in 1935-7, the state announced its acceptance of the principles of wage determination for Africans, and of narrowing the gap between skilled and unskilled wage levels. The liberals appeared to have won. The state had embraced the ideals of the Joint Councils, with their image of well-ordered chains of being, from the skilled artisan down to the poorest street-sweeper. The more able and willing Africans would be able to follow the proper avenues of ambition, from unskilled labour, through better paid employment in semi-skilled categories, right up to relatively highly paid craft work. The quantum leap from unskilled labourer's wages to skilled wages would gradually, but unerringly, be closed. As the state's regulation of labour as a whole expanded, so the regulation of wages would also be extended.

The new policy fitted the needs of a growing secondary industrial and commercial sector, where craft skills were no longer at a premium and where more and more semi-skilled posts were opening up. In addition, the dissemination of the theory that South African industry would gain from a larger internal black market also helped to popularise the notion that unskilled wages should be raised. Yet, although hundreds of thousands of blacks came under wage determinations before 1948, the wage gap between unskilled and skilled was not closed. The demands of the war effort, combined with pressure from farmers and mine-owners, discouraged the state from moving too quickly to alter existing wage structures. Instead, the Smuts government armed itself with draconian powers to ban strikes and settle disputes by arbitrary means. This was the last major change in the wage regulating system in this period. The War Measures of 1942, intended as a temporary expedient, became an essential part of the state's regulation of African wages.

It seems doubtful that the state ever really intended to push the wage-raising policy as far as the rhetoric of the late 1930s implied. As the NEC minority report recognised, low wages 'make possible and encourage certain forms of industry which could hardly be carried on without it'.[86] The state, ultimately, was not prepared to jeopardise going concerns to spread profits more evenly amongst disenfranchised workers. As we have seen, opposition to a high wage policy came from both outside and inside the state – externally from mineowners and farmers, and internally (in 1943, at least) from the Director of Native Labour. The NAD played a more equivocal part in this area than in other aspects of wage regulation, defending its own sphere of admin-istration while avoiding a politically contentious role in improv-ing black wages.

The task at hand belonged to the Department of Labour, which was more concerned with seeing jobs preserved for white workers and promoting the self-regulation of industrial relations under the IC Act. The former purpose could be served more simply and cheaply by widening the job market for machinists and supervisory staff. From 1935, the Department kept a much tighter rein on the Wage Board, which was no longer given the latitude it had enjoyed under FAW Lucas. Where Lucas had called for action on black wages, McGregor was more worried about driving businesses under. The government shared his anxiety, claiming that wage increases for urban Africans were inflationary. In consequence, a scheme begun with the express intention of raising black wages, came to be geared more nar-rowly towards preserving industrial peace. The Wage Board pleased nobody. Its procedures were complex to the point of absurdity, it struck fear into the owners of primary industry, and it left the mass of African workers submerged in poverty. As the next chapter shows, though, the problems of creating an alternative acceptable to all parties were more or less intractable.

7

THE STATE AND AFRICAN TRADE UNIONS

Introduction

By 1918, the state had considerable power over African workers under the masters and servants laws and the Native Labour Regulation Act.[1] While the government was to insist again and again over the next few years that black trade unions were not illegal, they had little opportunity to operate within the confines of existing industrial legislation. Official ideology held that black workers were not sufficiently civilised to run trade unions for themselves.[2] Inevitably, they would be dominated by communist subversives who would use them for their own devious, political ends. Instead, the government presented the NAD as the guardian of black interests. Under the NLR Act, the NAD had a duty to investigate the grievances of African workers in industry and in proclaimed labour districts, and to act as an intermediary between employers and employees in the event of a dispute.

Within the state, however, there developed a heated debate over official policy towards African trade unions. This chapter examines the reasons for this, including the organisation of black workers into trade unions, which sought to improve the degrading conditions in which most Africans lived and worked and the government's new industrial legislation, which was intended to bring stability to relations between white workers and their employers in the wake of the Rand Revolt of 1922. The question of official treatment of African trade unions was therefore intertwined with that of the wage regulating machinery discussed in Chapter 6. The two issues were even more closely linked in the 1930s, when African unions liaised unofficially with state officials to enforce wage determinations.

The debate was pursued largely by the Departments of Labour and Native Affairs. External bodies such as the SAIRR, white trade union organisations, the Chamber of Mines, the Department of Mines and, of course, African unions themselves made a significant contribution. The wider forces impinging on the debate involved ongoing industrialisation and urbanisation, increasing participation by blacks in unskilled and later in semiskilled jobs in industry and commerce, booms and slumps in the economy, and changes in the fortunes of the bureaucracy's political masters. As if this were not enough, officials also had to look to their own departmental interests, to protect themselves from adverse publicity and to predict the possible implications of changes in administrative and statutory regulation. The significance of all these different factors is discussed in the following pages.

Registered and Unregistered Unions, 1918-1930

The growth of black protest at the end of World War I was a serious worry for the state. The government was concerned about the prospect of African workers imitating their militant white counterparts, especially after the 1920 black mineworkers' strike and the 1922 Rand Revolt.[3] During the latter conflict, the NAD's sub-department of Native Labour took enormous care to prevent Africans from becoming 'infected' with the virus of revolt.[4]

Yet, despite these very real fears, the question of African unionisation did not become an issue in state circles until after the Pact government initiated its 'civilised labour' policy in 1924. In the latter half of the decade, the Departments of Labour and Native Affairs, the Native Affairs Commission and the Wage

Board kept up a heated debate on the role African trade unions should play in industrial relations and the forms of recognition that should be accorded to them.

The debate arose at this juncture for several reasons. Most importantly, the Industrial Conciliation Act established machinery for laying down wages and conditions in industry in consultation with registered trade unions. This was supplemented by the Wage Act of 1925, which created a Wage Board to perform a similar function in industries where no organised trade unions existed.[5] As the last chapter showed, the government expected these Acts to fulfil the additional aim of preventing secondary industry from being dominated by cheap black labour, and thus protecting another avenue of employment for 'poor whites'. Both Acts were openly intended to co-opt and control white workers. But the state had not appreciated the problems involved in regulating for one group of workers and not another. Neither Act allowed consultation with, or representation of, the mass of unskilled Africans, who by the mid-1920s, already formed the majority in secondary industry. Employers exploited the exclusion of 'pass-bearing' Africans from agreements under the IC Act, by replacing expensive white labour with cheaper African workers. This was not the case under the Wage Act, which contained no such racially-oriented restrictions. In that case, the presence of large numbers of unrepresented black workers operated to keep wages down generally, both in industries where determinations were applied, and in those where the Board felt a 'civilised' wage was impossible.

The second factor behind the debate on black unions involved the nature of the bureaucracy itself. The Pact government's victory and the inclusion in the cabinet of Labour Party members, FHP Creswell, Walter Madeley and Thomas Boydell, led to the creation of a new Department of Labour, backed by a consultative body called the Advisory Council of Labour. As explained in Chapter 2, several officials, including the later Secretary, Ivan Walker, had a history of active trade unionism and were well-disposed to the further development of organised labour.[6]

Although they were generally prejudiced in favour of white labour and shared many of the racist assumptions of society at large, their background and duties made them more willing than other officials to accept African trade unionisation. This contrasted with the more paternalistic attitudes prevailing in the NAD, where senior officers denied that Africans could run trade unions for themselves without corruption or subversion by white communists. The small, tight-knit formation of the Department of Labour may also have contributed to its comparatively early development of a recognisable position on this issue.[7] As the first Secretary for Labour, CW Cousins, wrote to his Minister:

> I think the assurance can be given that there is no member of this Staff, made up as it is of men and women brought into daily contact with the issues at stake, who would hold any other view than that suggested above.[8]

The rise of the ICU and, subsequently, the Federation of Non-European Trade Unions, was the other main cause of the debate on trade unions. The state as a whole was deeply concerned about the growth of interest in unions among Africans in the late 1920s, especially when the ICU was at the height of its power, from 1926 to 1927. The NAD kept a close eye on the organisation; the police harassed its officials; the white public was terrified by the prospect of revolutionary tendencies among African workers. In the light of subsequent events, the situation was not nearly as menacing as many then feared, but at the time, state officials believed they should act before further 'grave trouble' developed.[9]

The Department of Labour clearly wished to draw the teeth of the ICU by bringing it within bureaucratic structures designed to control organised labour in general.[10] Predictions that African trade unions would eventually dominate the industrial scene, and the desire to channel grievances in more controllable directions, were major features of the debate. However, this has to be qualified in several ways. For one, the Department of Labour's plans were not intended merely to emasculate the African trade union movement. Senior officials, such as the Secretary for Labour, CW Cousins, Under Secretary, E Muller, and W Free-stone, Divisional Inspector, believed black trade unions could be incorporated within official negotiating procedures, and were not simply trying to wrest the initiative from them.[11] Second, both the ICU and FNETU saw recognition as a real advantage. It was the prospect of African workers making immediate gains through their unions' incorporation within state structures, that ultimately led the Prime Minister himself to block recognition. For the Department of Labour, it was essential to prevent employers undercutting white workers by hiring blacks. The incorporation of blacks would help to protect white workers by increasing the cost of black labour and discouraging the displacement of whites by Africans. In this way, the Department of Labour pursued what its officials regarded as another of its main purposes.

Finally, the Department of Labour's position arose out of internal considerations as well as external ones. Officials in this tiny, newly-established department were as anxious to increase their own power and status within the state as they were to solve the problem of African trade unions. In this, their position was similar to that of the NAD, which was likewise eager to enhance its reputation as a branch of the public service. Unlike the NAD, though, Labour Department officials were not directly concerned about their image in the eyes of the African population.

The course of the debate between 1925 and 1930 was by no means a straight line, though various stages are discernible. The original impulse came in 1925 from the Economic and Wage (Mills) Commission, which called for general wage improvements for the lowest paid[12] and from the Department of Labour's own fears about the narrow definition of 'employee' in the IC Act, and the danger of displacement of whites by blacks.

The Labour Department's proposals for incorporating blacks were struck down by the Native Affairs Commission, which claimed they would cause the displacement of too many Africans and, more ominously, by the Prime Minister, General Hertzog, in his capacity as Minister of Native Affairs. He rejected incorporation of Africans under the Acts on the grounds that this would lead to higher prices for the white public, opposition from employers, 'violent agitation from natives ousted from industry' and catastrophe for white workers, who would be put on the same footing as blacks.[13]

By the time the issue was raised again, the position of African trade unions had come much more to the fore. The Conference of October 1927, between the NAD, NAC, Wage Board and Department of Labour, was partly a reaction to a visit by Clements Kadalie, the ICU leader, to the International Labour Organisation in Geneva. His trip had highlighted the bogeys of independent black unionisation and international criticism of South Africa.[14]

The conference was a free-for-all exchange of views between different branches of the state. The Secretary for Labour set the pace by calling for the inclusion of as many Africans as possible under the IC Act. He accepted that the industrial Acts had been framed to help white workers, but argued that they could be made to work for Africans, just as the Factories Act of 1918 already did.[15] With regard to unionisation, the Chief Inspector of Labour favoured incorporating Africans into established white unions. If any white unions refused to have black members, Africans could be given separate representation on industrial councils. If necessary, Inspectors of Labour could even organise African unions themselves – not to control them, but as a way of drawing black workers into established negotiating practices. Africans had to be encouraged to stand up for themselves. If they were afforded recognition, their position in industry would be strengthened and they would not face wholesale displacement. At any rate, Labour Department officials claimed, it was essential to bring blacks into conciliation before they became embittered.

These were similar to the arguments put forward by the Johannesburg Joint Council led by JD Rheinallt Jones, and in more vehement terms, by the ICU and (later) the Federation of

Non-European Trade Unions.[16] The DNL, HS Cooke, and members of the NAC, opposed them on the grounds that black workers would not get a fair deal on industrial councils. The white unions could not be trusted to put the African case fairly, and blacks whose wages had been raised would face replacement by whites. Much better, according to the DNL, to use the Wage Board to improve unskilled wages, but with an NAD official sitting on Wage Boards which affected African workers, to protect their interests. Trade unions for Africans were simply out of the question, since many blacks were migrants, the majority were illiterate, and public opinion (whites) would never accept it.

The NAD may have been trying to counteract what it saw as the Department of Labour's bias towards white workers. The Pact government's much-trumpeted 'civilised labour' policy threatened the NAD's legitimacy among African workers.[17] Moreover, white trade unions, especially on the Rand, would do little to help black workers unless the white unions saw immediate gains for themselves. Yet the DNL's fear of offending white public opinion and his insistence that whites and blacks had to be dealt with separately, suggests that his primary concerns were the needs of industrial employers and the power of his own department. The NAD had only recently extended its duties under the Native Administration Act of 1927; its officers now mooted an even larger part for themselves as the representatives of African workers on Wage Boards and industrial councils. At the conference, the DNL's immediate superior, JF Herbst, backed him up, although he did not take as much personal interest in labour matters as his successor, Douglas Smit. As a result of the NAD's rejection of the Department of Labour proposals, no settlement was reached on the main points under discussion. The only conclusion was that the NAD should have a consultative role in Wage Board cases which predominantly affected Africans.

Once the implications of excluding African workers from negotiating procedures became clear, the question of African industrial organisation was taken up at the political level.[18] The problems were raised in 1928, in the application of the South African Motor Drivers Union for registration under the IC Act. A lengthy correspondence ensued between Department of Labour officials, the Registrar of Trade Unions and the Department of Justice over whether an organisation representing coloureds and Africans could be registered. Registration was eventually prohibited on the recommendation of the law advisers, who used the legal principle of 'original intent' to argue that the Act was not applicable to blacks.[19]

As differences of opinion within the state reached a peak in late 1928, the NAD briefly offered to abandon its claim to represent Africans in industrial negotiations.[20] The SNA proposed that the Department of Labour should deal with all matters affecting Africans connected with the Wage and IC Acts and trade union organisation, except where these were statutorily administered by the DNL under the Native Labour Regulation Act. This about-turn seems to have arisen from a conflict between African postal workers and the Minister of Posts and Telegraphs in which the workers demanded representation by the ICU while the Minister claimed they should be represented by the NAD. A fierce editorial in *Imvo Zabantsundu* stated that the government stood for capital, and the NAD, as a part of the state, was a natural opponent of workers.[21] Caught in the middle, the SNA tried to pass the buck by giving the whole problem over to Labour in accordance with that department's earlier proposals.

Disappointed by its earlier failure to register the Motor Drivers Union, the Department of Labour received the NAD's 'epoch-making' minute with pleasure. In 1928, Labour Department officials drew up plans to amend the IC Act, to allow agreements to be extended to all workers in an industry. However, this was rejected internally as a betrayal of the principle of laying down wages and conditions only for those represented in negotiations.[22] Instead, the department sought to kill off the problems relating to industrial legislation by bringing all workers under the same laws. Wage settlements would ostensibly be colour-blind, with African workers incorporated into recognised, white-led trade unions. At one blow this would remove the threat of undercutting and displacement of white workers by blacks and prevent communist infiltration of independent black trade unions. Such a move would also allow the state to avoid the politically dangerous task of regulating wages by direct executive action through wage determinations.

From the start, Labour Department officials were doubtful that the suggestions would be put into effect.[23] The government's position was not fully spelt out until after the 1929 election. Despite a flurry of activity which saw senior Labour Department officials attending ICU conferences, and frequent articles in *The Star* on African industrial workers' unionisation, the NAD and the Department of Labour finally agreed in May 1929 that the 'time was not opportune' for a major change in administrative practice, at least until the government's policy was clearer and they had consulted various public bodies.[24] The collapse of the ICU, the eclipse of the Labour Party within the Pact government, and the onset of Depression, all served to encourage the Labour Department to back quietly away from the issue.

The first great debate on the recognition of trade unions ended with changes to the Wage Act regulations in 1929, and amendments to the Riotous Assemblies and IC Acts in 1929-30. The draconian nature of these laws demonstrates forcefully the limits of administrative power in determining policy within the state, and the Labour Party's lack of muscle in the Pact government. The alteration to the Wage Act regulations was reminiscent of what was known in the American Deep South as 'Jim Crow' – introduce a simple literacy requirement and so deny unlettered black people the rights to which they would otherwise have been entitled.[25] The amended IC Act authorised industrial councils to recommend wages and conditions for those outside the scope of the agreement.[26] This was openly intended to prevent employers displacing whites by blacks, by forcing them to pay the same wages to unrepresented workers. The idea of allowing black labour representation under the IC Act, either through white or African trade unions, or by NAD officials, was thus abandoned.

The repressive nature of both these changes was as nothing compared to the new Riotous Assemblies Act. As early as 1927, Hertzog had stated in parliament that the government would not ban Africans from forming legitimate trade unions. If African workers wished to organise there was nothing to stop them. The only restriction was that their unions could not be registered under the IC Act.[27] In theory, the Riotous Assemblies (Amendment) Act did not alter this, it merely made incitement to racial violence (by any party) a criminal offence. Nonetheless, as the Minister of Justice, Oswald Pirow, made clear, the Act was never intended for use against whites. It was aimed, rather, at the leaders of so-called subversive African organisations such as the ICU.[28] By introducing the Act, Pirow sought to achieve the Department of Labour's objective of control, not through the indirect means of co-option but via the direct route of coercion. The Act was a product of the Department of Justice, which in this period was increasingly staffed by nationalist civil servants with fascist sympathies.[29] Pirow was moved by repeated warnings from police spies of the activities of communist 'agitators', and by pressure from white farmers who feared ICU activities among agricultural labourers. There was considerable opposition in the white Press, from the white Trade Union Congress (led by the communist, Bill Andrews), from black trade unions, and from Church groups. Despite their criticisms, Pirow agreed only to minor limitations on his unprecedented powers under the Act.[30]

In this way, the hard-liners in the Pact government – especially Hertzog and Pirow – killed off the Department of Labour's plans to nurture Africans within white or separate trade unions. They also rejected, for the time being, the Wage Board Chairman's scheme for narrowing the skilled-unskilled wage gap through wage determinations. This reflected both the balance of power within the cabinet, where the Labour Party was definitely the junior partner (especially after the general election of 1929), and that between the civil service and the executive. In terms of the latter division, certain branches of the bureaucracy already had a more sophisticated concept of the role of a black proletariat in a white-dominated capitalist economy than did the Prime Minister, who viewed it in purely functional terms. But the argument was by no means over in 1930. Unlike Malan after 1948, Hertzog did not purge the bureaucracy of English-speaking, liberally-inclined officials, especially in the NAD, Labour and Public Health Departments. Despite the 1929-30 clamp-down, the state continued to seek some form of consensus among whites on race relations. In the process, it allowed a continued role in administration for the expression of different viewpoints.

The Lull before the Storm, 1930-1937

Partly as a result of severe state repression, the ICU and FNETU were shadows of their former selves by the early 1930s. African trade unions in the 1920s and early 1930s were stifled by a range of factors, including constant harassment under pass law regulations; the difficulties involved in organising semi-proletarianised, poverty-stricken workers; the lack of an educated, well-trained cadre of union leaders and shop stewards; internal ideological and personal differences; the hostility or disinterest of white unions; and the pressures of an economic slump. Only the bare bones of a structure survived on the Rand in the form of Gana Makabeni's Native Clothing Workers Union and Max Gordon's Laundry Workers Union.[31] At the Cape, Ray Alexander, James La Guma and others, worked among railway, harbour and factory employees to form communist-affiliated trade unions.[32] The state did not regard these organisations as a great threat and the question of how to administer African trade unions was shelved for a few years.

At the same time, changes in the South African economy were to have a major impact on the handling of trade unions after 1938. The economy entered a major growth phase from 1933, fuelled by devaluation of the South African pound, industrial protection and agricultural support. The permanent African proletariat around the major urban centres expanded and there was an increasing preponderance of African workers in unskilled and semi-skilled positions in secondary industry and commerce.[33] Between 1921 and 1936, the African population in the main industrial area on the Rand grew from 303 379 to 629 645 (see also Appendix 2). In the same period, the number of blacks employed in secondary industry in the country as a whole rose from 75 000 to 130 000, while the figures for white workers were 45 000 and 91 000 respectively.[34]

By 1937, the state was under pressure from all sides to find a more comprehensive way of dealing with black wage regulation. In the first place, African workers proved more and more willing to participate in strikes, regardless of their level of organisation in trade unions. This caused industrialists to turn to the state to control their demands and ensure that all sectors of industry and all parts of the country were equally affected by wage increases. On occasion, chambers of commerce and individual factory owners voiced general support for a 'high wage policy', though without specifying how this should be implemented. In this, they were partly influenced by the arguments of liberals and economists such as Rheinallt Jones and WM Macmillan, who contended that higher wages would increase the purchasing power of Africans and so benefit manufacturing concerns in the longer term.[35]

Finally, the government feared that the influx of Africans into the towns and the much lower wages paid to them, would eventually force white workers out of secondary industry altogether. In reality, this was highly unlikely, as the numbers of whites employed in industry also increased through the 1930s, albeit at a slower rate than those of Africans. However, the powerful white craft unions felt they were being undercut by mechanisation and the creation of semi-skilled jobs, from which they could not exclude blacks by controlling apprenticeships. The government was left with a choice. It could either extend the colour bar on the mines to other sectors and risk a backlash from employers and African workers or create machinery to narrow the gap between white and black wage levels. With JH Hofmeyr as Minister of Labour, the government chose the latter option, and

passed a new Wage Act in 1937.[36] Alongside this was the
redrafted IC Act of the same year, which allowed the Minister to
extend any industrial council agreement to those who were not
defined as 'employees' under that Act.

It was ironic that while in the political arena the state in the
late 1930s took drastic steps to extend segregation and restrict
black political rights, the same period saw the revival of the
debate on recognition of African trade unions. On the one hand,
the state responded to African urbanisation and proletarianisation by removing the few in the Cape who could vote to a separate voters' roll. On the other, the same processes provoked
discussion on how to incorporate blacks within the negotiating
structure. The reasons for this apparent contradiction lie in the
dynamics of African political and trade union mobilisation in the
later 1930s and in the workings of an ever more complex and
divided state.

The Recognition Debate, 1938-1948

As early as 1935, the Industrial Legislation (Van Reenen) Com-
mission foresaw the administrative problems in regulating
African wages under the forthcoming IC Act.[37] The Van Reenen
Report recommended including two officials (one from the
NAD) on each industrial council dealing with black wages and
conditions. The 1937 statute actually made provision for a
Labour Inspector to represent African interests at industrial
council meetings where necessary.[38] According to the Labour
Department, this was tantamount to non-discrimination before
the law. African workers had been brought under the IC Act, and
the only reason they were represented differently from whites
was because white unions refused to admit African members.[39]

Towards the end of 1938, the Department of Labour drew up
new plans, this time for administrative recognition of African
unions. In part, this was a response to the rise of two separate
trade union organisations on the Rand – Gana Makabeni's
Co-ordinating Committee of African Trade Unions and Max

Gordon's Joint Council of African Trade Unions. As Secretary of the African Commercial and Distributive Workers Union and several other unions, Gordon was in frequent contact with the Wage Board and Department of Labour Inspectors on the Rand. His role was to point to industries where wage determinations were necessary, and subsequently to assist in enforcing them.[40] A degree of unofficial recognition thus developed, at least at the level of individual wage determinations. In the late 1930s and 1940s, rising militancy among African workers, massive over-crowding and widespread poverty in the towns and the demands of wartime production, rendered this *ad hoc* strategy inadequate. These factors compelled the Native Affairs and Labour Departments to take black unions seriously and to come up with a strategy for dealing with them.

The Secretary for Labour's proposals encompassed official recognition of procedures already in operation. African unions could report to Divisional Inspectors on employment conditions, and assist the Labour Department in enforcing wage regulating instruments.[41] The unions would submit information on their leadership and membership to the Industrial Registrar, who also held such data on white unions. The NAD would attend consultative meetings between unions and Labour Department officials but would not form an integral link in the chain of communication. On the advice of their departmental secretaries, Smit and Walker, the Minister of Native Affairs, Deneys Reitz, and the Minister of Labour, Walter Madeley, approved the new rules. But there was strong opposition from the Secretary for Mines and the Transvaal Chamber of Mines, on the grounds that any form of recognition was the thin end of the wedge and would soon adversely affect the profitability of the gold mines.[42] At cabinet level, the Minister of Mines, Colonel Stallard, attacked the proposals, claiming they would encourage the spread of 'communistic agitation' to the mining industry.[43]

The communist bogey remained in the minds of administrators and politicians, despite the fact that CPSA influence in the trade union movement had never recovered from the collapse of

FNETU in the early 1930s. The CPSA supported Gordon's unions in their publication *Chain Breaker* but had little influence.[44] Few of the main union leaders on the Rand were CPSA members, though JB Marks of the African Mine Workers Union, and Ray Alexander of the Cape based Food and Canning Workers Union, were card-carrying communists. Meanwhile, the Commissioner of Police, as well as Smit at the NAD and Walker at the Labour Department, continued to see communists round every corner.[45] This may have been partly due to misinformation from the police, who seem to have regarded trade unionists by definition as communists (in September 1943, the Commissioner of Police reported there were communists at the head of most of the thirty African unions on the Rand).[46]

Consideration of the new rules proceeded through 1939 and into 1940, when the Secretary for Labour again circulated proposals akin to those of 1938. In parliament, 'Native' MP Margaret Ballinger brought the issue to a vote, but a massive majority rejected her motion to bring African workers under the IC Act.[47] CCATU was still lobbying for full recognition and Gordon tried to demonstrate his *bona fides* by sending the ACDWU's draft constitution to the Registrar of Trade Unions. By the end of 1940, however, the state had done nothing. This was largely because of opposition from the mining industry.[48] Far from recognising his organisation, the state detained Gordon in 1940 under the authority of the Minister of the Interior, HG Lawrence.[49]

It is difficult to assess what impact this initial failure to introduce partial recognition was to have on industrial relations in the 1940s. In particular, it is unclear whether the burgeoning African trade union movement would have accepted limited recognition in the changing conditions of the war. By 1945, African trade unions claimed a total membership of 155 000, of whom about half were employed on the Witwatersrand (including approximately 20 000 mineworkers). There was a total of about fifty unions, the vast majority representing workers in industrial and commercial undertakings.[50] The unions' growth and the fear they inspired in the state undoubtedly stiffened the resolve of some trade unionists.[51] Hard-liners in the Communist Party generally felt that any concession to state negotiating procedures was a betrayal of the principles of revolutionary socialism, and that even full recognition should be spurned. But the people who were organising on the Rand in this period, who confronted every day the grinding poverty of their members and the precariousness of their position in industry, could not so easily dismiss the advantages of accommodation within the existing power structure. According to the NAD, JCATU would have accepted recognition under the IC Act, while Makabeni's organisation was ready to compromise further as long as it could negotiate directly with the Labour Department.[52] If the state had registered African trade unions in the late 1930s, then in all probability, the organisations then in existence would have accepted the rules as a starting point, and the state would have avoided some of the violent confrontations of the early 1940s.

Senior Native Affairs and Labour Department officials were disappointed, but not deterred, by their failure to implement the 1938 proposals. The 'Native' parliamentary representatives, Rheinallt Jones, Margaret Ballinger and Donald Molteno, raised the recognition question in parliament and at meetings with civil servants whenever they had an opportunity.[53] The rise of a new, more united and powerful organisation, the Council of Non-European Trade Unions, also helped to pressure the bureaucracy to seek new solutions.[54] The Press, too, began to take up the issue *The Star* ran editorials calling for registration of black unions under 'vigorous oversight' by the NAD. It condemned the government's tardiness in dealing with the threat from unreasonable workers and 'agitators'. The communist newspaper *The Guardian*, put the case for full recognition. It claimed the whole labour movement supported this, and blamed Madeley for not convincing his more conservative cabinet colleagues.[55]

The whole question became increasingly difficult to handle in the early years of the war. On the one hand, the state sought to prevent disturbances in industrial production by whatever means necessary. Police broke up several strikes in the main

industrial areas and black strikers faced harsh treatment in the
courts. At the same time, the Smit Committee which reported to
Smuts on urban African conditions in March 1942, recommended a circumscribed form of recognition for black unions.[56]
The cabinet endorsed this and agreed that a NAD official should
be appointed to liaise with the unions. Unlike the Labour
Department proposals of 1940, the new regulations would have
allowed the Registrar to withhold recognition and give the trade
unions advice on their constitutions. For a while, it looked as if
the government would give the regulations weight by including
Africans in the definition of 'employee' in the IC Act. No decision was made on who would represent Africans on industrial
councils, though the government ruled out direct representation
by union officials.[57] In the end, however, the only action taken
was the introduction of War Measures 9 and 145 at the end of
1942. These prohibited strikes and provided for compulsory arbitration at the behest of the Minister of Labour.

Two years later, the question of trade union recognition was
still outstanding. The 'Native' parliamentary members held out
for an amendment of the definition of 'employee' to include
Africans. If a problem arose over open or parallel unions for
blacks and whites, the War Measure 145 could be changed to
allow African workers to claim arbitration as of right. This, they
suggested, should be accompanied by recognition of unions on
occupational rather than racial lines. By this means, the MPs
(including, after 1943, the prominent lawyer and former CPSA
member, Hyman Basner) hoped to protect black workers from
being manipulated by white trade unionists.[58] The Prime Minister, concerned about political opposition from the National Party
and the increasing radicalisation of the African trade union
movement, was unwilling to accede to their demands.[59] The
NAD, for its part, did not push hard for a settlement involving its
mediation on behalf of Africans, fearing that black workers
would not accept NAD-negotiated wage agreements.[60] The matter was allowed to drift while strikes, bayonet charges, mass
arrests and victimisation of union organisers continued unabated.

The DNL, EW Lowe, put the other point of view in 1943.[61] He was concerned at the way politicians and businessmen alike assumed that post-war expansion would be based on cheap, easily exploitable labour. This was not so, he argued. Africans were sick of miserable wages and conditions, and were ready to take action for themselves:

> The wholly unsatisfactory economic position of the Native wage-earner in the towns, the stress of hunger and malnutrition, the scandalous shifts to which he and his family are put to find the means to meet the cost of living – these are the very conditions to encourage the organisation of labour to which it is now readily turning.[62]

Lowe disputed the idea that African unionisation was the work of a few, ultra-left-wing subversives. Many leaders were educated and intelligent; Africans suffered many disabilities and there was a tendency to brand everyone who wanted to remove some of those handicaps a 'communist'. In any case, according to Lowe, employers were being forced to recognise unions whether or not the government did. It was now time for the state to come to terms with the African trade union movement. It had to begin improving industrial wages and conditions.[63]

Lowe was clearly out of step with his immediate superior, Douglas Smit. The SNA was aware of the political problems of introducing new regulations, given the opposition from the TCM and Department of Mines. The DNL, by contrast, was moved by different impulses. For one, his relative familiarity with black trade union organisation told him that it was wise to make concessions now, to pre-empt serious disruption. There were thirty-four strikes involving African workers in 1941 and fifty-eight in 1942, and the figure was rising.[64] Lowe was equally concerned that things were getting out of hand in administrative terms. By August 1942, there were thirty-two unions affiliated to CNETU. Union organisation had spread to the gold mines. Direct negotiations between employers and black unions meant that the NAD, and the sub-department of Native Labour in particular, could no longer control African workers in the industrial sector. Though Lowe did not see this as a problem because it might allow scope for agitators and subversives, it did create difficulties for a department whose *raison d'être* was to keep Africans separate from whites in rights, residence, and role in the economy. For the sake of departmental power and prestige the question of the recognition of African trade unions had to be answered. As Julius Lewin put it:

> It used to be said that a Minister's main function is to tell the permanent head of his department what the public will not stand. One might say that it is now the main duty of the well-informed official to tell his Minister and through him Parliament what the Africans will not stand.[65]

The third component in Lowe's argument was his disgust at the miserable plight of urban African families. This has to be placed in the context of his views on African advancement. Lowe was no guilt-ridden liberal – he did not support radical solutions or even equality of opportunity and he was concerned to safeguard industrial productivity. Yet, like most officials in his department, he did not believe the interests of employers and workers were necessarily exclusive. In any case, the welfare of African workers could and should be protected under a benevolent paternalism, and he as DNL had a duty to do something about it.

As the debate developed, Department of Labour officials encountered protests from white trade unions against the incorporation of Africans into negotiating procedures. As a long term policy, the Secretary for Labour still favoured the entry of blacks into established, white-led industrial unions, but by 1943, he acknowledged there was a danger that whites in the trade union movement would be swamped.[66] Like the DNL, Walker was reacting to both internal and external pressures. The external

ones came from the SATLC, which claimed that racially prejudiced members would oppose equal rights for Africans on
industrial councils. DF Malan's National Party also argued that
white workers' jobs were threatened by the government's plans
for African trade unions.[67] Internally, Labour Department officials began to wonder if the industrial council system could survive the incorporation of black workers. The IC Act was the
jewel in the crown of the department's industrial legislation.
Moreover, departmental officials felt a particular responsibility
to protect the interests of white workers. If incorporating Black
unskilled workers under the IC Act would create more problems
than it would solve, then its amendment would have to be
approached with caution.[68]

The Labour Department's fears of harming white workers'
interests may have helped to prevent too radical a revision of the
1938 proposals, which in turn may have discouraged black
unions and political representatives from accepting them. But the
main reason why the 1942-3 period proved fruitless was because
the workers themselves, by this time, would not be bought off by
minor concessions. African unions were now demanding full
recognition, and their case was publicised in both the left-wing
and mainstream Press.[69] At a conference between civil servants,
trade unionists and various leading liberals on this subject in
October 1943, Julius Lewin repeated that the unions wanted to
speak for themselves. Margaret Ballinger argued that the organisation of Africans on industrial lines was perfectly possible and
that they would not swamp existing industrial councils. ANC
President, AB Xuma, stressed the need for independent African
unions (at least for the time being) and Senator Basner agreed
that Africans must run things for themselves.[70] This was not a
rejection of involvement by such organisers as Max Gordon as
much as a response to SATLC proposals for whites to represent
Africans on industrial councils. The Trades and Labour Council
was at this time hopelessly split. Officially, it supported an
amendment of the definition of employee to include Africans,
but the bulk of its members were strongly opposed to full

African representation on industrial councils. Smit left the meeting with the impression that things had now gone too far for the easy solution of administrative recognition.

With industrial employers, trade unionists and white liberals all insisting on some form of recognition, the government could not be seen to be doing absolutely nothing. The Department of Labour duly took the initiative over the next few years. The 1938 proposals had collapsed because of protests from the mining industry; the African unions had rejected the 1942 offer because it did not go far enough. The Labour Department now attempted to refine previous formulae to produce a compromise settlement. They proposed separate statutory recognition for African trade unions through a new Native (Industrial) Bill.[71] A Central Native Mediation Board of officials from the Departments of Native Affairs, Labour and Commerce and Industries, would be created. Applications for the settlement of disputes would be directed to the Board, which, if it decided a dispute existed, would co-opt equal members of union and employers' representatives onto the Board. These representatives would negotiate in the presence of the permanent members. If they failed to reach agreement, the Board could make a compulsory award. The Labour Department would recognise one union for each industry. Africans would be prohibited from joining white unions, and strikes and lock-outs would also be banned. This would limit the influence of potential subversives, train Africans in negotiating procedures (presumably for the distant day when they would be allowed equal rights with whites) and meet public prejudices against race mixing. It would also satisfy the working principles of the Native Affairs and Labour Departments by preserving the concept of separate administration, while extending direct negotiation machinery for employers and workers.[72]

The Labour Department marketed the bill as a way of preventing blacks from dominating industrial councils through weight of numbers. Predictably, though, the bill did not satisfy all parties. Officials from the Department of Labour tried to convince the Gold Producers' Committee and the Minister of Mines that they would not be affected, despite the fact that Stallard's prophecy that you could not allow trade unions to operate in industry without them spreading to the mines had already come true.[73] Smuts, too, disagreed with the bill, which was announced by the acting Prime Minister, JH Hofmeyr, while Smuts was overseas.[74] As Minister of Labour, Hofmeyr had rejected the SATLC's calls for incorporation of Africans into collective bargaining procedures in 1937, but he appears to have accepted the Labour Department's compromise solution. Smuts, by contrast, had never been won over to the idea of direct negotiations with Africans. The Secretary for Labour, FLA Buchanan, did his best to convince him otherwise.[75]

Douglas Smit, former SNA and now Deputy Chairman of the NAC, agreed with Edgar Brookes that the penalties prescribed for strikers under the bill were far too heavy.[76] The NAC also argued for provision to be made for at least one African to sit on the Central Mediation Board. These were very mild criticisms. The NAC, like the NAD, had always supported separate administration for blacks. The NAD and the NAC both accepted the bill as upholding that principle and the new SNA, WJG Mears, joined Buchanan in pressing the cabinet to introduce it in parliament.[77]

There is evidence that the bill could have been a great success in winning African trade unions away from the radical leadership feared by the state. Already in anticipation of the new legislation, twenty-three out of thirty-three unions had left CNETU to form a rival organisation under DK Mfili and Daniel Koza, called the Transvaal Council of African Trade Unions. They sought recognition either under the IC Act or the Natives (Industrial) Bill.[78] If the bill had been passed, it is possible the state could have found trade unionists who would have co-operated with state structures, and yet still maintained the respect of the rank and file.[79]

In the event, the bill was never introduced. The Minister of Labour announced, late in the 1946 session, that there was no time for it in the government's busy schedule.[80] The following year, the bill was floated around various bodies and some thought was given to redrafting it, but the cabinet, worried about the impact of the 1946 mineworkers' strike on public opinion, remained undecided. This was not merely because of Smuts's lack of enthusiasm for African trade unions. Economic developments also played their part. The end of the war had alleviated the labour shortage and had further reduced the power of the African trade union movement. In his final months as Prime Minister, Smuts was more concerned with the threat from the Malanite nationalists than with the black labour movement.

The general election of 1948 finally brought down the curtain on the long debate. There was no possibility that the new Minister of Labour, Ben Schoeman, would countenance any recognition of African trade unions. The NAD's file on the subject closes with a terse note from Buchanan to Mears, asking him to take no further action pending instructions from the new regime.[81]

Conclusion

The way in which the South African civil service handled African trade unions, fits well with Weberian, Marxist and Poulantzian analyses of the role of bureaucracy in capitalist society. Weber and Marx both argue that 'the key to understanding bureaucratic power lies in its location within wider social and historical processes'.[82] For Weber, these pertain to the administrative and technical capabilities of bureaucracy required by modern industrialising societies; for Marx, they concern the class divisions of industrialising societies and the role of the bureaucracy in regulating class conflict. Both features are self-evident in the Native Affairs' and Labour Department's handling of trade union recognition. The degree of independence from their political masters demonstrated by senior officials, reflects the 'relative autonomy' which Poulantzas suggests is necessary to allow the bureaucracy to serve the ruling class as a whole, rather than a mere fraction thereof.[83] The solutions discussed by the two departments might well have served the long term interests of the ruling class by forestalling the development of revolutionary socialism. They were certainly a conscious attempt to mediate class conflict.

At the same time, to appreciate the full complexities of the debate one must return to Weber's description of the way bureaucracy functions. He pointed to some of the unanticipated consequences of bureaucratic organisation – ritualistic over-emphasis on rules, specialisation carried to extremes and self-protection for the sake of personal career advancement.[84] These factors are evident in, for example, the Labour Department's defence of industrial councils when they were threatened by white workers' race prejudice (over-emphasis on rules), and the NAD's fears of losing some of its duties through the transfer of functions to trade unions and other departments (career advancement). The NAD did not lose sight of its commitment to 'protecting' African workers in the fast-changing economic order. On occasion, its officers argued this point at length, as Lowe did in the early 1940s. But NAD officials also had to consider their broader commitment to a carefully-regulated workforce, as well as their own interests as professional administrators.

The course of the debate on African trade union recognition shows how difficult it was for bureaucrats to take all the factors into account. Even when the issues looked clearest, when the choice was either to accommodate the unions or lose control over a large, vital and growing movement, their political masters kept the administrators hamstrung. The politicians had their own short-term interests. If they could prevent labour unrest getting out of hand in the immediate future, then they would avoid handing a useful political issue to the opposition by recognising African unions. In 1929-30 and again in the 1940s, the cabinet dictated the limits of administrative power, and the government had other priorities than those which moved its chief civil servants.

8

CONCLUSION

Welfare, Repression and Ideology in African Labour Regulation

I set out in this book to achieve three things: to explain the development of labour regulation for African workers; to demonstrate the bureaucracy's central role in formulating, interpreting and mediating state interventions in labour relations; and to measure the strength of the working principles, or ethos, governing the actions of key departments, notably the NAD. Despite the growing literature on South African labour history, this constitutes the first general account of African labour regulation since Van der Horst's *Native Labour in South Africa* (1942).[1] It is also the first full-length analysis, drawing on theory and empirical research, of the civil service's position within the pre-1948 South African state.

South African labour regulation can be summarised in terms of welfare, repressive and ideological interventions. The first of these categories affected working conditions, injury and disease compensation, housing, social security, pensions and medical services. As Chapters 2 and 3 have shown, the development of state welfare initiatives was gradual and uneven. For the purposes of this section, they can be sub-divided into modifying clauses in repressive laws; so-called protective legislation which actually hurt black workers by restricting their rights; and genuine welfare activities.

Even the most repressive acts and regulations contained sections purporting to benefit Africans.[2] For example, the Native Labour Regulation Act (1911) made breach of contract by both employees and employers a criminal offence. Registration of contracts was supposed to prevent unscrupulous white employers from taking advantage of their workers' illiteracy and poor command of English or Afrikaans. The Native Commissioner or Pass Officer could ensure that Africans understood contracts and employers kept to them. But in the vast majority of cases which came before the courts, the employee was the one in the dock. Officials generally presumed white employers to be amenable to friendly persuasion and reason. In any case, judges were unlikely to sentence recalcitrant employers to more than small fines.

Legislation which was supposed to assist African workers but which actually hindered them includes interventions such as wage-regulating machinery (Chapter 6). It is very difficult to assess whether wage determinations benefited blacks in real terms, more than they held wages back by restricting free, collective bargaining. At least one economist has argued that during World War II, racial income levels narrowed and black wages rose at the cost of manufacturing profits.[3] On the other hand, rapid inflation and the rising importance of Africans in secondary industry would have been highly conducive to black trade unionisation if the government had not curbed this process. The fact that the state took it upon itself to improve unskilled wages after 1937 may have deflected African trade union activity just when it was about to blossom into a really effective force. Of course, wage regulation applied to white workers too, but the structural position of black employees was much weaker, and the chances of their benefiting from the legislation correspondingly less. Moreover, most black employees – including all those on the mines and farms – remained outside the wage-regulating machinery.

At the same time, genuine welfare initiatives edged their way into state regulation of labour, especially from the mid-1930s. Of course, the government's work in sub-economic housing, health care, unemployment insurance, compensation for accident and disease, and up-grading working conditions, should not be exaggerated. None of its programmes went nearly far enough. Whole sectors of employment (such as farming) were excluded, rates of compensation were minimal, hospitals and clinics were chronically under-funded. The South African government was primarily concerned with white workers as their political muscle was more immediate. In addition, many of these initiatives were motivated by the interests of the employer. Just as in Western Europe and North America, urbanisation and industrialisation brought increased government intervention to safeguard production and reproduction. This became all the more important as the uncontrolled growth of urban and peri-urban slums in the late 1930s and 1940s produced very great misery indeed. Yet by 1948, welfare in the broad sense had been accepted as a function of the state (Chapter 3). This supplemented the NAD's traditional function as 'protector of the natives'. It spread the positive side of African labour regulation among the Native Affairs, Labour, Social Welfare and Public Health Departments, in the process partially undermining the system of segregated administration for Africans. It also laid the foundations of a welfare infrastructure and went a little way towards balancing the repression and control of black workers.

The repressive element, examined explicitly in Chapters 4 and 5, and more obliquely in Chapters 6 and 7, is the most prominent aspect of labour regulation. From the 1920s onwards, the state built on pre-World War I legislation to compel African workers to fulfil contracts and obey the dictates of white employers. The Hertzog government updated the law on contracts for farm workers in the 1926 Masters and Servants (Transvaal and Natal) Amendment Act and the 1932 Native Service Contract Act. In the towns, the 1923 Natives (Urban Areas) Act (and later amendments) consolidated the attesting of contracts and criminalised contract-breakers. The Native Labour Regulation Act, meanwhile, continued to be enforced throughout the period.

Another key part of the state's repressive apparatus was its treatment of black trade unions as described in Chapter 7. These were never banned outright and some civil servants believed they should be given at least some of the rights accorded to white unions. But the state never granted African unions full recognition, which would have allowed them to negotiate on their own behalf under government-regulated procedures. On the contrary, when the Industrial and Commercial Workers' Union acquired mass support in the late 1920s, the state armed itself with legislative weapons against black leaders under the 1927 Native Administration Act and the 1929 Riotous Assemblies (Amendment) Act. The government again resorted to repression during World War II, when the police harassed trade union organisers such as Max Gordon, Daniel Koza and JB Marks.

Linked to this was official discouragement of strikes by Africans, whether on mines and farms, or in commerce and industry. The Native Labour Regulation Act made industrial action illegal for hundreds of thousands of mine labourers. In most cases, NAD officers tried to persuade strikers to return to work while official investigations were implemented. Needless to say, employers found these inquiries much less threatening than strikes. Under the Riotous Assemblies Act, government officials could also call in the police to break up mass pickets or union meetings. Short-staffed and usually heavily outnumbered, the police often used force to drive disaffected labourers back to work. They also routinely spied on union meetings. War Measures 9 and 145 of 1942 reinforced state powers to prohibit strikes and discipline participants.

Regulation of movement under pass and influx controls as described in Chapters 4 and 5 was the final, major component of repression. These terms covered a multitude of sins, involving socially-rooted fears of uncontrolled urbanisation, as well as the need to preserve a labour pool for farmers and mines recruiters. They were also intended to moderate competition between employers. The plethora of passes which African workers had to carry, testifies to a state struggling to control the movements of Africans through an endless paper chase of documents. The burden was heaviest on males travelling to the towns for the first time, but it affected all black workers in one way or another. Despite loopholes and overlaps, pass and influx controls inhibited African proletarianisation and worker solidarity. They also made it easier for farmers to keep hold of unwilling labour tenants. Moreover, they helped to channel 'clandestine' foreign migrants to six month contracts on farms in the northern provinces.

Ideological initiatives, including the justification of government policy and administrative procedure by direct and indirect means, pervaded the bureaucracy's work at every level. As senior civil servants well knew, the public image of a department, its standing within the state and their own career prospects, were closely tied to the popularity of the policies they implemented. This interlinkage was central to the way departments operated – they were anxious to back official initiatives which had the maximum prospective success rate and the minimum political risk. This was even more difficult for the NAD than for other departments, as it had to retain a degree of legitimacy with blacks, as well as with the politically dominant white community. In trying to cope with this dilemma, the NAD stressed the supposed harmony to be achieved through segregated administration and careful attention to each party's rights.

NAD propaganda, clumsy and amateurish as it often was, fed into the wider ideologies put about by the civil service, such as the notion of administration by experts and the concept of the state as mediator between competing interests. However, civil servants were denied access to the channels of communication enjoyed by their political masters. The frustration expressed by departments at the lack of public sympathy with their problems, underlines their inability to justify their role in labour regulation to their respective publics.

Bureaucracy, State and Labour

The relationship between the political and administrative spheres of government between 1918 and 1948 was many-layered. Both the Social and Economic Planning Council and the Centlivres Commission (discussed in Chapter 1) felt that civil servants held too much power within the central state. The Prime Minister and his cabinet still dictated policy objectives and had ultimate control of revenues, but public servants operated extensive regulations under the long administrative schedules attached to statutes. Often, civil servants held office for much longer than their ministers. They guided incoming political appointees in their responsibilities. They drafted bills, gave evidence to select and interdepartmental committees and commissions, attended meetings with and gave advice to their ministers, liaised with other departments and levels of government and conducted meetings with interest groups and members of the public. Furthermore, civil servants were responsible for the enforcement of laws passed in parliament, and where they regarded an act as unworkable, for whatever reason, they could use their delegated powers to alter the way the law was administered.

As Chapters 2 to 7 show, though, it is not enough simply to argue that South African civil servants had an important and hitherto largely unrecognised role in government. While stressing the overall significance of the administrators in African labour regulation, the preceding chapters have analysed the bureaucracy at the departmental level. This has highlighted the ways in which the influence of individuals or cadres of officials could fluctuate in importance, depending on their own abilities or those of their ministers, or according to prevailing trends in politics and economics. For example, in the Public Health Department in the 1940s, senior officials such as George Gale and Harry Gear found a sympathetic ear for their ideas on extending African health services in Henry Gluckman, Minister of Health from 1945 to 1948 (Chapter 3). In relation to the Labour Department the growth of secondary industry between 1933 and 1948 led to the extension of that department's functions. This in turn led to enhanced influence for officials who had wide experience of labour legislation, such as Ivan Walker, Secretary for Labour from 1932 to 1945 (Chapters 6 and 7). In the NAD, Douglas Smit wielded considerable influence over successive Ministers of Native Affairs during the war years, partly as a result of his long experience, his personal contact with the Prime Minister, and because the ministers appointed by Smuts lacked any special interest in the administration of Africans. On the other hand, in the Justice Department, Ministers Tielman Roos (1924-9) and Oswald Pirow (1929-33) had a much clearer idea of what they wanted to achieve in office. They were personally responsible for introducing the Masters and Servants (Transvaal and Natal) Amendment Act (1926) and the Native Service Contract Act (1932) (Chapter 5). They appointed officials who would best serve their interests and effectively bent the administrative machine to their own wills.

Broader chronological trends as well as individual relationships were important in the balance between politicians and administrators. The period 1918 to 1927 saw the establishment of the Public Health Department (1919) and the Labour Department (1924). It also witnessed the extension of the NAD's duties under the 1927 Native Administration Act. In this period also, both Smuts's and Hertzog's governments passed legislation which greatly expanded the work of the departments under discussion, as in the Factories Act (1918), Natives (Urban Areas) Act (1923), Industrial Conciliation Act (1924), Wage Act (1925) and the Native Taxation and Development Act (1925). The administrative powers created under these Acts significantly increased the bureaucrats' executive responsibilities.

The augmentation of bureaucratic power was taken further in the mid- to late-1930s, with the founding of the Social Welfare Department and the passing of the Natives' Trust and Land Act, the Native Representation Act (both 1936) and the Native Laws Amendment Act (1937). Despite the involvement of the Labour,

Public Health and Social Welfare Departments, by 1939, the separate administration of Africans had grown in accordance with the principles of Hertzogite segregation. It was during World War II that the SEPC and the Centlivres Commission claimed this process had gone too far.

Why did the bureaucracy assume such a significance in this period, especially in relation to labour and African administration? The answer lies partly in the rapid economic expansion and urbanisation which took place after World War I and particularly after 1933. As successive governments struggled to control these processes, they found it necessary to delegate powers to officials. In addition, Hertzog's segregation policies, which were meant to meet the challenge to white supremacy in a new, more urban, industrial age, were partially based on the creation of separate administrative machinery for Africans. However, officials themselves increasingly found that new economic realities made separate administration almost impossible. In secondary industry, health and social welfare, segregated administration could not be maintained as rigidly as many Hertzogite and Malanite nationalists would have liked.

Despite such difficulties, the administrators acted as a stabilising force during a difficult time for the South African state. Politically, by treating Africans as an administrative 'problem' and claiming that 'native' administration was not a political issue, the state sought to draw off criticism from both white liberals and the right wing. Economically, the latitude granted officials under the law permitted them to deal with new situations as they arose, to take account of regional diversity and to hold powers in abeyance when special circumstances so required. For example, the Public Health Act could be used to deal with the appallingly poor living conditions for workers on eastern Transvaal farms in the 1930s. Farmers could be given special recruiting rights near the border at times of acute farm labour shortages (Chapter 5), or pass offenders in towns could be treated more leniently, to increase industrial productivity and limit black protest, as in the early years of World War II (Chapter

4). By operating in this way, the bureaucracy may be said to have acted as an autonomous *corps intermédiaire*, softening the state's more rigid, dictatorial tendencies and absorbing the criticisms of disparate public groups.

Raymond Williams's concept of residual, dominant and emergent cultures provides a further way of observing this process. The dominant political culture of the period was segregation. It was supported by all the major political parties and given expression in numerous laws. Nevertheless, some officials, especially in the NAD, adhered to a protectionist or paternalist tradition which had its roots in Cape liberalism and Cape African administration.[4] This 'residual' element helped to perpetuate the dominant code of segregation. It limited the harshest and most resented effects of segregation, and so restricted popular African opposition. We shall return to this concept in the following section.

The third and final theoretician whose work illuminates this topic is Max Weber. Weber's depiction of a bureaucracy which functions for its own benefit and that of its constituent parts, is highly applicable to the South African civil service from 1918-1948. As the Centlivres Report recognised, officials were not purely concerned with the common weal or with the needs of a particular group or sector; they were also moved by more personal matters, such as power and prestige. Of course, this is not an easy point to prove, as public servants were hardly likely to compromise themselves by admitting to venal self-interest in official memoranda. But it helps to explain the frequent conflicts and crises which arose in intra- and inter-departmental relations. The state could usually pull together to give effect to a particular government policy, but it was not the well-oiled, efficient machine depicted in some of the Marxist structuralist literature.[5]

In crude Marxist terms, the state is created to serve the interests of capital. In South Africa between 1918 and 1948, the state certainly succeeded in ensuring the conditions in which businesses could thrive. At the same time, the peculiar racial configuration of South African society compelled the state to discriminate in favour of its white electorate and to place white interests above those of people of colour. Arising from a combination of these two factors, the labour regulation system was harsh and unyielding in its repressive dimensions and highly discriminatory in its welfare functions. Yet the manner in which labour regulation developed cannot be explained merely by reference to these two factors. As this study shows, the state bureaucracy was crucially important in formulating and implementing policy with regard to African labour. Its significance has been underestimated by historians and political scientists alike. The role of individual departments of state is central in explaining the uneven and haphazard way in which labour regulation evolved over these years. In analysing the South African state, it is essential to move beyond a crude, 'totalised' view, and to comprehend the inner functions of the state, as well as the people who worked within its corridors.

1948 and After

Both African labour regulation and the state bureaucracy altered considerably between 1918 and 1948. At the end of World War I, South Africa's labour legislation effectively only covered black migrants to the Rand gold mines. The nineteenth century bequeathed an array of pass controls and masters and servants laws, but these were well out of date by 1918. Thirty years later, African labour regulation extended to every sector of the economy, with the partial exception of agriculture. Working conditions, wages, health, housing, injury and disease compensation, movement, pensions and unemployment insurance, were all covered in one way or another. Nonetheless, one could not truthfully say that workers were better off in 1948 than they were in 1918. Over the intervening decades, the black population had been hard hit by landlessness and overcrowding. The overall African population nearly doubled, from 6 927 403 in 1921, to 12 671 403 in 1951.[6] In the same period, the proportion of urban-based Africans had increased from 14 per cent to 27.2 per cent (see Appendix 3). Untold numbers in urban areas were without proper accommodation. They were subject to hunger, malnutrition and all the misery that goes with life in a squalid and unfamiliar environment. Factory inspectors and wage regulation had some impact in improving overall conditions and wage levels, at least for those in industrial and commercial employment. On the other hand, health and welfare measures had only minimal effects on a worsening situation. The number of Africans working on white farms increased by more than 100 per cent, from 254 623 in 1917-18, to 592 488 in 1952, as people left the overcrowded reserve areas in search of employment and as white commercial farming expanded.[7] Wages in agriculture remained very low and the vast majority of farm workers were unaffected by official legislation. On the mines, there were significant advances in health and safety through the 1920s and 1930s, but wage increases ran below the rate of inflation as mineowners, supported by the state, kept labour costs down.[8]

The root of the problem for African workers lay more in the nature of South African economic development than in the state's interventions. Rapid transition from a pre-capitalist to a capitalist economy, accelerated growth in the population, dislocation of social groupings and the influx to the slums and shanties of the towns, were the chief causes of African poverty and misery. In addition, African workers were more hurt than helped by the panoply of labour legislation that existed by 1948. The negative aspects of labour regulation – control over movement, the instability of urban life, enforcement of contracts under the criminal code, restrictions on trade unions and industrial action, effective exclusion from skilled work under the Apprenticeship Act and from promotion on the mines under the Mines and Works Act, far outweighed the limited positive interventions in wages, conditions, health and welfare.

However, it should be stressed that the planning and reforms of the period from the mid-1930s to 1948 had at least laid the groundwork for a more enlightened system of labour regulation. While there was no obvious turning point in state interventions, the government was compelled by the force of economic and social change to begin to address overcrowding, homelessness, poverty, lack of sanitation and malnutrition among Africans. These issues became more pressing during World War II, when Smuts's coalition was anxious to raise morale amongst all races and to persuade its citizens that they were marching towards a better, brighter post-war South Africa. On the other hand, the government was constrained by Malanite nationalist opposition to public spending on the black majority, as well as by the need to ensure an obedient black workforce for the sake of the war effort.[9]

The extent to which the Smuts government had built the foundations for a South African 'welfare state' by 1948, may be partly ascribed to the ceaseless pressure in this direction from white liberals (both inside and outside parliament), as well as from African trade unions and political organisations. It also arose from the work of civil servants, especially in the NAD, but also in Public Health and Labour, who sought to improve conditions for African workers. In 1948, there remained a residue of paternalist notions of administration. These dictated that white authorities had a duty to protect Africans from the harsh effects of contact with whites, to prevent exploitation by white employers and to provide for the destitute.

This concern, and the powerful administrative positions in which some of its proponents found themselves, continued to exert an influence on the government down to 1948. Officials such as Smit, Mears, Brink, Buchanan, Gale and Gear, voiced their concerns within the dominant political culture of segregationism, using the public institutions of the day to remind the government of its responsibilities towards the black majority. Their limited successes show the extraordinary ability of the pre-apartheid South African state to absorb the views of different interests and to balance them to preserve stability, continuity and the legitimation of existing structures of authority.

The victory of the National Party in 1948 brought an end to this state of affairs. Whereas previously segregation was the dominant political culture, after 1948 the government adhered to the more rigid form of racial separation and discrimination known as apartheid. Within a few years it had tightened up on influx control, passes and trade unions, and cut back on wage regulation, health facilities and social welfare for Africans. Posel has shown that apartheid was not a monolithic concept, developed and enforced as part of a 'grand plan'. The incoming National Party adapted its policies to fit a range of competing capitalist interests and to take account of the fluctuating strength of African resistance. Even so, as Posel writes, the incoming government 'built Apartheid into a monstrously labyrinthine system which dominated every facet of life in South Africa'.[10] The 1960s saw the extension of social engineering as the nationalists under HF Verwoerd tightened their grip on state power and whittled away the rights of Africans outside the homelands.

In the civil service, the residual culture of protectionism slowly faded. The old dominance of English-speakers and anglicised Afrikaners, which was maintained in most departments through the Smuts and Hertzog era, disappeared. The new language of administration was Afrikaans, as shown by the small percentage of English language files in the State Archives after about 1950. The incoming government did not dismiss long-standing public servants, but National Party supporters, many of them Broederbonders, were placed in key positions. One such was the new Secretary for Native Affairs in 1948, WM Eiselen. By 1968, there were 415 Broeder public servants, fifty-nine of whom were Secretaries or Assistant Secretaries of civil service departments.[11] The Native Affairs Department took on a new role as the vanguard of apartheid policy-making within the state. This was especially true for the 1960s, when apartheid ideologues took a firm grip on the renamed Bantu Affairs Department and considerably extended the department's power and status. It was not until the mid-1970s, as international pressures mounted and mass strikes and protests erupted in the urban areas, that the state was forced to take the first faltering steps on the road to reform.

The reforms begun in the late 1970s under Prime Minister BJ Vorster and continued by his successor in office, PW Botha, were considerably speeded up following President FW de Klerk's dramatic unbanning of the ANC on 2 February 1990. Influx controls and pass laws are now a thing of the past. Laws relating to health care, working conditions, pensions, unemployment and other aspects of labour regulation have gradually lost their racially discriminatory character. The chief labour union federations are set to play an important role in the economic life of the `new' South Africa and are forming new relationships with the Government of National Unity, constituted in April 1994. The public service, too, is undergoing changes, with a commitment to apolitical, non-discriminatory administration of the law.

Despite the encouraging signs, the forging of a new order will encounter enormous difficulties. Although the political and economic face of South Africa has been transformed since 1948, there is a danger that some of the same problems which arose in the pre-apartheid period, will recur in the post-apartheid era. First, there is a danger that a civil service which is still predominantly staffed by Afrikaans-speaking, National Party supporting bureaucrats will frustrate the intentions of a future, non-racial government. As this study has shown, bureaucratic power can quickly take on a life of its own. Department of state, branches of departments and individual officials can develop sectional interests which are at odds with policies propounded at cabinet level. One way of overcoming this is to place government appointees in key administrative positions, but this runs directly counter to the goal of creating an apolitical public service. The threat of a serious chasm between the administrative and political spheres may well be greater in the 'new' South Africa than it ever was in the pre-1948 period.

At the same time, although trade unions are much more powerful now than they ever were before 1948, there remains the possibility that workers' interests will be neglected in post-apartheid South Africa. As in the 1918-1948 period, the exact relationship between the new government, the major political parties and the trade unions, remains unclear. In a country with runaway population growth, forty per cent unemployment and a crisis-hit economy, there is a danger that the unions will be side-lined as the state struggles to solve the massive problems it faces. As workers resort to strike action to defend the gains of the last decade and to further improve pay and conditions, they threaten to undermine the entire Reconstruction and Development Pro-gramme.

The greatest worry of all is that the dismantling of apartheid will prove to be more apparent than real. Long before the term 'apartheid' was invented, the South African state was severely restricting the rights of black workers and overseeing a highly exploitative relationship between capital and labour. It is to be hoped that as South Africa enters a new phase in its history, the state pays heed to workers' needs and builds the foundations for a humane but productive relationship between the state, business and labour.

NOTES

CHAPTER 1

1. H Bradford, *A Taste of Freedom: The ICU in Rural South Africa, 1924-30* (New Haven, 1987); B Hirson, *Yours for the Union: Class and Community Struggles in South Africa, 1930-1947* (Johannesburg, 1989).
2. J Lewis, *Industrialisation and Trade Union Organisation in South Africa, 1924-55: The Rise and Fall of the South African Trades and Labour Council* (Cambridge, 1984); I Berger, Solidarity Fragmented: Garment Workers of the Transvaal, 1930-60, in S Marks and S Trapido (eds), *The Politics of Race, Class and Nationalism in Twentieth Century South Africa* (London, 1987).
3. E Straus, *The Ruling Servants: Bureaucracy in Russia, France and Britain* (London, 1961).
4. For a broad review of South African historiography, see K Smith, *The Changing Past: Trends in South African Historical Writing* (Johannesburg, 1988).
5. WM Macmillan, *Complex South Africa: An Economic Foot-Note to History* (London, 1930), pp 141-2.
6. CW de Kiewiet, *A History of South Africa, Social and Economic* (London, 1941); ST van der Horst, *Native Labour in South Africa* (London, 1942).
7. GV Doxey, *The Industrial Colour Bar in South Africa* (London, 1961); D Hobart Houghton, *The South African Economy* (Oxford, 3rd Edition, 1973).
8. Van der Horst, *Native Labour*, p 185.
9. WH Hutt, *The Economics of the Colour Bar* (London, 1964); R Horwitz, *The Political Economy of South Africa* (London, 1967); M Lipton, *Capitalism and Apartheid: South Africa, 1910-1984* (New York, 1984).

10. F Engels, *The Origin of the Family, Private Property and the State* (1884; trans New York, 1968), pp 155-7.

11. L Althusser, *Lenin and Philosophy and Other Essays* (London, 1971), p 169.

12. N Poulantzas, *Political Power and the Social Classes* (1968; trans London, 1974), p 137.

13. H Wolpe, Capitalism and Cheap Labour Power: From Segregation to Apartheid, *Economy and Society* 1974, Vol 1 No 4. pp 425-55.

14. Ibid. p 445.

15. M Lacey, *Working for Boroko: The Origins of a Coercive Labour System in South Africa* (Johannesburg, 1981).

16. R Davies, D Kaplan, M Morris and D O'Meara, Class Struggle and the Periodisation of the South African State, *Review of African Political Economy* 1976, No 7, pp 4-30.

17. FA Johnstone, *Class, Race and Gold: A Study of Class Relations and Racial Discrimination in the South African Gold Mining Industry* (London, 1976).

18. Ibid. pp 86-8.

19. R Davies, *Capital, State and White Labour in South Africa, 1900-1960: An Historical Materialist Analysis of Class Formation and Class Relations* (Brighton, 1979); D Yudelman, *The Emergence of Modern South Africa. State, Capital and the Incorporation of Organized Labour on the South African Goldfields, 1902-1939* (Westport, 1983).

20. S Greenberg, *Race and State in Capitalist Development* (New Haven, 1980).

21. Ibid. p ix.; K Marx and F Engels, *The German Ideology* (1854-6; trans Moscow, 1964).

22. Greenberg, *Legitimating the Illegitimate: State, Markets and Resistance in South Africa* (New Haven, 1987).

23. Ibid. p 106.

24. AH Jeeves, *Migrant Labour in South Africa's Mining Economy: The Struggle for the Gold Mines' Labour Supply, 1890-1920* (Kingston, Montreal and Johannesburg, 1985); JS Crush, *The Struggle for Swazi Labour, 1890-1920* (Kingston and Montreal, 1987); JS Crush, AH Jeeves and D Yudelman, *South Africa's Labor Empire: A History of Black Migrancy to the Gold Mines* (Cape Town, 1991).

25. EC Webster, *Cast in a Racial Mould: Labour Process and Trade Unionism in the Foundries* (Johannesburg, 1985).

26. J Lewis, *Industrialisation and Trade Union Organisation in South*

Africa, 1924-55: The Rise and Fall of the South African Trades and Labour Council (Cambridge, 1984).

27. *Yours for the Union.*

28. B Bozzoli, *The Political Nature of a Ruling Class: Class, Capital and Ideology in South Africa, 1890-1933* (London, 1981).

29. DC Hindson, *Pass Controls and the Urban African Proletariat in South Africa* (Johannesburg, 1989); see also his The Pass System and the Formation of an Urban African Proletariat in South Africa. A Critique of the Cheap Labour Power Thesis (University of Sussex Doctoral Thesis, 1983).

30. *Pass Controls*, p 109.

31. S Dubow, *Racial Segregation and the Origins of Apartheid in South Africa, 1919-1936* (London, 1989).

32. Ibid.

33. D Posel, *The Making of Apartheid, 1948-1961. Conflict and Compromise* (Oxford, 1991).

34. Ibid. p 7.

35. Ibid. p 5.

36. Marks and Trapido, *Race, Class and Nationalism*, p 1.

37. J Selby, *A Short History of South Africa* (London, 1973), pp 214-5.

38. EA Walker, *A History of Southern Africa* (London, 1957), p 573.

39. JC Smuts, *Towards a Better World* (New York, 1944), pp 12-13. See also AG Smurthwaite, 'The Policy of the Smuts Government towards Africans, 1919-1924' (Master's Dissertation, University of South Africa, 1975).

40. WK Hancock, *Smuts vol 2: The Fields of Force, 1919-1950* (Cambridge, 1968), p 115.

41. K Ingham, *Jan Christian Smuts. The Conscience of a South African* (Johannesburg and London, 1986), p 191.

42. TRH Davenport, *South Africa: A Modern History* (3rd edn, London, 1987), pp 319-25.

43. Yudelman, *Emergence of Modern South Africa*, pp 214-43.

44. *Cape Times*, 6 June 1934. See also NM Stultz, *Afrikaner Politics in South Africa, 1934-1948* (Berkeley, 1974), pp 23-39; and Davenport, *South Africa*, p 305.

45. R de Villiers, Afrikaner Nationalism, in M Wilson and LM Thompson (eds), *The Oxford History of South Africa vol II*, (Oxford, 1971), p 423. On the nationalist opposition, see also PN Furlong, *Between Crown and Swastika: The Impact of the Radical Right on the Afrikaner*

Nationalist Movement in the Fascist Era (Johannesburg, 1991).
46. WH Worger, *South Africa's City of Diamonds. Mine Workers and Monopoly Capitalism in Kimberley, 1867-1895* (New Haven, 1987); RV Turrell, *Capital and Labour on the Kimberley Diamond Fields, 1871-1890* (Cambridge, 1987).
47. P Richardson, *Chinese Labour in the Transvaal* (London, 1982).
48. W Beinart, P Delius, S Trapido (eds), *Putting a Plough to the Ground: Accumulation and Dispossession in Rural South Africa, 1850-1930* (Johannesburg, 1986).
49. RP 18, *Annual Report of the Government Mining Engineer*, 1962.
50. For statistics on the number of workers in mining, industry and commerce, see Appendices 5-7.
51. Hobart Houghton, *South African Economy*, p 122.
52. UG 40-1941, *The Industrial and Agricultural Requirements Commission 4th Interim Report*, para 89.
53. *Union Statistics for Fifty Years, 1910-1960* (Pretoria, 1960), S-3. See also Appendix 4.
54. A Giddens, *Emile Durkheim: Selected Writings* (Cambridge, 1972).
55. A Giddens, *Studies in Social and Political Theory* (New York, 1977), p 258.
56. Ibid. p 260.
57. M Weber, *Economy and Society* (trans New York, 1968); Weber, *The Theory of Social and Economic Organization* (trans New York, 1947).
58. D Schuman, *Bureaucracies, Organizations and Administration. A Political Primer* (New York, 1976), p 56.
59. R Sebris, Bureaucracy and Labour Relations, *Civil Service Journal* 1978, Vol 19 No 2, p 28.
60. Posel, *The Making of Apartheid*, p 20; see also D Held and J Krieger, Accumulation, Legitimation and the State: The Ideas of Claus Offe and Jurgen Habermas, in D Held (ed), *States and Societies* (Oxford, 1983), p 488.
61. UG 15-1944, *Social and Economic Planning Council Report No 3. Aspects of Public Service Organisation and Employment*, p 2. See also EH Brookes, The Public Service, in EH Brookes (*et al*), *Coming of Age. Studies in South African Citizenship and Politics* (Cape Town, 1930), pp 333-55.
62. UG 15-1944, *Social and Economic Planning Council Report No 3*, p 2.
63. R Williams, *Culture and Society* (London, 1958), p 329.
64. R Williams, *Marxism and Literature* (London, 1977), pp 122-3.

Dubow, in his *Racial Segregation and the Origins of Apartheid*, argues that the dominant administrative ethos in the NAD came from the Transkei, where such figures as Charles and Frank Brownlee were active (pp 99-103). A corps of Transkeian administrators was established in the later nineteenth century, and was wedded to the ideals of 'progress' and 'individualism'. From the 1880s, this was gradually transformed into a more cautious ethos, based on 'benevolent paternalism'. This involved close personal contact and sympathy with the African's problems, 'a conscious paternalism, whereby the function of the native administrator was gradually to wean his subjects over to "civilisation" ' (p 101). The paternalism was certainly still present in the NAD's handling of labour regulation between 1918 and 1948, though the lack of opportunity for personal contact, and the need to pay attention to other interests, significantly distorted the old 'Transkeian tradition'.

65. On the 'Reconstruction' period, see D Denoon, *A Grand Illusion: The failure of imperial policy in the Transvaal Colony during the period of reconstruction, 1900-1905* (London, 1973). Denoon notes that Milner believed in the 'Englishman's aptitude and special experience in the work of governing and directing more backward nations' (p 39). However, as Denoon shows, the vast majority of imperial appointments did not survive beyond the restoration of self-government (Ch 7).

66. CM van den Heever, *General JBM Hertzog* (Johannesburg, 1946).

67. Dubow, *Racial Segregation and the Origins of Apartheid*, p 80.

68. *Union Year Book* Vol 3 (1910-18), p 107; *Union Year Book* Vol 24 (1948), pp 80-1.

69. MH de Kock, *An Analysis of the Finances of the Union of South Africa* (Cape Town, 1928), p 27.

70. UG 6-1921, *Fifth Report of the Public Service Inquiry Commission* (Chairman: TL Graham), para 1865.

71. Ibid. para 1876.

72. EH Brookes, The Public Service, pp 335-40.

73. SC 8-1948, 17-1948, 8-1949, *Reports of the Select Committee on Delegated Legislation*.

74. UG 53-1946, *Fifth Report of the Public Service Enquiry Commission* (Chairman: A vd S Centlivres), para 409.

75. Ibid. para 318.

76. Ibid. paras 447, 459.

77. Ibid. para 396.
78. Ibid. para 348.
79 . Ibid. paras 453-4.
80. UG 15-1944, *Social and Economic Planning Council Report No 3*, para 30.
81. UG 53-1946, *Fifth Report of the Public Service Inquiry Commission*, para 405.
82. UG 54-1947, *Sixth Report of the Public Service Enquiry Commission*, paras 513-9.
83. Ibid. Ch XVII, paras 821, 830-6, 848.
84. I Wilkins and H Strydom, *The Super-Afrikaners: Inside the Afrikaner Broederbond* (Johannesburg, 1978).
85. H Gibbs, *Twilight in South Africa* (London, 1949), p 212.
86. *Sunday Times*, 25 February 1945.

CHAPTER 2

1. The GNLB systematised and greatly expanded work already being done under the Coloured Labourers' Health Ordinance of 1905.
2. *Statutes of the Union of South Africa*, Act 12/1911, Secs. 6-9. Act 15/1911 prohibited recruiting of Africans under eighteen for the mines.
3. D Yudelman, *The Emergence of Modern South Africa* (Westport, 1983), pp 142,220.
4. Ibid. p 175.
5. UG 34-20, *Final Report of the Low Grade Mines Commission* (Kotze Commission), para 108.
6. Ibid. para 182.
7. Ibid. para 152.
8. CPSA A1882. Kotze's Evidence to the Economic and Wage Commission 2 September 1925, pp 770-2.
9. *Union Year Book* Vol 4 (1910-1920), p 579; Vol 13 (1930-1); Vol 21 (1940), p 817. In the same period, the total number of employees had risen from 309 118 (1920), to 352 938 (1930), to 480 139 (1939). The death rate per thousand rose from 2.21 in 1920 to 2.46 in 1930, and then dropped to 1.72 by 1939.
10. E Rosenthal (compiler), *The Southern African Dictionary of National Biography* (London and New York, 1966), p 294.
11. CPSA AD1769. Lucas Papers. Summary of Pirow's Evidence to be

submitted to the Low Grade Ore Commission of Enquiry by the GME, 22/9/30. Pirow did not explain how he would surmount the old problem of training Africans to fill semi-skilled positions, without stationing them permanently on the mines. On an earlier phase in this debate, see AH Jeeves, *Migrant Labour in South Africa's Mining Economy: The Struggle for the Gold Mines' Labour Supply* (Montreal and Kingston, 1985), p 32.

12. CPSA A1280. Kotze's Evidence to the Unemployment Commission (1930), para 5047-8.

13. UG 36-25, *Report of the Mining Regulations Commission*. The commission was chaired by William Pittman. The report argued that the ratio of whites to blacks had fallen from 1:7.7 in 1911, to 1:10.1 in 1923.

14. MNW MM2489/25 pt 1, Minutes of meeting between South African Association of Employees, SAMWU and the Minister of Mines and Industries, 24 November 1925.

15. MNW MM2489/25 pt 1, Secretary for Mines and Industries to GME, 30 December 1925.

16. MNW MM2489/25 pt 1, Inspector of Mines, Johannesburg, to GME, 13 January 1926. A misfire is an accidental explosion occurring during blasting.

17. MNW MM2489/25 pt 1, Notes on meeting between Witwatersrand White Miners' Association, Secretary for Mines and Industries, and Ministers of Labour and Mines and Industries, 5 December 1925.

18. See RH Davies, *Capital, State and White Labour in South Africa, 1900-1960* (Brighton, 1979) and Yudelman, *Emergence of Modern South Africa*.

19. Yudelman, *Emergence of Modern South Africa*, p 231. Yudelman expresses surprise at Kotze's 'very unusual' move from the bureaucracy into private business.

20. CPSA A1882, Cooke's Evidence, p 1389.

21. *Statutes of the Union of South Africa*, Act 21-1923, Sec 11(a).

22. CPSA AD1438, Cooke's Evidence to Native Economic Commission (Holloway Commission), 4 May 1931, p 7212.

23. GNLB 291/18/78, Report of the Public Service Commission Inspectors on the sub-department of Native Labour, 1922, pp 4-6.

24. GNLB 291/18/78, DNL to SNA, 27 November 1923.

25. S Dubow, *Racial Segregation and the Origins of Apartheid in South Africa*, pp 81-6.

26. *Rand Daily Mail*, 27 February 1923, 28 February 1923, 1 March 1923.
27. Pritchard had no intention of living out his retirement by the fireside. He put his experience as DNL to work in his new career as a labour recruiter for the Natal sugar and cotton estates. According to Public Health Department officials, he used his 'very accurate knowledge of the care of Natives in Natal' to exploit loopholes in housing regulations. GES 539/13, Assistant Health Officer, Durban, to Secretary for Public Health, 9 March 1925.
28. GNLB 291/18/78, DNL to SNA, 8 October 1923.
29. GNLB 291/18/78, DNL to SNA, 27 February 1924.
30. CPSA AD1438, Cooke's Evidence to the Holloway Commission, 4 May 1931, p 7278.
31. CPSA A1882, Cooke's Evidence to the Mills Commission, 27 August 1925, para 1399.
32. CPSA AD1438, Cooke's Evidence to the Holloway Commission, 4 May 1931, p 7274.
33. CPSA AD1438, Cooke's Evidence to the Holloway Commission, 4 May 1931, p 7228.
34. CPSA AD1438, Cooke's Evidence to the Holloway Commission, 4 May 1931, p 7230.
35. NTS 697/408C, C Potgieter to O Pirow, Acting Minister of Mines, 12 August 1932.
36. NTS 697/408C, DNL to SNA, 27 August 1932.
37. NTS 697/408C, Memorandum by DNL (AL Barrett) on Simmer and Jack Compound, 5 October 1934.
38. GN 1988, Sec 18, 30 November 1911. On the GNLB's fear of antagonising mine management, see also JJ Baker, 'The Silent Crisis': Black Labour, Disease, and the Economics and Politics of Health on the South African Gold Mines, 1902-1930 (Queen's University Doctoral Thesis, 1989), pp 57-68.
39. *Report and Recommendations of the Departmental Committee appointed by the Hon. Minister of Native Affairs to Enquire into the Alleged Shortage of Native Labour in the Natal Province* (Wheelwright, 1918).
40. See GES 24/5, documents on maltreatment of native labourers on the Natal sugar estates, 1921-4.
41. GNLB 64/23/9, Return of Assaults Committed Upon and Hardships Suffered By Natives for the Month of May, 1923, 3 July 1923.
42. See, for example, GNLB 69/23/154, INL, Springs, to DNL, 19 February 1923.

43. Some protection against underground violence was afforded by the recruiters, who feared that a bad reputation would make it difficult to recruit for a particular mine.
44. *Statutes of the Union of South Africa*, Act 15/1911, Sec 14.
45. C van Onselen, *Chibaro* (London, 1976), p 157.
46. WG James, The Group With the Flag: Class conflict, mine hostels and the reproduction of a labour force in the 1980s. Paper presented at the African Studies Institute, Johannesburg, February 1989.
47. '... it is the policy of the Company to avoid any expenditure, especially on the surface, unless it can be justified as being absolutely necessary for, and assisting in the continued working of the Mines'. NTS 697/408C, General Manager, New Consolidated Gold Fields, to DNL, 27 October 1932.
48. UG 30-38, *Department of Labour Report for 1937*, p 3.
49. Ibid. p 3.
50. *Union Year Book* Vol 8 (1925), pp 228-9.
51. *Union Government Gazette*, 2 May 1919, 18 February 1920, 19 November 1920, 10 February 1922, 22 August 1924.
52. TK Djang, *Factory Inspection in Great Britain* (London, 1942), pp 31-41. See also MNW MM2426/22, AAM Anderson, 'Notes on the welfare of workers in South African factories compared with the United Kingdom', 30 July 1922.
53. *Union Year Book* Vol 9 (1926-7), p 1030.
54. *Statutes of the Union of South Africa*, Mines and Works (Amendment) Act (Act 22-1931); Factories (Amendment) Act (Act 26-1931).
55. M Weber, *The Theory of Social and Economic Organization* (New York, 1947), p 337.
56. UG 45-41, *Department of Labour Report for 1940*, p 2.
57. ARB 1132, Women's Section, TAU to Secretary for Labour, 23 August 1935; Secretary for Justice to Secretary for Labour, quoting the Cape Kongres van die Vroue-Landbouvereniging, 11 December 1935. See also U.G. 30-1938, *Department of Labour Report for 1937*, p 5.
58. On the Wage Board in the 1930s and 1940s, see Chapter 6, sections on The Native Service Contract Act and Farm Labour After 1939.
59. ARB 1132, Secretary for Labour to SNA, 1 February 1944.
60. UG 45-41, *Department of Labour Report for 1940*, p 4.
61. ARB CF2/0, General Secretary, SATLC, to Minister of Labour, 31 January 1939.

62. ARB CF2/0, Prepared answer to Parliamentary Question, 14 February 1939.
63. Djang, *Factory Inspection*, pp 75-6.
64. *Statutes of the Union of South Africa*, Act 41/1939.
65. *Union Year Book*, Vol 23 (1946), p 22.
66. During World War II, the government also adopted a more lenient exemptions policy than that contained in the 1918 Act. State Archives, K302 (Van Eck Commission Papers), Box 10. Department of Labour Memorandum on 2nd Interim Report of the Industrial and Agricultural Requirements Commission.
67. *Union Year Book* Vol 23 (1946), p 27.
68. *Statutes of the Union of South Africa*, Act 22/1941 (Factories, Machinery and Building Work Act), Sec 3.
69. See Chapter 7.
70. Wits A1882, Director of the Industries Division Evidence to the Mills Commission, 24/8/25, para. 567.

CHAPTER 3

1. D Harvey, *Consciousness and the Urban Experience. Studies in the History and Theory of Capitalist Urbanization* (Baltimore, 1985), p 51:
   That there is a relationship of some sort between working and living, and that by manipulating the latter a leverage can be exerted on the former, has not escaped the notice of the capitalist class. A persistent theme in the history of the advanced capitalist countries has been to look for those improvements in the living place that will enhance the happiness, docility and efficiency of labour.
2. Ibid. p 47.
3. Acts 15/1911, 25/1914, 40/1919.
4. On industrial diseases, see RM Packard, Tuberculosis and the Development of Industrial Health Policies on the Witwatersrand, 1902-32, *Journal of Southern African Studies* 13(2), 1987, pp 187-209; E Katz, Silicosis on the South African Gold Mines, in F Wilson and G Westcott (eds), *Hunger, Work and Health* (Johannesburg, 1980), pp 187-224; G Burke and P Richardson, The Profits of Death: A Comparative Study of Miners Phthisis in Cornwall and the Transvaal, *Journal of Southern African Studies* 4(2), 1987, pp 147-171; JJ Baker, 'The Silent Crisis': Black Labour, Disease, and the Eco-

nomics and Politics of Health on the South African Gold Mines, 1902-1930 (Queen's University Doctoral Thesis, 1989).

5. Jeeves, *Migrant Labour in South Africa's Mining Economy*, pp 260-4.
6. SC 3-1940, *Report of the Select Committee on the Operation of the Workmen's Compensation Act, 1934*, pp vii-viii.
7. See, for example, Public Health Department Report on Silicosis on the Witwatersrand Goldmines, July 1928. GES 9/17A: File on TB in Mine Natives, 1922-9.
8. *Rand Daily Mail*, 23 September 1922.
9. D Harvey, *The Limits of Capital* (Oxford, 1982), pp 34; 77.
10. *Statutes of the Union of South Africa*, Act 15/1911, Sec 22.
11. Cape Acts 40/1905, 41/1906; Natal Acts 12/1896, 18/1906; Transvaal Acts 36/1907, 11/1910.
12. The gold mines' tight-fistedness prevented the Bureau from providing adequate numbers of doctors for inspections. As its Chairman, W Watkins-Pitchford, argued in 1925, one doctor for 10 000 labourers was not even an approximation of the sort of care whites could expect. GNLB 50/5, Minutes of meeting re Medical Officers for Mine Natives, 18 December 1925.
13. NTS 224/280 pt 1, TCM to DNL, 29 December 1927.
14. NTS 224/280 pt 1, DNL to SNA, 21 April 1931. Miners' Phthisis Act 40-1919, Sec 66, defined:
    – 'Ante-primary stage' silicosis as 'physical signs of damage to the lungs short of definite physical signs of silicosis... such damage has supervened during and in consequence of employment in a scheduled mine'.
    – In 'primary stage' silicosis, 'definite and specific physical signs are or have been present', and the miner's capacity for work has been impaired (though not seriously or permanently).
    – In 'secondary' silicosis, 'definite and specific physical signs of silicosis are or have been present', and the miner's capacity for work has been seriously and permanently impaired.
    – Tuberculosis cases expectorate the tubercle bacillus; and have 'closed tuberculosis such that working capacity is seriously impaired', and they have to be removed from the mine.
15. *Statutes*, Acts 35/1925; 47/1946; 59/1934; 30/1941; 27/1945.
16. SC 12-1931, *Report of the Select Committee on the Report of the Miners' Phthisis Commission*; SC 13-1931, *Report of the Select Committee on the Subject of the Workmen's Compensation Bill*; SC 14-1932, *Report of the*

Select Committee on the Report of the Miners' Phthisis Commission of Enquiry; SC 15-1934, *Report of the Select Committee on the Subject of the Workmen's Compensation Bill.*

17. NTS 224/280 pt 1, DNL to SNA, 16 September 1927.
18. Cooke wanted to set figures of £60 for permanent, partial incapacity, and £120 for permanent, total incapacity. These were to be maximum figures; lesser sums would be assessed on the basis of disability in relation to total incapacity. If the worker died, 'dependants' would be understood to include partners and children of a customary union. NTS 224/280 pt 1, DNL to SNA, 31 December 1927 (signed by HG Falwasser).
19. NTS 224/280 pt 1, TCM to DNL, 29 December 1927; DNL to SNA, 31 December 1927. Cooke subsequently expressed doubts about the value of compounds and rations for African labourers: DNL to SNA, 21 April 1931.
20. ARB 1050-20, SNA to Minister of Native Affairs, 15 March 1932.
21. ARB 1050-20 (no date).
22. NTS 224/280 pt 2, DNL to SNA, 21/1/35. The DNL noted that in practical terms, compensation paid to Africans was approximately one quarter of that paid to whites.
23. *Statutes*, Act 59/1934, Sec 70. No compensation was payable if the worker was found to be guilty of 'serious and wilful misconduct'.
24. SC 13-1931, *Report of the Select Committee on the Subject of the Workmen's Compensation Bill*; SC 15-1934, *Report of the Select Committee on the Subject of the Workmen's Compensation Bill.*
25. ARB 1050-20, DNL's Memorandum on WC Bill, 11 March 1932.
26. NTS 224/280 pt 2, SNA to DNL, 28 May 1934.
27. The DNL was irritated by the control exercised in country areas by NCs and Magistrates, who lacked his expertise. NTS 224/280, DNL to SNA, 24 September 1937.
28. See Note 12.
29. GNLB 50/6, DNL to TCM Consultant, HO Buckle, 30 November 1929.
30. GNLB 50/6, General Manager, GPC, to DNL, 3 December 1939, 24 January 1930.
31. GNLB 50/6, SNA to DNL, 17 April 1930.
32. ARB 1050-20, DNL's written evidence to the Select Committee (13-1931), 13 May 1931.
33. S Marks, Industrialization, Rural Health and the 1944 National

Health Services Commission in South Africa, in S Feierman and J Jansen (eds) *The Social Basis of Health and Healing in Africa* (Los Angeles, forthcoming).

34. See, for example, articles in *Race Relations*: JD Rheinallt Jones, Social Work and the Non-European, vol 3(4) (1936), pp 84-6; E Batson, The Social Services and the Poverty of the Unskilled Worker, vol 6(4)(1939), pp 156-60; E Batson, The Social Services: Discrimination and Counteraction, vol 7(2) (1940), pp 18-23.

35. Marks presents evidence from Public Health Department files that EH Cluver was as concerned as his predecessors to keep the costs of health services down (Marks, Industrialization, p 31). In liberal circles, though, he was regarded as an improvement. See Bishop of Pretoria to Smit, Wits Archives, AD843 (Rheinallt Jones Papers), 16 June 1938.

36. White Paper (1945), *Silicosis Bill, 1945. Explanatory Memorandum*, pp 6-8.

37. *Statutes*, Act 47/1946, Sec 71.

38. White Paper (1945), *Silicosis Bill, 1945. Explanatory Memorandum*, p 7.

39. JD Rheinallt Jones, Social Work and the Non-European, *Race Relations* 3(4), 1937, pp 84-6.

40. *Rand Daily Mail*, 27 March 1935. On liberals and health issues, see also D Duncan, Liberals and Local Administration in South Africa: Alfred Hoernlé and the Alexandra Health Committee, 1933-1943, *International Journal of African Historical Studies*, 23(3), 1990, pp 475-493.

41. See MS Swanson, The sanitation syndrome: bubonic plague and urban native policy in the Cape Colony, 1900-1909, *Journal of African History*, XVIII(3), 1977, pp 387-410.

42. WE Leuchtenburg, The Great Depression, in C Vann Woodward, *A Comparative Approach to American History* (Washington, 1974), pp 325-343: 329-30.

43. V George, *Social Security and Society* (London, 1973), p 23.

44. GES 593/13, Memorandum by P Targett Adams, Regarding Urban and Rural Native Locations and their Sanitary, Medical and Economic Arrangement and Control, 26 July 1921.

45. GES 593/13, Adams to Secretary for Public Health, August, 1921.

46. *Union Year Book*, Vol 13 (1930-1), p 209.

47. GES 82/33, Report of the Commission of Enquiry on the City of Johannesburg Public Health and Native Affairs Departments, 27 November 1935. The Slums Act (53/1934) laid down regulations

for the expropriation and evacuation of slum properties. Fifty-seven separate authorities had made use of the Act by 1946. See *Union Year Book*, Vol 23 (1946), pp 166-7.

48. GES 593/13, Secretary for Public Health to Secretaries, Cape Eastern Public Bodies, 12 December 1936.
49. *Union Year Book*, Vol 20 (1939), pp 208-9.
50. *Report of the Inter-Departmental Committee on the Social, Health and Economic Conditions of Urban Natives* (Smit Report) (1942), paras 91-4.
51. Smit Report, paras 97-100.
52. UG 8-40, *Report of the Committee to consider the Administration of Areas which are becoming urbanised but which are not under Local Government Control, 1938-9* (Chairman: Sir Edward Thornton); Smit Report, Appx 1, paras 174-180.
53. *Statutes*, Acts 49/1944; 45/1945.
54. SC 10-1944, *Report of the Select Committee on Social Security*, p iii.
55. Smit Report, para 14.
56. UG 58-1948, *Department of Public Health. Report for Year Ending 30 June, 1947.* UG 45-1949, *Department of Health. Report of the National Housing and Planning Commission, 1947, 1948.*
57. E Hellmann, Urban Areas, pp 245-6, in E Hellmann (ed), *Race Relations Handbook* (Oxford, 1949).
58. UG 9-1943, *Social and Economic Planning Council, Report No 1. Re-employment, Reconstruction and the Council's Status.*
59. UG 14-1944, *Report of the Social Security Committee and Report No 2 of the Social and Economic Planning Council, Entitled: Social Security, Social Services and the National Income.*
60. Waterson was promoted again in 1946 to Minister of Mines.
61. JD Rheinallt Jones, Social Welfare, in Hellmann (ed), *Handbook of Race Relations*, p 423.
62. *Statutes*, Act 48/1944. The rates for whites were £60, £54 and £48 respectively.
63. NTS 24/349A pt 2, Memorandum on Social Benefits for Natives, 1947.
64. White Paper (1945), *Memorandum on Poor Relief.*
65. White Paper (1945), *Memorandum on the Government's Proposals Regarding Some Aspects of Social Security.*
66. NTS 133/362, Secretary for Labour to SNA, 15 March 1946.
67. White Paper (1945), *Memorandum on the Government's Proposals Regarding Some Aspects of Social Security*, p 6.

68. *Statutes*, Act 53/1946.
69. NTS 133/362, Comment on Unemployment Insurance Bill, by GE Barry, 10 March 1946.
70. *Union Year Book*, Vol 23 (1946), p 494. During the war, the mines faced increased pressure on production costs, which intensified their opposition to paying unemployment insurance.
71. NTS 133/362, Minutes of the NAC Discussion on the Unemployment Insurance Bill, 4 April 1946.
72. See Chapter 4, section on Urban Areas.
73. NTS 133/362, SNA's Draft Memorandum for Secretary for Labour on the Unemployment Insurance Bill: Tribal Natives (no date).
74. NTS 133/362, Secretary for Labour to SNA, 15 March 1946.
75. *Statutes*, Act 53/1946, Sec 2.
76. UG 9-1943, *Social and Economic Planning Council, Report No 1*, para 45.
77. WA Friedlander, *Introduction to Social Welfare* (Englewood Cliffs, New Jersey, 3rd edn, 1968), pp 39-40.
78. UG 22-32, *Report of the Native Economic Commission* (Chairman: JE Holloway), paras 251-334. On the repatriation of sick workers from the gold mines, see Baker, 'The Silent Crisis', pp 126-130.
79. Ibid. Addendum by FAW Lucas, paras 60-3.
80. Marks, Industrialization, pp 13-14.
81. Smit Report, paras 54-60.
82. *House of Assembly Debates*, Vol 34, Col 4602, 12 May 1939.
83. UG 30-1944, *Report of the National Health Services Commission* (Gluckman Report), p 25.
84. UG 30-1944, *Report of the National Health Services Commission*, p 20-1.
85. Ibid. para 34.
86. *Statutes*, Act 15/1911, Sec 2.
87. GES 7/26A, Assistant Health Officer, Durban, to Secretary for Public Health, on the establishment of a clinic for mine labourers at Vryheid, 4 February 1928; GES 24/5, documents on maltreatment of native labourers on the Natal sugar estates, 1921-4.
88. GES 4/5A, A de V Brunt (for Secretary for Public Health) to the Secretary, OFS Municipal Association, 18 July 1935.
89. For example, GES 4/5A, Secretary for Public Health to Secretary, OFS Municipal Association, 18 July 1935; Secretary for Public Health to Secretary, Municipal Association of the Transvaal, 25 February 1938.

90. *Union Year Book*, Vol 18 (1937), p 204; *Union Year Book*, Vol 23 (1946), p 179.
91. For an account of the National Health Services Commission, see H Gluckman, *Abiding Values. Speeches and Addresses* (Johannesburg, 1970).
92. *Union Year Book*, Vol 15 (1932-3), p 958. In the 1930s, the TCM did provide small grants for rural mobile clinics from unclaimed moneys in the deferred pay fund.
93. Smit Report, Appx 1, paras 14-30.
94. GES 1/62, 1/62B, on medical health services, 1936-40, 1943-52; GES 3/62 on hospitals, 1938-40.
95. Marks, Industrialization, p 30.
96. Ibid. p 41.
97. GES 1/62, Notes of meeting of subcommittee of Provincial Consultative Committee, held in Pretoria on 7 November 1938.
98. *House of Assembly Debates* Vol 61, 20 May 1947, col 4981-5 (speech by MDC de W Nel). Nel put the total revenue of the Union for the previous year at £140m, of which Africans contributed £12m.
99. *House of Assembly Debates* Vol 61, 2 June 1947, col 6273.
100. SC 10-44, *Report of the Social Security Committee*, para 44.
101. UG 30-44, *Report of the National Health Services Commission*, p 176.
102. *House of Assembly Debates* Vol 51, 6 February 1945, col 831 (speech by Minister of Welfare and Demobilisation).
103. G Gale, Health Services, in Hellmann, *Race Relations Handbook*, p 411. See also his The Aftermath in Gluckman, *Abiding Values*, pp 495-518. Gale resigned from the Civil Service to become Dean of the Durban Medical School in 1952. In 1955, he left the country altogether to take up the Professorship of Preventive Medicine at Makerere Medical School, Uganda.
104. See Harvey, *Consciousness and the Urban Experience*, who argues that bourgeois reform can ensure social stability and a 'relatively well-satisfied workforce' (p 52).

CHAPTER 4

1. E Kahn, Pass Laws, in E Hellmann (ed), *Handbook of Race Relations* (Cape Town, 1949), pp 271-91.
2. Except in the minds of a few, increasingly marginalised extremists, pass laws are now a dead issue in South Africa. In the 1980s, they

were borne away on a tide of reform, perhaps the greatest achievement of the decade, as the National Party groped its way towards a
new political and economic dispensation. Africans are now permitted to travel freely. On 1 February 1991, the government
announced its intention to abolish the last bastion of influx control,
the Group Areas Act.

3. For a functionalist explanation of passes, see Hindson, *Pass Controls
   and the Urban African Proletariat in South Africa*, p 97. See also his
   The Pass System and the Formation of an Urban African Proletariat
   in South Africa. A Critique of the Cheap Labour Power Thesis
   (University of Sussex Doctoral Thesis, 1983). Hindson argues that
   passes and influx controls provided for 'differentiated labour
   power', thus alleviating tensions between competing business
   interests (*Pass Controls*, p 58). In his *Legitimating the Illegitimate:
   State, Markets and Resistance in South Africa* (Berkeley, 1987), Stanley
   Greenberg argues that labour/influx controls were rudimentary
   before 1937. From 1939-48, the government favoured a free market
   in labour supply, and resisted farmers' demands for tighter pass
   laws. The Native Laws (Fagan) Commission (1946-8) recognised a
   need for orderly urbanisation, but proposed voluntary bureaucratic procedures such as labour bureaux (pp 33-7).

4. For example, E Kahn, Pass Laws, expresses approval of passes for
   identification purposes.

5. JUS 1/264/32, Clerk of Court, Umgeni, to Additional Magistrate,
   Umgeni, 14 August 1918.

6. JUS 1/264/18, Note by Justice official [W.E. Bok?], 19 September
   1918.

7. JUS 1/264/18, Secretary for Justice to Magistrate, Bergville, 19 June
   1933.

8. See Chapter 5.

9. D O'Meara, *Volkscapitalisme: Class, Capital and Ideology in the Development of Afrikaner Nationalism, 1934-1948* (Johannesburg, 1983).
   On the Native Service Contract Act, see Chapter 5. The Act had
   plenty of muscle, but was difficult to enforce. Often farmers could
   not identify their absent servants, while urban employers evaded
   regulations to retain their labour. For political reasons, penalties for
   violations under the NSC Act fell on the workers, rather than on
   employers, which would have been one way of making it more
   effective.

10. GNLB 301/19/72, HO Buckle, Transvaal Chamber of Mines, to DNL, 8 May 1920.

11. *Rand Daily Mail*, 5 February 1923.

12. *House of Assembly Debates* vol 48, col 3068, 14 March 1944.

13. Ibid. col 3086.

14. The vast bulk of pass law arrests – 39 000 out of 42 000 in 1931 – were in the Transvaal. FAW Lucas's Addendum in UG 22-32, *Report of the Native Economic Commission*, para 359.

15. UG 41-1922, *Report of the Inter-Departmental Committee on the Native Pass Laws*.

16. *Rand Daily Mail*, 5 February 1923.

17. GNLB 301/19/72, DNL to Secretary, Natal Navigation Collieries and Estates Co, 12 October 1925.

18. Hindson argues to the contrary in his *Pass Controls*, p 44.

19. UG 22-1932, para 722.

20. *Report of the Inter-Departmental Committee on the Social, Health and Economic Conditions of the Urban Natives* (Smit Report), para 304. By the late 1960s, there were over 650 000 convictions annually.

21. UG 42-1941, *Report of the Native Affairs Commission, 1939-40*, p 63; Smit Report paras 302-8; UG 28-48, *Report of the Native Laws Commission* (Fagan Report), para 43. HA Fagan had been Minister of Native Affairs under Hertzog. In contrast to some of his successors between 1939 and 1948, he had a fairly clear idea of the way pass laws should operate. See his *Our Responsibility* (Stellenbosch, 1960), in which he argues that Smuts's defeat in 1948 was partly due to white discontent at 'the alleged laxity of the Government in dealing with influx' (p 21); and his *Co-existence in South Africa* (Cape Town, 1963), which argues that blacks should be members of a watchdog committee to 'keep a constant eye' on the pass laws (p 121).

22. CPSA AD1756, Evidence to the Native Economic Commission, pp 1316-9 (Welsh); pp 2801-2 (Lowe and Barrett).

23. State Archives, Pretoria, K357, Evidence to the Godley Committee, Box 1, 2 March 1920; Box 2, 27 January 1920.

24. *Statutes of the Union of South Africa*, Act 25-1945.

25. *The Star*, 27 February 1945.

26. NTS 465/280, Acting DNL, JM Brink, to SNA, 9 February 1945.

27. See, for example, TRH Davenport, The Triumph of Colonel Stallard: The Transformation of the Natives (Urban Areas) Act between 1923 and 1937, *South African Historical Journal*, 2 (1970), pp 77-96.

28. S Dubow, *Racial Segregation and the Origins of Apartheid* (Oxford, 1989), sees urban influx and pass controls as a 'defensive strategy' aimed at consolidating white power in a time of social and economic change (p 180).

29. To quote Hindson, *Pass Controls*, p 46:

     The paramount concern of African urban policy in the 1920s and 1930s was to hold together a rapidly disintegrating system of reproduction of labour power. In urban areas, influx control and residential segregation aimed to limit the undermining effects of migrants' competition on the wages and living conditions of urban Africans. This was to be done by limiting the numbers of Africans entering the towns and expelling the unemployed and redundant. The conditions of reproduction of employed urban Africans could be secured by providing family housing and services at subsistence levels.

     For a more middle-of-the-road approach, see, P Maylam, The Local Evolution of Urban Apartheid: Influx Control and Segregation in Durban, c 1900-1951 (Paper Presented to the History Workshop Conference, Johannesburg, February 1990).

30. UG 22-1932, para 549.

31. See Chapter 6. Industrial employers of the 'advancement school' occasionally advocated a high wage policy, without explaining how this could be implemented. It involved the vague appropriation of Fordist models of industrial society, by which workers would be given adequate wages to buy the mass-produced output of the factories in which they worked. The idea was first developed in the Ford Motor Company in the USA See D Clawson, *Bureaucracy and the Labour Process. The Transformation of U.S. Industry, 1860-1920* (New York, 1980).

32. E Hellmann (ed), Urban Areas in *Handbook*, p 240.

33. Report of the Departmental Committee Appointed to Enquire into and Report Upon the Question of Residence of Natives in Urban Areas and Certain Proposed Amendments to the Natives (Urban Areas) Act No 21 of 1923 (Young-Barrett Report), 1937.

34. *Statutes of the Union of South Africa*, Act 21-1923.

35. NTS 209/313, Regulations under Sec 23(1) of Act 12-1923.

36. NTS 209/313, Godley to SNA, 9 April 1924.

37. NTS 209/313, Town Clerk, Pretoria, to Acting SNA, 23 October 1923.

38. UG 22-1932, Annexure 15.

39. NTS 11/313, Municipal Association of Natal to SNA, 13 February 1930; NTS 99/362 pt 1, Municipal Association of Transvaal to SNA, 31 January 1930.
40. See Appendices 2 and 3. Also, UG 15-1923, *Third Census of the Population of the Union of South Africa*; UG 21-1938, *Sixth Census of the Population of the Union of South Africa*.
41. See TRH Davenport, African Townsmen? South African Natives Urban Areas Legislation Through the Years, *African Affairs*, 68, 271 (1969), pp 100-1.
42. UG 22-1932, para 544.
43. Ibid. para 549.
44. Young-Barrett Report, paras 41-5.
45. NTS 99/362, Minister's speech for second reading of Native Laws Amendment Bill (no date).
46. NTS 581/313, PG Caudwell's Report on Natives in the Cape Peninsula, 30 April 1941.
47. NTS 581/313, Minutes of Conference of Cape Peninsula Local Authorities, Convened by SNA, 7 May 1941.
48. UG 40-1941, *Fourth Interim Report of the Industrial and Agricultural Requirements Commission*, para 187.
49. NTS 585/313. The file documents the efforts of Smit and Mears to persuade the Secretary for Finance and other departments to implement recommendations in the Smit Report.
50. Hellmann, Urban Areas, in Hellmann (ed), *Handbook*, p 240.
51. *Cape Times*, 21 January 1942.
52. P van der Byl, *Top Hat to Velskoen*, (Cape Town, 1973), p 220.
53. *House of Assembly Debates* vol 51, 2 March 1945, col 2696. As Van der Byl said, it was the officials who would most welcome the elucidation of the legislation.
54. *Senate Debates* 26 March 1942, col 1570. On migrancy to the gold mines generally, see Crush, Jeeves and Yudelman, *South Africa's Labor Empire*.
55. See Opening Quotation.
56. *Statutes of the Union of South Africa*, Act 15-1911.
57. See Chapter 2.
58. *Statutes of the Union of South Africa*, Act 18-1921. The wage advances were already falling, largely because of the rising participation rate in the migrant labour system. By 1916, a majority of Union mine-workers were unrecruited 'voluntaries'.

59. Proclamations 175-1921, 231-1923.
60. H Rogers, *Native Administration in the Union of South Africa* (Johannesburg, 1933), p 211.
61. UG 7-1919, *Native Affairs Department Report for 1913-18*, p 9.
62. By 1930, eighty white farming districts in the Cape, all but two in the Free State, and twenty-five in the Transvaal were closed in whole or in part to outside recruiters. In other districts, recruiting was limited to locations and Crown lands, areas set apart for African occupation, missions, reserves, and private property with the written consent of the owner. GN209 of 17 February 1924, as amended.
63. Jeeves, *Migrant Labour in South Africa's Mining Economy*. Crush, *The Struggle for Swazi Labour*. At the same time, ruthless competition for recruited labour for the farms was just taking off in the 1920s. Regulation in this area was much less rigid: farmers and their 'bona fide servants' were not required to carry labour agents' licences. See Chapter 5.
64. The Native Recruiting Corporation operated for the Chamber of Mines in South Africa and the High Commission Territories; the Witwatersrand Native Labour Association recruited in Mozambique and in tropical areas. See Crush, *The Struggle for Swazi Labour*.
65. MNW MM2489/25, FHP Creswell, Acting Minister of Mines and Industries, Notes on an Interview with the President of the Chamber of Mines, 18 February 1926. See also M Creswell, *An Epoch of the Political History of South Africa in the Life of Frederick Hugh Page Creswell* (Cape Town, 1956).
66. CPSA A1280, Evidence to the Unemployment Commission, 1921, p 773.
67. *The Star*, 23 November 1925.
68. MNW MM2489/25, Creswell, Memorandum on the Restriction on the Importation of Portuguese Natives, 17 September 1927.
69. MNW MM2489/25, Secretary for Mines and Industries to GME, 18 January 1926.
70. CPSA A1280, Creswell's Evidence to the Unemployment Commission, 1921, p 776.
71. MNW MM2489/25, Arthur French, President of the Gold Producers' Committee, to Minister of Native Affairs, 11 February 1927.
72. MNW MM2836, Meeting of Departmental Heads on the Mozambique Convention, 1 September 1921.

73. MNW MM2489/25, DNL to SNA, 4 March 1927.
74. MNW MM2489/25, DNL to SNA, 10 March 1926. There were three types of labour from the Union and the Protectorates: 1) 'recruited', who selected their mine before leaving home; 2) 'voluntary new', who went direct from their home to the mine; and 3) 'local', who, after working for one employer, presented themselves for employment on another mine. There were four categories of East Coast labour: 1) those engaged on open contracts, who were sent to a particular mine; 2) 'specials', who had already worked on the mine, and returned to the same employer within nine months; 3) 'voluntary new' (as above); and 4) 'local' (as above). GNLB 220/13/100, DNL to GME, 13 January 1926.
75. MNW MM2489/25, W Gemmill, General Manager, NRC. Report on Nine Month Contracts, 11 March 1926.
76. MNW MM2489/25, ER Garthorne, Memorandum on Recruiting of Native Labour for the Mines, 14 January 1926. Dubow notes that Garthorne was one of the chief 'intellectual mandarins' of the NAD from his promotion to Under Secretary in 1925. See Dubow, *Racial Segregation and the Origins of Apartheid*, p 80.
77. UG 34-1920, *Report of the Low Grade Mines Commission* (Kotze Report), para 103; UG16-1932, *Report of the Low Grade Ore Commission* (Pienaar Report), p 11.
78. GES 41/12A, W. Gemmill, Report on Experiment with Tropicals on Mines, 2 March 1937. For the thirty-seven months before 31 January 1937, the death rate of 'tropical' labour was 14.4 per 1 000. This compared to 11.02 for Bechuana 'non-tropicals'; 9.47 for Mozambicans; and 6.87 for all African mineworkers. See also UG 44-1946, *Native Affairs Department Report for 1944-5*, p 89.
79. As Jeeves has shown, Gemmill was exceptionally important in shaping mining industry policy throughout this period. See Jeeves, William Gemmill and South African Expansion, 1920-1950. Paper presented to the History Workshop Conference, Johannesburg, February 1987.
80. MNW MM3361/28, Acting Inspector of Mines, Natal, to GME, 1 November 1928.
81. NTS 389/280, Theron and Co to DNL, 7 September 1938.
82. NTS 389/280, Note by SNA, 31 January 1939.
83. NTS 445/280 pt 1, Minutes of Meeting of Minister of Native Affairs, SNA and Natal Coal Owners' Association, 10 November 1943.

84. *Report and Recommendations of the Departmental Committee appointed by the Hon. Minister of Native Affairs to Enquire into the Alleged Shortage of Native Labour in the Natal Province* (Wheelwright Report), 1918, p 9.
85. *House of Assembly Debates*, vol 6, 1926, col 393.
86. NTS 445/280, Minister of Native Affairs to the Prime Minister's Private Secretary, 4 June 1943.
87. NTS 338/280 pt 1; NTS 338/280/2; NTS 245/280 pt 1.
88. See Chapter 5, Farm Labour after 1939.
89. Posel, *The Making of Apartheid, 1948-1961*.

CHAPTER 5

1. C Bundy, *The Rise and Fall of the South African Peasantry* (London, 1979); W Beinart, *The Political Economy of Pondoland* (Johannesburg, 1982); P Delius, *The Land Belongs To Us* (Johannesburg, 1983); W Beinart, P Delius, S Trapido (eds), *Putting a Plough to the Ground: Accumulation and Dispossession in Rural South Africa, 1850-1930* (Johannesburg, 1986); T Keegan, *Rural Transformations in Industrializing South Africa. The Southern Highveld to 1914* (London, 1986). See also D Duncan, The State Divided: Farm Labour Policy in South Africa, 1924-1948, *South African Historical Journal*, Vol 24 (1991), pp 67-89.
2. Bradford, *A Taste of Freedom*, p 23.
3. Ibid. p 25.
4. For a thorough study of white farming in the 1920s and 1930s, see A de V Minnaar, South African White Agriculture and the Great Depression (1929-1934) (Doctoral Thesis, University of South Africa, 1988). See also D Cooper, Agriculture: its Problems and Prospects, in R Schrire (ed), *Critical Choices for South Africa: An Agenda for the 1990s* (Cape Town, 1990), pp 341-68: p 343; D Hobart Houghton, *The South African Economy* (London, 1965), pp 65-6.
5. *Union Statistics for Fifty Years* (Pretoria, 1961), Table I-11.
6. *Report of the Farm Labour Committee*, 1939 (Chairman: JF Herbst), para 226. The Native Trust and Land Act (No 18-1936) differentiated between 'squatters' (which it took to mean sharecropping and rent-paying tenants only) and 'labour tenants'. A sharecropper rented land in return for a portion of his produce; a labour tenant rented land in return for labour on the owner's land. However, the

term 'squatter' continued to be used in official circles and by the general public to refer to labour tenants. See ST van der Horst, *Native Labour in South Africa* (London, 1942), p 286.

7. For a contrary view, see Bradford, *A Taste of Freedom*, p 288, note 7. Bradford argues that the Agriculture Department was out of touch with small, Afrikaans-speaking farmers. This may have been true of other areas of farming, but not of labour, where the department supported the farmers' demands.

8. For a description of Kemp, see LE Neame, *Some South African Politicians* (Cape Town, 1929).

9. See, for example, *Cape Times* (editorial), 10 May 1932; *Imvo Zabantsundu*, 16 February 1932; UG 26-1932, *Report of the Native Affairs Commission for the Years 1927-31*, pp 21-3.

10. See section on the NAD v the Department of Agriculture.

11. For example, LDB R4545, SNA to Secretary for Agriculture, 17 April 1930.

12. NTS 442/280, Minutes of NCs' Conference, 26 May 1943.

13. LDB R4545, Director of Veterinary Services to Secretary for Agriculture, 8 November 1928. For a full account, see Bradford, *A Taste of Freedom*, pp 171-3.

14. LDB R4545, Additional NC, Pretoria, to SNA, 17 January 1930.

15. LDB R4545, SNA to Secretary for Agriculture, 17 April 1930.

16. LDB R4545, Director of Veterinary Services to Secretary for Agriculture, 2 May 1930. Farmers across the country complained that government agencies paid African labourers too highly, especially on road and railway construction.

17. LDB R4545, Kemp to EG Jansen (Minister of Native Affairs), 15 May 1930.

18. The idea of administrative action to supply 'unemployed' Africans to farmers had been mooted by a previous SNA in 1916. See NTS 161/280 pt 1, SNA to DNL, 27 March 1916. The proposed 1928 scheme would have involved cooperation between farmers' associations and NAD officials in finding labour and ensuring standardised pay and conditions. LDB R2989 pt 1, SNA to Secretary for Agriculture, 14 May 1928.

19. LDB R2989 pt 1, SNA to H Howard, Rietfontein, 3 April 1928.

20. LDB R2989 pt 2, SNA to Secretary for Agriculture, 10 June 1930.

21. NTS 10/280, SNA to NC, Potgietersrus, 30 November 1926.

22. See Chapter 4, the section on the pass laws. Departmental reports

from 1920, 1935, and 1942, chaired by GA Godley, JM Young/AL Barrett, and DL Smit respectively, all took a moderate line on passes. See also JM Young's evidence to the NAC, 7 February 1939, in Smuts Papers, Box 129, No 18; H Rogers, *Native Administration in South Africa* (Johannesburg, 1933); GNLB Vol 320, 301/19/72, Memorandum on the Consolidation of Union Pass Laws, 1925.

23. LDB R3710, Minutes of External Relations Committee, 22 May 1934. The government always resisted the demands of Natal and Zululand farmers for the right to recruit labour in Mozambique. However, in 1934, the government made an agreement with the Portuguese to permit the employment of illegal immigrants from Mozambique on South African farms, provided that fees and taxes were paid to the Portuguese authorities. Thousands of workers from southern Mozambique were employed in Natal, Zululand and the eastern Transvaal. See *House of Assembly Debates* vol 24, col 2513, 5 March 1935.

24. LDB R737, Eshowe District Farmers Association to Minister of Agriculture, 10 July 1945.

25. This conflicts with Bradford, *A Taste of Freedom*, p 53, who contends that the NAD was increasingly willing to embrace repression. See also M Morris, Apartheid, Agriculture and the State, SALDRU Working Paper No 8 (University of Cape Town, 1977), p 12.

26. LDB R2989 pt 1, Secretary for Agriculture to SNA, 2 August 1928. Inspectors operated on the Natal sugar plantations from the 1920s, but lacked powers of enforcement as the NLR Act did not apply there.

27. GES 131/38, SNA to Secretary for Public Health, 12 February 1937.

28. NTS 10/280, Chief NC, Natal, to SNA, 5 September 1923.

29. LDB R3710, Memorandum on Native Wages on Farms (no date).

30. For example, LDB R2989 pt 2, Secretary for Agriculture to Departments of Mines and the Interior and the Railways and Harbours Administration, asking them not to permit recruiting where it would interfere with farmers' labour requirements, 12 May 1939.

31. *House of Assembly Debates* vol 29, col 3785, 24 March 1937, speech by Lt-Col PA Froneman, MP for Senekal.

32. LDB R3710, Acting Secretary for Agriculture to G Schroeder, Glencoe, Natal, 5 July 1937.

33. LDB R2989, Memorandum on Native Labour Problems by SJ de Swardt, 6 September 1938.

34. *Report of the Native Farm Labour Committee, 1937-1939* (Herbst Committee), 1939. In replies to a questionnaire sent to NCs and Magistrates in Natal and the Transvaal, thirty-eight supported improving conditions. Sixteen recommended tighter controls over farm labourers.
35. The evidence presented in this section completely contradicts Lacey, *Working for Boroko*. She argues that the Hertzog government steadily and purposefully built up legislative support for farmers in their search for labour. Lacey treats labour tenancy as 'the pillar of the Nationalists' farm labour policy' (p 158). 'The long battle between the mines and farms since the 1890s was at an end', she writes: 'Hertzog's intervention had given rural labour supplies to the farmers' (p 180). In *Volkscapitalisme*, O'Meara argues the opposite: that the Pact government wanted to end labour tenancy and turn all rural Africans into wage labourers (p 27). The truth lies somewhere between the two. Most white politicians agreed that the ultimate goal was a system of modern, capital-intensive agriculture with purely wage labour; but in the short term, there were important elements which accepted the need for interim support for the many farmers (especially outside the Cape) who depended on squatters.
36. Bradford, *A Taste of Freedom*, pp 53-4.
37. JUS 1/103/29, Secretary for Justice to Magistrate, Johannesburg, 17 March 1925.
38. Transvaal Provincial Division, 243/1921.
39. JUS 1/103/29 (sub), Memorandum by Secretary for Justice on the Masters and Servants (Transvaal and Natal) Amendment Bill, 14/1/26 (Transvaal Provincial Division, 388/1923). The case was interpreted as an authority.
40. NTS 13/362, Reply to Senator Opperman's question to Minister of Native Affairs, 12 March 1924.
41. JUS 1/103/29 (sub), Secretary for Justice's Memorandum, 14 January 1926.
42. JUS 1/103/29 pt 3, Minister of Justice to Secretary for Justice, 19 October 1925. For a description of Roos, see Neame, *Some South African Politicians*, pp 19-20.
43. JUS 1/103/29 pt 1, SNA to Secretary for Justice, 18 December 1923.
44. Young later became co-chairman of the Young-Barrett Committee, and a member of the NAC. Bok had been Secretary for Justice since

the end of the Great War. He was not a close confidant of the Minister's and resigned in 1930 to become a Judge of the Supreme Court. J Van Rensburg, *Their Paths Crossed Mine* (Johannesburg, 1956), p 42.

45. JUS 1/103/29 pt 2, SNA to Secretary for Justice, 23 October 1925, 25 November 1925.

46. JUS 1/103/29 pt 3, Minister of Justice to Secretary for Justice, 2 July 1928. For farmers' support for stronger measures to control farm labour, see *House of Assembly Debates* vol 18, col 654, 4 February 1932, speech by SF Alberts, MP for Magaliesberg.

47. *House of Assembly Debates* vol 18, col 650, 4 February 1932, speech by General Smuts, MP for Standerton.

48. Ibid. vol 18, col 1335-1336, 22 February 1932, speech by JH Hofmeyr, MP for Johannesburg North.

49. Lacey, in *Working for Boroko*, insists that the South African Party opposed the bill on behalf of mining magnates. However, as she herself admits, the parliamentary opposition did not attack the bill on the grounds that it would affect the mines' labour supply. The mines did not send a delegation to the Select Committee on the bill, nor do they appear to have made any written or oral protest over the bill.

50. For example, NTS 13/362, Oswald Pirow to Minister of Native Affairs on the subject of greater control over 'Native squatters', 28 January 1925.

51. Van Rensburg was the third ardent Nationalist to hold the office of Secretary for Justice since WE Bok, the others being Charles Pienaar and 'Toon' van den Heever. Van Rensburg was promoted from Under Secretary on 26 January 1933. *Union Year Book* No 14; Van Rensburg, *Their Paths Crossed Mine*, p 54; B Sachs, *Personalities and Places* (Johannesburg, 1965), pp 9-23.

52. Van Rensburg, *Their Paths Crossed Mine*, p 63.

53. The Free State was covered by clauses 1, 7, 8, and 10. These concerned the sale or lease of land in contravention of the 1913 Natives Land Act, and the provision of information to Magistrates about Africans living on land outside the locations. *Statutes of the Union of South Africa*, Act 24/1932.

54. *Cape Times*, 29 December 1930; *Imvo Zabantsundu*, 16 February 1932. See also UG 26-32, *Native Affairs Commission Report for 1927-1931*.

55. *Ilanga Lase Natal*, 11 March 1932; *Umteteli wa Bantu*, 12 March 1932.

56. NTS 61/362, Memorandum by Rogers to Chief Clerk, 29 September 1932.

57. JUS 1/103 29 pt 3, Johannesburg Joint Council of Europeans and Natives, 'General Hertzog's Solution of the Native Question. Memorandum No 5', para 33.
58. S Dubow, Holding 'A Just Balance between White and Black': The Native Affairs Department in South Africa c 1920-1933. *Journal of Southern African Studies* 12(2), April 1982, pp 217-239.
59. NTS 61/362, DNL to SNA, 15 June 1933.
60. NTS 61/362, NAD General Circular 1/1934; Magistrate, Umtata, to SNA, 15 January 1934.
61. NTS 61/362, Additional NC, Louis Trichardt, to SNA, 6 February 1934.
62. NTS 61/362, NC, Far East Rand, to Chief NC, Johannesburg, 19 January 1934.
63. JUS 1/103/29 pt 4, Attorney-General, Natal, to Secretary for Justice, 27 June 1934; Secretary for Justice to Attorney-General, 17 July 1934; GDC Lumsden for Secretary for Justice, to Magistrate, Howick, 5 November 1934. Mnyeza won the case on appeal. The Justice Department decided it could not upset the Appellate Division decision because of the unclear wording of the Act. Instead, it referred the case to the NAD for possible amendment of the Act.
64. G.N. 1505/1934, 1839/1934.
65. NTS 61/362, Handwritten note by SNA, 31 July 1934.
66. NAD General Circular No. 22/1938, 9 July 1938.
67. JUS 1/103/29 pt 7, Allison (Under Secretary for Native Affairs) to Secretary for Justice, 4 October 1938.
68. White Paper 1/1942, p 1. Smit was the author of the paper.
69. NTS 56/293 pt 1, Waterberg District Farmers Association to Minister of Native Affairs, 5 May 1928.
70. On the municipalities' lack of co-operation on influx control, see *House of Assembly Debates* vol 31, col 713, 1 March 1938. More generally, see TRH Davenport, The Triumph of Colonel Stallard: The Transformation of the Natives (Urban Areas) Act between 1923 and 1937, *South African Historical Journal* No 2, (1970) pp 77-96.
71. NTS 90/362, Memorandum on Native Trust and Land Act. O'Meara states that the purpose of the Act was to eradicate labour tenancy (*Volkscapitalisme*, p 231). It is true that in the long term all branches of the state supported a progression to a purely cash-based system. But in the short term, there was no intention of pro-

hibiting labour tenancy. Even sharecropping was only to be phased out over thirty years.

72. NTS 643/280, Minutes of Native Farm Labour Conference, 15 September 1944. As O'Meara points out, the government also feared opposition from African peasants. *Volkscapitalisme*, p 231.

73. When the Van Eck Report discusses agricultural development, it includes the reserve areas. UG 40-1941, *4th Interim Report of the Industrial and Agricultural Requirements Commission*, paras 186-7.

74. For example, *House of Assembly Debates* vol 29, col 3783-3785, 24 March 1937, speech on the labour problem on Free State farms by Lt-Col PA Froneman, MP for Senekal; vol 54, col 8276, 28 May 1945, speech by JJ Serfontein, MP for Boshof.

75. On the influx to urban areas and the problems it created, see Chapter 4, sections on Pass Laws and Urban Areas.

76. For example, NTS 61/362, Farm Labourers and the War, article for NAD Bulletin, 9 October 1940. The article was intended to encourage labourers to stay on the farms for the sake of the war effort.

77. NTS 61/362, Letaba District Liaison Committee to SNA, 16 August 1941; Handwritten note, 18 September 1941.

78. NTS 643/280, Minutes of Native Farm Labour Committee, 15 September 1944.

79. LDB 3710, Report of the Interdepartmental Farm Labour Committee, 10 December 1942.

80. NTS 643/280. The meetings took place on 17 August 1944 and 15 September 1944 respectively. There were further meetings between NAD officials and the SAAU on 31 October 1944 and 13 November 1944.

81. NTS 643/280, SNA to Minister of Native Affairs, 23 February 1945.

82. NTS 378/280, DNL to SNA, 6 October 1939; Acting SNA to Secretary for External Affairs, 21 July 1942. The NAD had first requested this in 1937. The farms were already receiving other mine rejects under an agreement with the TCM.

83. NTS 338/280, SNA to Transvaal Agricultural Union (no date). The scheme was first introduced in 1937.

84. LDB R2989, Secretary for Agriculture to Secretary for Justice, 16 October 1942.

85. NTS 469/280 pt 2, SNA's Memorandum to Minister of Native Affairs, 23 February 1945.

86. NTS 463/280 pt 2, Notes on NAD's actions re SAAU recommendations (no date).
87. NTS 463/280 pt 2, Minister of Native Affairs to Prime Minister, 9 October 1945.
88. NTS 463/280 pt 2, SNA's notes on meeting with Minister of Native Affairs and Prime Minister, 23 February 1945.
89. NTS 463/280 pt 2, Minutes of NAD meeting with SAAU Special Farm Labour Committee, 31 October 1944.
90. *The Guardian*, 6 September 1945.
91. NTS 463/280 pt 2, Minutes of NAD meeting with SAAU Special Farm Labour Committee, 1 November 1948.
92. NTS 646/280, DNL to SNA, 18 May 1948.
93. H Bradford, Getting Away with Slavery: Capitalist Farmers, Foreigners and Forced Labour in the Transvaal, c 1920-1950, Paper presented to the History Workshop Conference, University of the Witwatersrand, Johannesburg, February 1990, argues that De Beer, who had eastern Transvaal connections, was bribed by farmers (p 13).
94. R First, Bethal Case-Book, in *Africa South*, Vol 2 No 3, April-June 1958, pp 14-25; M Scott, *A Time to Speak* (London, 1958). See also Bradford, Getting Away with Slavery.
95. NTS 741/280 (216), DM Mtonga to Nyasaland government representative, Johannesburg, 10 June 1948. The NAD's lack of success in the long term is chronicled in many newspaper articles highlighting the miserable plight of farm labourers across South Africa. For example, 18 Families Forced into the Cold – *The Star*, 6 June 1989; 'Working on the Land is Not Child's Play – Some Farmers Pay as Little as 13 Cents an Hour' – *Saturday Star*, 24 June 1989; 'Torture on Farm Claim' – *The Sowetan*, 28 June 1989.
96. Bradford, Getting Away with Slavery, p 14.
97. NTS 463/280 pt 2, Minutes of NAD meeting with SAAU Special Farm Labour Committee, 1 November 1948.
98. Smit exerted a considerable influence over Van der Byl in terms of policy-making. On the relationship between Smit and Van der Byl, see Van der Byl, *Top Hat to Velskoen*, and MM Bell, The Politics of Administration. A Study of the Career of Dr DL Smit with special reference to his work in the Native Affairs Department, 1934-45. (Masters' Dissertation, Rhodes University, 1978).

CHAPTER 6

1. *Statutes of the Union of South Africa*, Act 29-1918.
2. Ibid. Act 26-1922. For a detailed discussion of the Apprenticeship Act, see ST van der Horst, *Native Labour in South Africa* (London, 1942), pp 240-5, and J Lewis, *Industrialisation and Trade Union Organisation in South Africa, 1924-55. The rise and fall of the South African Trades and Labour Council* (Cambridge, 1984), pp 24-8.
3. RH Davies, *Capital, State and White Labour in South Africa, 1900-1960: an historical materialist analysis of class formation and class relations* (Brighton, 1979), p 362.
4. On Smuts, see WK Hancock, *Smuts. The Fields of Force, 1919-50* (Cambridge, 1968); NTS 166/338, Smit Memorandum, 7 January 1943. Also, O Pirow, *James Barry Munnik Hertzog* (Cape Town, 1957), pp 94 and 129.
5. NTS 35/362 pt 1, E Muller for Secretary for Labour to SNA, 23 December 1925.
6. CPSA A71 (Lucas Papers), FAW Lucas, Memorandum on the Determination of Wages in South Africa, p 9.
7. CPSA A71 (Lucas Papers), Memorandum on the Determination of Wages in South Africa, p 5.
8. *Statutes*, Act 11-1924.
9. Ibid. Act 27-1925.
10. On the Wage Board, 1925-37, see IM Phillips, The 'Civilised Labour Policy' and the Private Sector: The Operation of the South African Wage Act, 1925-37 (Doctoral Thesis, Rhodes University, 1984). Phillips wrote at a time when state files from 1937 onwards (and certain pre-1937 files) were not available. This leads to rather a distorted view, as the later period saw the fruition of some of the schemes advocated by Labour officials from 1925-37. Furthermore, the debate conducted within the State did not focus on the Wage Act alone: officials, unionists and employers could scarcely separate the two Acts in their minds. However, his conclusions are solid – the Wage Act entrenched racial discrimination between workers; employers at first opposed but later accepted the Act once they realised it brought stability to labour relations; and the Board served to secure jobs for whites through the Depression but failed to provide in full the benefits originally anticipated by pro-Pact white workers (pp 432-44).

11. NTS 35/362 pt 1, Secretary, NAC, to SNA, 2 February 1926.
12. NTS 35/362 pt 1, SNA to Secretary for Labour, 23 February 1926. Herbst emphasised that he was quoting the Minister's views, not his own.
13. G.N. 1607, 15 September 1925.
14. NTS 35/362 pt 1, GA Godley, for SNA, to Secretary for Labour, 6 February 1926.
15. NTS 35/362 pt 1, Secretary for Labour to SNA, 3 August 1926.
16. UG 14-1926, *Report of the Economic and Wage (Mills) Commission*, p 194. Those employed in agriculture were to be excluded from the Commission's recommendations.
17. B Bozzoli, *The Political Nature of a Ruling Class. Capital and Ideology in South Africa, 1890-1933* (London, 1981), (pp 193-4).
18. Phillips, 'Civilised Labour Policy', p 442.
19. CPSA A71 (Lucas Papers), Memorandum on the Determination of Wages in South Africa, p 8.
20. 'Civilised Labour Policy', p 437.
21. *Rand Daily Mail*, 22 November 1927.
22. ARB 1069/5 pt 1, Memorandum on the Wage Act by CW Cousins for F McGregor (no date).
23. IL Walker, B Weinbren, *2 000 Casualties. A History of the Trade Unions and the Labour Movement in the Union of South Africa* (Johannesburg, 1961), pp 168-9. Walker and Weinbren single out 'such efficient and social-minded public servants' as CW Cousins, Frank McGregor, HF Cuff, MS Tobias and RH Miller 'for the highest commendation in developing industrial legislation'.
24. ARB LC1103, Minutes of Conference between the NAD, NAC, Department of Labour and Wage Board, 25-7 October 1927, 25 November 1927.
25. NTS 35/362 pt 1, SNA to DNL, 21 November 1929.
26. ARB LC1103, Secretary for Labour to Minister of Labour, 30 November 1927.
27. ARB LC1103, Under Secretary for Labour (IL Walker) to Secretary for Labour, 10 August 1929. See Chapter 7, section on Registered and Unregistered Unions.
28. *Social and Industrial Review*, 16 November 1928.
29. ARB LC1103, Minutes of Conference between the NAD, NAC, Department of Labour and Wage Board on the Regulation of Native Interests in Industry, 25-7 October 1927, 25 November 1927,

pp 7-9; Conference Annexure 'C', Statement by the Wage Board on the Relationship of the Wage Act to Native Workers, p 2. ARB 1764 pt 2, Wage Board Report for 1 March 1929 to 31 December 1931, pp 48-50; Wage Board Report for 1 January 1932 to 31 December 1933.

30. In the late 1920s, employers generally resented wage determinations, protesting that they would be driven out of business, or forced to pass on costs to customers; ARB 1764 pt 2, Wage Board Report for 1 March 1929 to 31 December 1931 pp 49-50; SAS vol 1075 ref: P12/46/6, Report on the 12th Annual Congress of the FCI, 10-11 September 1929, p 10. By the mid-1930s, the FCI, led by its General Secretary, HJ Laite, had clearly accepted aspects of the 'advancement' argument: Laite told the Select Committee on the Wage Bill in 1937 (SC 5-37), that his Executive Council approved the bill and registered its support for it. The FCI's chief complaint to the Select Committee was that the Wage and IC Acts were not fully enforced on all employers (p 18).

31. Report of the Wage Board, 1 March 1929 to 31 December 1931, p 48.

32. ARB 1069/5 pt 4, Wage Bill AB 39-1936: General Comments by Interested Organisations and the Press, p 2.

33. UG 22-1932, *Report of the Native Economic (Holloway) Commission*, paras 993-1010.

34. Ibid. para 1005.

35. NTS 35/362 pt 1, SNA to DNL, 21 November 1929; UG 22-1932, paras 1000-2.

36. UG 22-1932, para 1040.

37. Ibid. paras 1010-17.

38. *Statutes*, Act 21-1930. See also Report of the Wage Board, 1 March 1929 to 31 December 1931, p 8.

39. Report of the Wage Board, 1 January 1932 to 31 December 1933, p 2.

40. 'Civilised Labour Policy', pp 441-4.

41. ARB LC1103, Minutes of Conference between NAD, NAC, Department of Labour and Wage Board, 25-27 October 1927, p 12.

42. NTS 35/362 pt 2, Chief Magistrate, Transkeian Territories, to SNA, 17 December 1929.

43. NTS 35/362 pt 1, Chief Native Commissioner, Natal, to SNA, 25 November 1929.

44. According to FCI figures, industrial wage increases for 1934-5 amounted to £4 062 132 for whites, and £1 222 864 for 'non-

Europeans'. In the same period, employment figures had risen by 13 739 whites, and 22 607 'non-Europeans'. See ARB C1066, Report of the 20th Annual Convention of the FCI, 25 October 1937.

45. NTS 35/362 pt 2, SNA's Notes on Discussion with DNL, 19 September 1934.
46. NTS 35/362 pt 2, DNL to SNA, 6 September 1934.
47. UG 37-1935, *Report of the Industrial Legislation (Van Reenen) Commission*, para 95.
48. CPSA A71 (Lucas Papers): In his 1935 pamphlet, Put an End to Poverty, Lucas condemned the persistence of sweated labour and shocking conditions for workers.
49. Ibid. para 141.
50. Ibid. para 113.
51. ARB 1069/5 pt 4, Gold Producers' Committee, Statement to the Select Committee Considering the Bills to Amend the Industrial Conciliation and Wage Acts (no date).
52. *Cape Times*, 19 April 1937.
53. WE Leuchtenberg, The Great Depression, in C Vann Woodward (ed), *A Comparative Approach to American History* (Washington, 1968), pp 325-44: p 331.
54. Ibid, p 307-8.
55. 'Civilised Labour Policy', p 438.
56. *Cape Times*, 19 March 1937.
57. *Statutes*, Act 36-1937.
58. Ibid. Act 44-1937.
59. The TLC was still complaining about this in 1948. See ARB 1069 pt 10, Memorandum on Resolutions at the 18th Annual Congress of the Trades and Labour Council, April 1948.
60. ST van der Horst, *Native Labour in South Africa* (London, 1942), presents the employers' viewpoint that they were not making large dividends which could be passed from shareholders to workers without affecting output and growth. Employers, she contends, did not combine to depress wages in manufacturing and commerce (p 261).
61. NTS 44/362, SNA's Notes on Interviews with F McGregor, Chairman, Wage Board, 24 June 1943.
62. ARB 1069 pt 10, Memorandum on Resolutions Passed at the 18th Annual Congress of the TLC, April 1948, p 6.
63. Davies argues that the changes were merely intended to improve

the efficiency of the civilised labour policy. In *State, Capital and White Labour*, p 266.

64. ARB 1183/12-41, JJ Scheepers, Chief Clerk, 'C' Division, to Secretary for Labour, 3 July 1945.

65. ARB 1183/12-44, Report of the Arbitrators on Johannesburg Municipal Undertaking, 27 June 1947, p 1. WM 145 of 1942 remained in place after the war. The Industrial Conciliation (Natives) Bill of 1947 was based on the principles of WM 145, but was never introduced in parliament (See Chapter 7). The nationalists finally introduced their own solution to the problem in the Natives (Settlement of Disputes) Act, 1953.

66. ARB 1183/12-44, Report of the Arbitrators on Johannesburg Municipal Undertaking, 27 June 1947, p 10.

67. UG 45-41, *Department of Labour Report for 1940*, p 31.

68. UG 62-48, *Department of Labour Report for 1946*, p 32. See also A Spandau, South African Wage Board Policy: An Alternative Interpretation, in *South African Journal of Economics*, 40(4), 1972; N Nattrass, Wages, Profits and Apartheid: 1939-1960. Paper presented to the History Workshop, University of the Witwatersrand, February 1990.

69. ARB 1069 pt 10, Comments on the Memorandum Submitted by the National Executive Committee of the SATLC (no date), p 7.

70. ARB 1069 pt 9, Ray Alexander, Secretary, Food and Canning Workers' Union, to Minister of Labour, 23 November 1946.

71. ARB 1069/5 pt 5, Secretary, Wage Board, to Secretary for Labour, 22 January 1942.

72. ARB 1069 pt 9, Secretary, Food and Canning Workers' Union, to Secretary for Labour, 3 February 1947.

73. *House of Assembly Debates*, vol 44, col 5582, 8 April 1942; vol 45, col 1177, 9 February 1943; vol 54, col 8913, 4 June 1945.

74. ARB 1069 pt 10, Comments on the Memorandum Submitted by the National Executive Committee of the SATLC (no date), p 6.

75. ARB COM1/40, Minutes of the Conference of Engineering Industrial Councils, November 1942, p 1.

76. Lewis, *Industrialisation and Trade Union Organisation*, pp 132-55.

77. ARB 1069/5 pt 5, Secretary, Low Veld (North-East) Farmers' Association, to Minister of Labour, 20 April 1948.

78. NTS 44/362, SNA's Notes of Interview with F McGregor, Chairman, Wage Board, 24 June 1943. Smit and McGregor discussed setting up a committee to 'ensure a satisfactory division of labour as

between the different areas'. The committee was to include representatives of the farming community.

79. ARB 1055 pt 4, Secretary, Federated Chamber of Industries, to Minister of Native Affairs, 14 February 1946.
80. ARB 1069 pt 7, Minutes of a Conference of Divisional Inspectors, 6-9 November 1944, p 2.
81. ARB 1069/5 pt 5, Secretary, Wage Board, to Secretary for Labour, 22 January 1942.
82. NTS 44/362 pt 2, Acting DNL to SNA, 14 June 1943. The mining industry was struggling to maintain output for the war effort, and to cope with the loss of white manpower to the armed forces. Mining was declared an essential service, but 8 500 miners enlisted with permission, and 3 000 without permission (*Union Year Book*, 1946, vol 23, pp 6-7). Mine labourers' wages were addressed in the Lansdown Commission, appointed in February 1943. The *Report of the Witwatersrand Mine Native Wages Commission* (UG 21-1944), published in April 1944, recommended increases of 5d per shift for surface workers, and 6d per shift for underground labourers, plus cost of living allowance, boot allowance, Sunday pay and overtime. In fact, surface workers were given raises of 4d per shift, and underground workers 5d per shift, plus overtime. See B Hirson, *Yours for the Union: Class and Community Struggles in South Africa, 1930-1947* (Johannesburg, 1989), pp 174-5.
83. NTS 44/362 pt 2, SNA to Chairman, Wage Board, 19 June 1943.
84. NTS 44/362 pt 2, SNA's Notes of Interview with F. McGregor, Chairman, Wage Board, 24 June 1943.
85. Johannesburg Joint Council of Natives and Europeans, Memorandum No 3: *The Native Worker in Industry*, p 11.
86. UG 22-32, para 1011.

CHAPTER 7

1. See Chapter 6 for a more detailed discussion of issues relating to the Wage and IC Acts. For broader reflections on the relationship between the state and organised African labour, see D Duncan, The State and African Trade Unions, 1918-1948, *Social Dynamics*, 18(2), (1992).
2. NTS 35/362/1 pt 1, Minister Van der Byl's notes on trade unions (no date).

3. FA Johnstone, The IWA on the Rand: Socialist Organising among Black Workers on the Rand, 1917-1918 and RH Davies, The 1922 Strike and the Political Economy of South Africa in B Bozzoli (ed), *Labour, Townships and Protest: Studies in the Social History of the Witwatersrand* (Johannesburg, 1979). RH Davies, *Capital, State and White Labour in South Africa, 1900-1960.* (Atlantic Highlands, NJ, 1979). This was not a new worry for the state. In the 1913 white mine-workers' strike, the prospect of whites allying with African mine labourers, had caused the Minister of Native Affairs, FS Malan, to appoint a commission under HO Buckle (Magistrate for Johannesburg) to investigate native grievances. The government assured Africans of protection in the event of future white labour unrest. See UG 37-14, *Report of the Native Grievances Commission.*

4. GNLB 125/19/48, sundry documents.

5. *Statutes of the Union of South Africa*, Acts 11/1924, 27/1925.

6. IL Walker, B Weinbren, *2 000 Casualties: A History of Trade Unions and the Labour Movement in the Union of South Africa* (Johannesburg, 1961), p 168.

7. *Union Year Book* Vol 19, 1925-6 p 116.

8. ARB LC1103, Secretary for Labour to Minister of Labour, 15 November 1928.

9. ARB LC1103, CW Cousins, Memorandum on Natives under Industrial Laws of the Union, 2 September 1927, p 6.

10. Bradford, *A Taste of Freedom*, p 171; Davies, *Capital, State and White Labour*, p 160.

11. ARB LC1103, Conference between NAD, NAC, Department of Labour and Wage Board on the Regulation of Native Interests in Industry, 25-27 October 1927, 25 November 1927.

12. UG 14-26, *Report of the Economic and Wage Commission.* Report 1 (Stephen Martin, Henry Clay and John Martin), Conclusions and Recommendations, para 101.

13. NTS 35/362 pt 1, SNA to Secretary for Labour, 23 February 1926.

14. ARB LC1103, Secretary for Labour to SNA, 2 August 1927.

15. See Chapter 2, section on Factories, Shops and Offices.

16. *The Star*, 2 September 1929.

17. ARB LC1103, Minutes of Conference, 25-27 October 1927.

18. *Rand Daily Mail*, 22 November 1927.

19. ARB 1054/316, Secretary for Justice to Secretary for Labour, 16 April 1928.

20. ARB LC1103, SNA to Secretary for Labour, 16 November 1928.
21. *Imvo Zabantsundu*, 27 November 1928.
22. ARB LC1103, Under Secretary for Labour to Secretary for Labour, 10 August 1929.
23. ARB LC1103, Handwritten notes by Secretary for Labour and Minister of Labour, 20 November 1928 and 23 November 1928.
24. ARB LC1103, Secretary for Labour to SNA, 8 May 1929.
25. ST van der Horst, *Native Labour in South Africa* (Oxford, 1942), p 254.
26. Ibid. p 246.
27. ARB 1054/316, Secretary for Labour to Minister of Labour, 3 May 1928.
28. *Cape Times*, 8 January 1930.
29. On the Department of Justice, see Chapter 5, section on The Native Service Contract Act.
30. *The Daily Representative*, 11 January 1930.
31. B Hirson, *Yours for the Union*, pp 39-49.
32. HJ and RE Simons, *Class and Colour in South Africa, 1850-1950* (1st edn, Harmondsworth, 1969), pp 458-9.
33. *Union Year Book* Vol 18, 1937, p 444.
34. *Statistics for Fifty Years, 1910-1960* (Pretoria, 1961), p 13. See also Appendices 3 and 6.
35. JD Rheinallt Jones, The Worker in Industry in EH Brookes (*et al*), *Coming of Age. Studies in South African Citizenship and Politics* (Cape Town, 1930); WM Macmillan, *Complex South Africa: an economic footnote to history* (London, 1930).
36. Simons and Simons, *Class and Colour*, p 515.
37. *Report of the Industrial Legislation Commission*, 1935, para 389.
38. *Statutes of the Union of South Africa*, Act 26/1937, Sec 27(a).
39. NTS 35/362 pt 3, SNA to WG Ballinger, 14 January 1938.
40. AL Saffery, African Trade Unions and the Institute, *Race Relations* vol VIII, 1941, pp 28-32.
41. NTS 35/362/1 pt 1, Secretary for Labour to SNA, 10 November 1938.
42. NTS 35/362/1 pt 1, Secretary for Mines to Secretary for Labour, 8 August 1940.
43. Col CF Stallard was Minister of Mines from 6 September 1939 to 5 December 1945. *Union Year Book* Vol 30, 1960.
44. Hirson, The Making of the African Working Class, pp 62-7.

45. NTS 35/362/1 pt 1, SNA's Memorandum for Minister of Native Affairs, 2 November 1939.

46. NTS 35/362/1/ pt 3, Commissioner, SAP, to SNA, 27 September 1943. On the differing approaches of the NAD, Labour Department and the SAP to industrial action by Africans in this period, see D Duncan, State Bureaucracy and African Labour in South Africa: the Transvaal Milling Workers' Strike of 1944, *Canadian Journal of African Studies*, 25(3), (1992).

47. *Cape Times*, 19 April 1939.

48. NTS 35/362/1 pt 1, SNA to Minister of Native Affairs, 6 December 1941. The SNA specifically stated that nothing was done in 1939 because of opposition from the TCM. See also NTS 35/362/1 pt 1, Secretary for Mines to SNA, 8 August 1940; NTS 35/362/1 pt 2, SNA to TCM, 9 February 1942, and GPC to SNA, 24 February 1942. In the last letter, the GPC argued that the only valid reason for recognition was if it removed the people who were currently controlling the African unions. Also, NTS 35/362/1 pt 3, Memorandum by Minister of Mines (no date).

49. Lawrence appears to have genuinely feared white 'agitators' leading African trade unions. See *Cape Times*, 13 January 1939, transcript of Lawrence's speech to the SAIRR.

50. *Cape Times*, 19 March 1943.

51. NTS 35/362/1 pt 3, Minutes of Conference, 27 October 1943.

52. NTS 35/362/1 pt 1, SNA's Memorandum for Minister of Native Affairs, 2 November 1939.

53. NTS 35/362/1 pt 1, SNA to Minister of Native Affairs, 6 December 1941.

54. CPSA AD843 (Rheinallt Jones Papers), CNETU to SAIRR, 4 April 1946.

55. *The Star*, 10 December 1942, 5 December 1939 and 15 July 1943; *The Guardian*, 10 December 1942.

56. *Report of the Inter-departmental Committee on the Social, Health and Economic Conditions of Urban Natives*, Appendix 1, para 37.

57. NTS 35/362/1 pt 2, SNA to Secretary for Labour, 10 April 1942.

58. NTS 35/362/1 pt 3, Minutes of Conference on Native Trade Unions, 26 January 1943.

59. NTS 35/362/1 pt 3, Secretary for Labour to SNA, 22 August 1945.

60. CPSA A836 (McGregor Papers), SATLC Memorandum on Recognition of African Trade Unions, 9 November 1945, p 2; FCI, Report of

Ad Hoc Labour Legislation Committee on 'Native Trade Unions', 5 October 1946; SAIRR Memorandum on the Statutory Recognition of African Trade Unions, 24 January 1947, p 5.

61. Lowe was the former Chief Native Commissioner for the Northern Areas. He succeeded BW Martin as DNL on 1 July 1940. *Union Year Book* Vol 22, 1941, p 1131.
62. NTS 35/362/1 pt 2, DNL to SNA, 15 August 1941.
63. NTS 35/362/1 pt 3, DNL to SNA, 18 October 1943. In the 1970s, employers came to see recognition of black trade unions as the only way to ensure order in labour relations. See S Friedman, *Building Tomorrow Today. African Workers in Trade Unions, 1970-1984* (Johannesburg, 1987).
64. *Cape Times*, 19 March 1943.
65. J. Lewin, The Recognition of African Trade Unions, *Race Relations*, vol X 1943, pp 111-116.
66. NTS 35/362/1 pt 3, SNA's note on meeting of Ministers of Native Affairs and Labour with 'Native' parliamentary representatives, 26 January 1943.
67. NTS 35/362/1 pt 3, Minutes of Conference on Native Trade Unions, 26 January 1943.
68. NTS 35/362/1 pt 3, Madeley and Walker, statements at meeting on 26 January 1943 (see note 67).
69. *Cape Times*, 19 April 1939.
70. NTS 35/362/1 pt 3, Minutes of Conference on Native Trade Unions, 27 October 1943.
71. NTS 35/362/1 pt 4, Memorandum on Native (Industrial) Bill, 10 April 1946.
72. NTS 35/362/1 pt 3, Secretary for Labour to SNA, 22 August 1945. In an article written in 1976 and published in 1981, D Lewis argues that the bill demonstrated the state's weakness in the face of 'rising dominated classes' and a 'fluid power bloc' (The South African State and African Trade Unions, *Africa Perspective* Vol 18, p 52). L Welcher rightly contests this interpretation in his 1978 thesis. Employers certainly disagreed on the best means of controlling workers, but the state was not in retreat from a divided and defeated black trade union movement in the late 1940s. See Welcher, The Changing Relationship between the State and African Trade Unions in South Africa: 1939-1953 (University of the Witwatersrand Honours Dissertation, 1978) p 20-1.

73. For unionisation on the gold mines, see TD Moodie, The Moral Economy of the Black Miners' Strike of 1946. *Journal of Southern African Studies* (1986) 13(1).
74. *Cape Times*, 22 November 1946.
75. NTS 35/362 pt 4, Secretary for Labour to SNA, 27 April 1947.
76. NTS 35/362 pt 4, Smit's notes on the Native (Industrial) Bill, 3 May 1947.
77. NTS 35/362/1 pt 4, SNA to Minister of Native Affairs, 2 July 1947.
78. NTS 35/362/1 pt 4, INL to DNL, 12 November 1947.
79. NTS 35/362/1 pt 4, Memorandum on meeting of Department of Labour and Transvaal Council of African Trade Unions, 11 December 1947.
80. *House of Assembly Debates* vol 57, col 6362.
81. NTS 35/362/1 pt 5, Secretary for Labour to SNA, 20 July 1948.
82. D Beetham, *Bureaucracy* (Minneapolis, 1987), p 92.
83. N Poulantzas, The Problems of the Capitalist State, *New Left Review* 58 (1969), p 73. BC Smith, *Bureaucracy and Political Power* (Brighton, 1988), p 73.
84. H Cohen, *The Demonics of Bureaucracy* (Ames, Iowa, 1965), p 15.

CHAPTER 8

1. S van der Horst, *Native Labour in South Africa* (London, 1942).
2. See H Rogers, *Native Administration in the Union of South Africa* (Johannesburg, 1933). Rogers describes each Act in turn, balancing the negative clauses for Africans against the positive ones.
3. N Nattrass, Wages, Profits and Apartheid: 1939-1960. Paper presented to the History Workshop, University of the Witwatersrand, February 1990.
4. See TRH Davenport, The Cape Liberal Tradition to 1910, in J Butler, R Elphick and D Welsh (eds), *Democratic Liberalism in South Africa. Its History and Prospect* (Cape Town, 1987), pp 21-34; S Dubow, *Racial Segregation and the Origins of Apartheid in South Africa, 1919-1936* (Oxford, 1989), pp 119-125.
5. For example, Lacey, *Working for Boroko*, pp 207-43; S Greenberg, *Race and State in Capitalist Development*, pp 151-61.
6. *Union Statistics for Fifty Years, 1910-1960. Jubilee Issue* (Pretoria, 1960), G-2.
7. Ibid. G-3; J Nattrass, *The South African Economy: Its Growth and*

Change (Cape Town, 1981), p 65.

8. Nattrass, *South African Economy*, p 139.
9. D O'Meara, *Volkscapitalisme*, pp 171-5.
10. D Posel, *The Making of Apartheid, 1948-61. Conflict and Compromise*, (Oxford, 1991), p 1.
11. JHP Serfontein, *Brotherhood of Power. An Expose of the Secret Afrikaner Broederbond* (London, 1979), p 136.

APPENDIX 1

Cabinet Ministers and Senior Officials in the Central Administration

A. Ministers

Department of Native Affairs:

–23/9/13	L. Botha
–3/9/19	J.C. Smuts
–30/6/24	J.B.M. Hertzog
–19/6/29	E.G. Jansen
–30/3/33	P.G.W. Grobler
–3/6/38	H.A. Fagan
–6/9/39	D. Reitz
–11/1/43	P.V.G. van der Byl
–4/6/48	E.G. Jansen

Department of Justice:

–23/9/13	N.J. de Wet
–30/6/24	T.J. Roos
–19/6/29	O. Pirow
–30/3/33	J.C. Smuts
–6/9/39	C.F. Steyn
–9/11/45	H.G. Lawrence
–4/6/48	C.R. Swart

Department of Agriculture

–23/9/13	H.C. van Heerden
–19/3/20	F.S. Malan

–10/3/21   T. Smartt
–30/6/24   J.C.G. Kemp

Department of Agriculture and Forestry
–7/1/35   D. Reitz
–8/11/38   W.R. Collins
–6/3/44   J.G.N. Strauss
–4/6/48   S.P. le Roux

Department of Mines and Industries
–20/12/12   F.S. Malan
–30/6/24   F.W. Beyers
–30/8/29   A.P.J. Fourie

Department of Mines
–30/3/33   P. Duncan
–4/12/36   J.H. Hofmeyr
–8/11/38   D. Reitz
–6/9/39   C.F. Stallard
–5/12/45   S.F. Waterson
–15/1/48   J.H. Hofmeyr
–4/6/48   E.H. Louw

Department of Public Health
–1/7/19   T. Watt
–10/3/21   P. Duncan
–30/6/24   D.F. Malan
–30/3/33   J.H. Hofmeyr
–4/12/36   R. Stuttaford
–6/9/39   H.G. Lawrence
–9/11/45   H. Gluckman
–4/6/48   H.J. Stals

Department of Labour
–30/6/24   F.H.P. Creswell
–12/11/25   T. Boydell
–19/6/29   F.H.P. Creswell
–30/3/33   A.P.J. Fourie
–4/12/36   J.H. Hofmeyr

–20/7/38	H.G. Lawrence
–6/9/39	W.B. Madeley
–9/11/45	C.F. Steyn
–4/6/48	B.J. Schoeman

Department of Social Welfare

–1/10/37	J.H. Hofmeyr
–26/9/38	H.A. Fagan
–6/9/39	W.B. Madeley
–9/11/45	H.G. Lawrence
–15/1/48	C.F. Steyn
–4/6/48	A.J. Stals

B. Senior Officials

[For certain years, the exact date of commencement of service is unavailable. Dates give thus: (1918) constitute the year an official is first mentioned in that position in the *Union Year Book*. The *Year Book* was not published from 1942-5. Consequently,there may have been officials who served for brief periods during the war who are not listed below].

Department of Native Affairs

Secretary
E. Barrett (1920)
J.F. Herbst (1/4/23)
D.L. Smit (2/7/34)
W.J.G. Mears (21/3/45)

Under Secretary
E. Barrett (1918)
G.A. Godley (1920)
E.R. Garthorne (1925)
J.S. Allison (1/11/29)
H. Rogers (4/12/39)
F. Rodseth (21/3/45)
C.J. Lever (1948)

DNL
S.A.M. Pritchard (1918)
H.S. Cooke (1/2/24)
A.L. Barrett (1/1/32)
B.W. Martin (1/8/36)
E.W. Lowe (1/7/40)
C.P. Alport (1943?)
J. Brink (25/2/46)
P.G. Caudwell (1948)

Department of Justice

Secretary
W.E. Bok (1918)
C.I. Pienaar (1/2/30)
F.P. van den Heever (1/8/31)
J.F.J. van Rensburg (26/1/33)
C.H. Blaine (1/12/36)
W.G. Hoal (18/9/39)
A.E. Wollaston (1/9/46)
A.E.M. Jansen (14/7/48)

Under Secretary
D.D. Keay (1918)
S.A. McCormick (1/1/29)
J.F.J. van Rensburg (10/4/31)
D.L. Smit (26/1/33)
C.H. Blaine (9/7/34)
J.G. Jeffery (1/12/36)
L.D. Durham (2/1/41)
A.E.M. Jansen (25/4/44)
J.C. Steyn (1/8/48)

Department of Agriculture (and Forestry)

Secretary
F.B. Smith (1918)
P.J. du Toit (1920)
G.N. Williams (1/8/26)

P.R. Viljoen (1/5/33)
C.H. Neveling (26/7/45)

Under Secretary
P.J. du Toit (1918)
A. Holm (1918)
G.N. Williams (1920)
E.J. Macmillan (1920)
F.E. Geldenhuys (1/9/26)
P.R. Viljoen (16/1/31)
M.J.A. Joubert (19/5/33)
G.A.W. Schneider (1/4/35)
W.L. du Plessis (12/2/40)
J.J. Adams (17/12/42)
M.S. du Toit (20/8/46)
F.J. van Biljon (27/7/45)

Department of Mines (and Industries)

Secretary
H. Warington Smyth (1918)
H. Pirow (Acting – 1926-7)
L.P. van Zyl Ham (1/9/28)
J.F. Muller (6/2/40)

Under Secretary
F.M. Blundell (1918)
F.A. Nixon (1/4/24)
J.F. Muller (24/10/34)
A.A. Eales (6/2/40)
V.H. Osborn (1946)

GME
R.N. Kotze (1918)
H. Pirow (1/12/26)
H.E. Barrett (1/6/37)
H.S.H. Donald (18/3/42)
D.G. Malherbe (11/5/46)

Department of Public Health

Secretary
> J.A. Mitchell (1/7/19)
> E.N. Thornton (9/4/32)
> E.H. Cluver (10/6/38)
> P. Allan (1/7/40)
> G.W. Gale (1/7/46)

Under Secretary
> A. de V. Brunt (1/10/32)
> A. Stuart (22/8/39)
> H.F. Cuff (2/5/41)
> N.A.G. Reeler (4/5/45)

Senior Assistant Health Officer (later promoted to Deputy Chief Health Officer)
> G.A. Park Ross (1/10/19)
> F.C. Wilmott (1/10/19)
> W.A. Murray (9/4/32)
> E.H. Cluver (20/12/34)
> P. Allan (8/9/37)
> H.S. Gear (19/1/39)
> A.J. van der Spuy (19/1/39)
> B.M. Clark (5/12/38)
> A.L. Ferguson (1/11/46)
> J.J. du Pre le Roux (1/1/45)

Assistant Health Officer
> L.G. Haydon (1918)
> E.N. Thornton (1/4/20)
> H.F. Sheldon (1920)
> P. Targett Adams (1922)
> G.A. Park Ross (1/10/19)
> F.C. Wilmott (1/10/19)
> W.A. Murray (24/9/23)
> E.H. Cluver (22/9/26)
> A.J. van der Spuy (1/12/27)
> G.D. Laing (1926-7)

        L. Fourie (3/12/29)
        F.W.P. Cluver (21/2/31)
        P. Allan (27/1/35)
        H.S. Gear (29/5/35)
        B.M. Clark (29/11/37)
        J.H. Loots (1/9/38)
        J.J. du Pre le Roux (17/1/39)
        A.L. Ferguson (19/1/39)
        G.W. Gale (1/11/39)
        P.C. Eagle (21/1/44)
        C.A.M. Murray (1/11/44)
        W.A. Smit (1/11/48)
        K.D. Winterton (1/7/47)
        C.J.G. Hunter (1/3/48)
        N.S. Turnbull (30/6/48)

Department of Labour

Secretary
        C.W. Cousins (25/7/24)
        I.L. Walker (4/5/32)
        F.L.A. Buchanan (7/11/45)
        A.D. Lee (1/8/48)

Under Secretary
        E.H.W. Muller (1925)
        I.L. Walker (18/9/29)
        W.D. Norval (1/4/33)
        J.H. Lewis (7/11/45)
        L.E. Orkin (7/11/45)

Chief Inspector of Labour
        I.L. Walker (1925)
        T. Freestone (1/1/45)

Chief Inspector of Factories
        H.C. Fowler (1/8/24)
        C.H.C. Clutterbuck (1/10/34)
        F.W. Joubert (10/2/39)
        H.O. Smith (12/10/47)

Labour Adviser
    T.G. Strachan (1/10/29)

Commissioner for Workmen's Compensation
    J.F. Malherbe (15/10/34)
    M.S. Tobias (1/8/40)
    A.D. Lee (23/12/43)
    J.H. Lewis (1/8/48)

Department of Social Welfare

Secretary
    G.A.C. Kuschke (1/10/37)

Under Secretary
    D.D. Forsyth (1/10/37)
    A.C. van der Horst (13/7/39)
    F. Brummer (1/2/46)

APPENDIX 2

Statistics on Population

Source: *Statistics for Fifty Years*, G-2

Population of all ages:	All Races	Africans
1921	6 927 403	4 697 285
1936	9 587 863	6 595 597
1946	11 415 925	7 830 559
1951	12 671 452	8 560 083

Economically active population, 15 years and over:		
1921	–	–
1936	–	–
1946	4 586 886	3 270 899
1951	4 592 587	3 110 004

APPENDIX 3

Urban African Population by Per Centage

Source: *Statistics for Fifty Years*, A-10

	All Races	Africans
1911:	24.7	12.6
1921:	27.9	14.0
1936:	32.4	18.4
1946:	38.4	23.7
1951:	42.6	27.2

Total Urban and Rural African Population in 1951:
Total Urban: 2 328 534   Total Rural: 6 231 549

APPENDIX 4

Source: *Statistics for Fifty Years*, G-3

Numbers of Farm Employees:

	All Races	Africans
Av. Jul. 1917-Jun.1918:	488 062	358 973
At 31 Aug. 1925:	689 165	435 185
At 31 Aug. 1930:	749 197	475 909
Av. Sep. 1936-Aug.1937:	969 410	658 412
At 31 Aug. 1952:	929 275	801 211

APPENDIX 5

Numbers Employed in Mining

Source: *Statistics for Fifty Years*, G-4

	All Races	Africans
1918:	291 113	255 897
1919:	288 623	250 593
1920:	306 554	265 540
1921:	276 098	242 408
1922:	253 116	226 969
1923:	288 469	256 404
1924:	302 482	269 215
1925:	300 554	266 912
1926:	341 033	301 132
1927:	349 850	309 230
1928:	356 748	318 057
1929:	345 711	306 640
1930:	349 031	312 123
1931:	329 073	294 415
1932:	307 167	275 140
1933:	330 874	295 398
1934:	362 710	323 035
1935:	400 274	355 563
1936:	429 400	381 714
1937:	438 934	388 415
1938:	459 727	405 806

1939:	464 359	408 706
1940:	502 008	444 242
1941:	522 766	464 333
1942:	517 398	458 825
1943:	463 557	406 361
1944:	453 560	398 366
1945:	462 392	409 337
1946:	464 426	411 758
1947:	457 425	405 639
1948:	438 598	386 521

APPENDIX 6

Numbers Employed in Private Industry

Source: *Statistics for Fifty Years*, G-6

	All Races	Africans
1917-18	134 211	51 870
1918-19	123 975	–
1919-20	155 008	–
1920-21	160 035	–
1921-22	152 343	–
1922-23	152 530	–
1923-24	162 203	–
1924-25	169 676	55 638
1925-26	139 478	59 593
1926-27	147 286	63 046
1927-28	152 522	65 796
1928-29	161 349	69 830
1929-30	162 329	69 895
1930-31	–	–
1931-32	–	–
1932-33	141 906	55 407
1933-34	176 510	72 339
1934-35	207 652	89 613
1935-36	240 078	107 674
1936-37	263 978	119 463

1937-38	274 456	126 648
1938-39	275 852	126 067
1939-40	282 779	130 597
1940-41	311 007	149 031
1941-42	331 303	164 793
1942-43	344 143	176 442
1943-44	366 111	189 580
1944-45	399 112	207 797
1945-46	423 824	218 896
1946-47	455 663	234 117
1947-48	505 522	262 835
1948-49	556 779	292 366

APPENDIX 7

Numbers Employed in Retail, Wholesale and Service Establishments,1946-7 and 1952

Source: *Statistics for Fifty Years*, G-14

	All Races	Africans
Retail, 1946-7:	142 169	60 176
Retail, 1952:	159 340	68 055
Wholesale, 1946-7:	71 113	31 054
Wholesale, 1952:	93 404	42 940
Service, 1946-7:	82 522	42 870
Service, 1952:	89 867	49 189

BIBLIOGRAPHY

A. Primary Sources

1. Official Sources (Unpublished).

A. STATE ARCHIVES (PRETORIA); CENTRAL ARCHIVES DEPOT.

–ARB Archives of the Department of Labour
–GES Archives of the Department of Public Health
–JUS Archives of the Department of Justice
–LDB Archives of the Department of Agriculture
–MNW Archives of the Department of Mines
–NTS Archives of the Department of Native Affairs
–SAS Archives of the South African Railways and Harbours Administration
–TES Archives of the Treasury
–VWN Archives of the Department of Social Welfare

B. STATE ARCHIVES (PRETORIA); TRANSVAAL ARCHIVES DEPOT.

–GNLB Archives of the Government Native Labour Bureau.

C. UNPUBLISHED REPORTS

'Report of the Departmental Committee Appointed to Enquire into and
Report upon the Question of Residence of Natives in Urban Areas
and Certain Proposed Amendments to the Natives (Urban Areas)
Act No.21 of 1923)' (Young-Barrett, 1937)

D. Unpublished Evidence to Government Commissions and Committees

–University of the Witwatersrand, Church of the Province of South Africa Archives

A1280 Unemployment Commission, 1920-1
AD1438 Native Economic Commission, 1930-2
AD1756 Native Laws Commission, 1946-8
A1882 Economic and Wage Commission, 1925

–State Archives, Pretoria

K53 Miners' Phthisis Commission, 1920-1
K71 Miners' Phthisis Act, 1918
K30 Industrial and Agricultural Requirements Commission, 1939-45
K303 Social Security, 1943-4
K356 Native Labour (Farm) Committee, 1937-8
K357 Native Pass Laws
K389 Native Affairs Commission, 1932-6

2. Newspapers

Cape Times
Daily Mail
Daily Representative
Forum
The Guardian
Ilanga Lase Natal
Imvo Zabantsundu
Natal Witness
Rand Daily Mail
The Star
Sunday Times
Umteteli wa Bantu
Die Vaderland

3. Private Papers

–University of the Witwatersrand, Church of the Province of South
　　Africa Archives.

A71	– F.A.W. Lucas
A836	– F. McGregor
AD1178-9	– A.L. Saffery
A1207	– H. Gluckman
AD1623	– R.F.A. Hoernle
AD843	– SAIRR

–State Archives, Pretoria.

A1	– J.C. Smuts
A32	– J.B.M. Hertzog

B. Published Government Sources

1. White Papers (W.P.)

3-1923	1909 Transvaal-Mozambique Convention
4-1924	Old Age Pensions (Treasury Memorandum)
1-1933	Gold Mines – Proposed Levy on Excess Profits
2-1939	Government's Proposals on the Agricultural Position.
4-1941	Poor Relief
1-1942	Native Affairs Department – Policy and Activities
5-1942	Bill to Control Rents and Consolidate Law Thereto
1-1945	Workmen's Compensation (Amendment) Bill, 1945
3-1945	Social Security – Government's Proposals on
6-1945	Silicosis Bill, 1945
–1945	Poor Relief
1-1947	National Housing. A Review of Policy and Progress
19-1947	Native Laws Amendment Bill, 1947

2. Select Committee (S.C.) Reports

1-18	*Factories Bill*
3-18	*Gold Mining Industry*

16-20	*Housing Bill*
3-21	*Report of the Miners' Phthisis Commission*
3-23	*Native Registration and Protection Bill*
5-23	*Industrial Conciliation Bill*
12-25	*Masters and Servants (Transvaal) Amendment Bill*
14-25	*Wage Bill*
6A-29	*Natives (Urban Areas) Act, 1923, Amendment Bill, 2nd. Report*
9-30	*Industrial Conciliation Amendment Bill*
7-31	*Native Service Contract Bill*
13-31	*Workmen's Compensation Bill*
14-32	*Report of the Miners' Phthisis Commission of Enquiry*
15-34	*Workmen's Compensation Bill*
9-36	*Unemployment Insurance Bill*
5-37	*Industrial Conciliation and Wage Bill*
3-40	*Operation of the Workmen's Compensation Act, 1934*
10-44	*Social Security*
10-45	*Natives (Urban Areas) Consolidation Bill*
11-46	*Unemployment Insurance Bill*
8-48	*Delegated Legislation*
17-48	*Delegated Legislation*
8-49	*Delegated Legislation*

3. Official Publications

– *Union Statistics for Fifty Years – jubilee issue 1910-1960* (Pretoria, 1960)
– *Statutes of the Union of South Africa, 1910-1948*
– *Senate Debates*
– *House of Assembly Debates*
– *Union Year Books, 1918-1948*
– *Union Government Gazette, 1918-1948*
– *Social and Industrial Review* (Department of Labour)
– *Farming in South Africa* (Department of Agriculture)

4. Annual Departmental Reports and Reports of Commissions and Committees

U.G. 37-1914, *Report of the Native Grievances Commission* (Buckle)
Report and Recommendations of the Departmental Committee appointed by the Hon. Minister of Native Affairs to Enquire into the Alleged Shortage

of Native Labour in the Natal Province, (Wheelwright, 1918)

U.G. 7-1919, *Native Affairs Department Report for 1913-18*

U.G. 34-1920, *Final Report of the Low Grade Mines Commission* (Kotze)

U.G. 6-1921, *Fifth Report of the Public Service Enquiry Commission* (Graham)

U.G. 41-1922, *Report of the Inter-Departmental Committee on the Native Pass Laws* (Godley)

U.G. 15-1923, *Third Census of the Population of the Union of South Africa* (enumerated 3/5/21).

U.G. 36-1925, *Report of the Mining Regulations Commission* (Pittman)

U.G. 14-1926, *Report of the Economic and Wage Commission* (Mills)

U.G. 16-1932, *Report of the Low Grade Ore Commission* (Pienaar)

U.G. 22-1932, *Report of the Native Economic Commission* (Holloway)

U.G. 26-1932, *Native Affairs Commission Report for 1927-1931*

U.G. 37-1935, *Report of the Industrial Legislation Commission* (van Reenen)

U.G. 21-1938, *Sixth Census of the Population of the Union of South Africa* (enumerated 5/5/36).

U.G. 30-1938, *Department of Labour Report for 1937*

Report of the Native Farm Labour Committee, 1937-1939 (Herbst, 1939)

U.G. 8-1940, *Report of the Committee to consider the Administration of Areas which are becoming Urbanised but which are not under Local Government Control, 1938-9* (Thornton)

U.G. 40-1941, *The Industrial and Agricultural Requirements Commission, 4th Interim Report* (van Eck)

U.G. 42-1941, *Report of the Native Affairs Commission, 1939-40*

U.G. 45-1941, *Department of Labour Report for 1940*

Report of the Inter-Departmental Committee on the Social, Health and Economic Conditions of Urban Natives (Smit, 1942)

U.G. 9-1943, *Social and Economic Planning Council, Report No.1. Re-employment, Reconstruction and the Council's Status*

U.G. 14-1944, *Report of the Social Security Committee and Report No.2 of the Social and Economic Planning Council, Entitled: Social Security, Social Services and the National Income*

U.G. 15-1944, *Social and Economic Planning Council Report No.3. Aspects of Public Service Organisation and Employment*

U.G. 21-1944, *Report of the Witwatersrand Mine Native Wages Commission* (Lansdown)

U.G. 30-1944, *Report of the National Health Services Commission* (Gluckman)

U.G. 44-1946, *Native Affairs Department Report for 1944-5*

U.G. 53-1946, *Fifth Report of the Public Service Enquiry Commission* (Centlivres).

U.G. 54-1947, *Sixth Report of the Public Service Enquiry Commission* (Centlivres)

U.G. 28-1948, *Report of the Native Laws Commission* (Fagan)

U.G. 58-1948, *Department of Public Health. Report for Year Ending 30 June, 1947*

U.G. 62-1948, Department of Labour Report for 1946

U.G. 45-1949, Department of Health. Report of the National Housing and Planning Commission, 1947, 1948

R.P. 18, *Annual Report of the Government Mining Engineer, 1962*

C. Secondary Works

1. Books

Althusser, L., *Lenin and Philosophy and Other Essays* (London, 1971).

Beetham, D., *Bureaucracy* (Minneapolis, 1987).

Beinart, W., *The Political Economy of Pondoland* (Johannesburg, 1982).

Beinart, W., Delius, P., and Trapido, S. (eds.), *Putting a Plough to the Ground. Accumulation and Dispossession in Rural South Africa, 1850-1930* (Johannesburg, 1986).

Bozzoli, B. (ed.), *Labour, Townships and Protest: Studies in the social history of the Witwatersrand* (Johannesburg, 1979).

Bozzoli, B., *The Political Nature of a Ruling Class: Class, Capital and Ideology in South Africa, 1890-1933* (London, 1981).

Bradford, H., *A Taste of Freedom. The ICU in Rural South Africa, 1924-1930* (New Haven, 1987).

Braverman, H., *Labour and Monopoly Capital* (London, 1974).

Brookes, E.H. (*et al.*), *Coming of Age. Studies in South African Citizenship and Politics* (Cape Town, 1930).

Bundy, C., *The Rise and Fall of the South African Peasantry* (London, 1979).

Carnoy, M., *The State and Political Theory* (Princeton, 1984).

Clawson, D., *Bureaucracy and the Labour Process. The Transformation of U.S. Industry, 1860-1920* (New York, 1980).

Cohen, H., *The Demonics of Bureaucracy* (Ames, Iowa, 1965).

Creswell, M., *An Epoch of the Political History of South Africa in the Life of Frederick Hugh Page Creswell* (Cape Town, 1956).

Crush, J.S., *The Struggle for Swazi Labour, 1890-1920* (Kingston and Montreal, 1987).

Crush, J.S., Jeeves, A.H. and Yudelman, D., *South Africa's Labor Empire: A History of Black Migrancy to the Gold Mines* (Cape Town, 1991).

Davenport, T.R.H., *South Africa. A Modern History* (3rd edn., London, 1987).

Davies, R.H., *Capital, State and White Labour in South Africa, 1900-1960. An Historical Materialist Analysis of Class Formation and Class Relations* (Brighton, 1979).

De Kiewiet, C.W., *A History of South Africa, Social and Economic* (London, 1941).

De Kock, M.H., *An Analysis of the Finances of the Union of South Africa* (2nd edn., Cape Town, 1928).

Delius, P., *The Land Belongs to Us* (Johannesburg, 1983).

Denoon, D., *A Grand Illusion. The failure of imperial policy in the Transvaal Colony during the period of reconstruction, 1900-1905* (London, 1973).

Djang, T.K., *Factory Inspection in Great Britain* (London, 1942).

Doxey, G.V., *The Industrial Colour Bar in South Africa* (London, 1961).

Draper, H., *Karl Marx's Theory of Revolution. Vol.1, State and Bureaucracy* (New York, 1977).

Dubow, S., *Racial Segregation and the Origins of Apartheid in South Africa, 1919-1936* (London, 1989).

Engels, F., *The Origin of the Family, Private Property and the State* (trans. New York, 1968).

Fagan, H.A., *Our Responsibility* (Stellenbosch, 1960)

Fagan, H.A., *Co-existence in South Africa* (Cape Town, 1963).

Foucault, M., *The Order of Things* (New York, 1970).

Foucault, M., *Discipline and Punish* (New York, 1978).

Friedlander, W.A., *Introduction to Social Welfare* (Englewood Cliffs, N.J., 3rd. edn. 1968).

Friedman, S., *Building Tomorrow Today. African Workers in Trade Unions, 1970-1984* (Johannesburg, 1987).

Furlong, P.J., *Between Crown and Swastika: The Impact of the Radical Right on the Afrikaner Nationalist Movement in the Fascist Era* (Johannesburg, 1991).

George, V., *Social Security and Society* (London, 1973).

Gibbs, H., *Twilight in South Africa* (London, 1949)

Giddens, A., *Emile Durkheim. Selected Writings* (Cambridge, 1972).

Giddens, A., *Studies in Social and Political Theory* (New York, 1977).

Gluckman, H., *Abiding Values. Speeches and Addresses* (Johannesburg, 1970).

Gramsci, A., *Selections from Prison Notebooks* (New York, 1971).

Greenberg, S., *Race and State in Capitalist Development* (New Haven, 1980).

Greenberg, S., *Legitimating the Illegitimate. State, Markets and Resistance in South Africa* (New Haven, 1987).

Hancock, W.K., *Smuts. The Fields of Force, 1919-1950* (Cambridge, 1968).

Harvey, D., *Consciousness and the Urban Experience. Studies in the History and Theory of Capitalist Urbanization* (Baltimore, 1985).

Held, D. (ed.), *States and Societies* (Oxford, 1983).

Hellmann, E. (ed.), *Race Relations Handbook* (Oxford, 1949).

Hindson, D.C., *Pass Controls and the Urban African Proletariat in South Africa* (Johannesburg, 1987).

Hirson, B., *Yours for the Union. Class and Community Struggles in South Africa, 1930-1947* (Johannesburg, 1989).

Hobart Houghton, D., *The South African Economy* (3rd. edn., Oxford, 1973).

Holloway, J., and Picciotto, S. (eds.), *State and Capital: A Marxist Debate* (London, 1978).

Horwitz, R., *The Political Economy of South Africa* (London, 1967).

Hutt, W.H., *The Economics of the Colour Bar* (London, 1964).

Ingham, K., *Jan Christian Smuts. The Conscience of a South African* (Johannesburg and London, 1986).

Jeeves, A.H., *Migrant Labour in South Africa's Mining Economy. The Struggle for the Gold Mines' Labour Supply, 1890-1920* (Kingston, Montreal and Johannesburg, 1985).

Johnstone, F.A., *Class, Race and Gold. A Study of Class Relations and Racial Discrimination in the South African Gold Mining Industry* (London, 1976).

Jordan, Z.A., *Economy, Class and Social Revolution* (London, 1971).

Keegan, T., *Rural Transformations in Industrializing South Africa. The Southern Highveld to 1914* (London, 1986).

Lacey, M., *Working for Boroko: The Origins of a Coercive Labour System in South Africa* (Johannesburg, 1981).

Lenin, V.I., *The State and Revolution* (trans. Peking, 1965).

Lewis, J., *Industrialisation and Trade Union Organisation in South Africa, 1924-55. The Rise and Fall of the South African Trades and Labour Council* (Cambridge, 1984).

Lipton, M., *Capitalism and Apartheid* (New York, 1984).

Macmillan, W.M., *Complex South Africa: An Economic Foot-Note to History* (London, 1930).

Marks, S. and Trapido, S. (eds.), *The Politics of Race, Class and Nationalism in Twentieth Century South Africa* (London, 1987).

Marx, K., and Engels, F., *The German Ideology* (trans. Moscow, 1964).

Miliband, R., *The State in Capitalist Society* (London, 1969).

Miliband, R., *Marxism and Politics* (London, 1977).

Mouffe, C. (ed.), *Gramsci and Marxist Theory* (London, 1979).

Neame, L.E., *Some South African Politicians* (Cape Town, 1929).

O'Meara, D., *Volkscapitalisme. Class, Capital and Ideology in the Development of Afrikaner Nationalism, 1934-1948* (Johannesburg, 1983).

Posel, D., *The Making of Apartheid, 1948-1961: Conflict and Compromise* (Oxford, 1991).

Poulantzas, N., *Political Power and the Social Classes* (trans. London, 1974).

Poulantzas, N., *State, Power and Socialism* (trans. London, 1980).

Richardson, P., *Chinese Labour in the Transvaal* (London, 1982).

Rius, *Marxism for Beginners* (New York, 1976).

Rogers, H., *Native Administration in the Union of South Africa* (Johannesburg, 1933).

Rosenthal, E. (compiler), *Southern African Dictionary of National Biography* (London and New York, 1966).

Sachs, B., *Personalities and Places* (Johannesburg, 1965).

Schrire, R. (ed.), *Critical Choices for South Africa: An Agenda for the 1990s* (Cape Town, 1990).

Schuman, D., *Bureaucracies, Organizations and Administrations: A Political Primer* (New York, 1976).

Scott, M., *A Time to Speak* (London, 1958).

Selby, J., *A Short History of South Africa* (London, 1973).

Serfontein, J.H.P., *Brotherhood of Power. An Expose of the Secret Afrikaner Broederbond* (London, 1979).

Simons, H.J. and Simons, R.E., *Class and Colour in South Africa, 1850-1950* (1st. edn., Harmondsworth, 1969).

Smith, B.C., *Bureaucracy and Political Power* (Brighton, 1988).

Smith, K., *The Changing Past: Trends in South African Historical Writing* (Johannesburg, 1988).

Strauss, E., *The Ruling Servants. Bureaucracy in Russia, France – and Britain?* (London, 1961).

Stultz, N.M., *Afrikaner Politics in South Africa, 1934-1948* (Berkeley, 1974).

Turrell, R.V., *Capital and Labour on the Kimberley Diamond Fields, 1871-1890* (Cambridge, 1987).

Van der Byl, P.G.V., *Top Hat to Velskoen* (Cape Town, 1973).

Van der Horst, S.T., *Native Labour in South Africa* (London, 1942).

Van Onselen, C., *Chibaro: African Mine Labour in Southern Rhodesia, 1900-1933* (London, 1976).

Van Rensburg, J., *Their Paths Crossed Mine* (Johannesburg, 1956).

Vann Woodward, C. (ed.), *A Comparative Approach to American History* (Washington, 1974).

Walker, I. and Weinbren, B., *2 000 Casualties. A History of the Trade Unions and the Labour Movement in the Union of South Africa* (Johannesburg, 1961).

Weber, M., *The Theory of Social and Political Organization* (trans. New York, 1947).

Weber, M., *Economy and Society* (trans. New York, 1968).

Webster, E.C., *Cast in a Racial Mould: Labour Process and Trade Unionism in the Foundries* (Johannesburg, 1985).

Wilkins, I. and Strydom, H., *The Super-Afrikaners. Inside the Afrikaner Broederbond* (Johannesburg, 1978).

Williams, R., *Culture and Society* (London, 1958).

Williams, R., *Marxism and Literature* (London, 1977).

Wilson, F., and Westcott, G. (eds.), *Hunger, Work and Health* (Johannesburg, 1980).

Worger, W.H., *South Africa's City of Diamonds. Mine Workers and Monopoly Capitalism in Kimberley, 1867-1895* (New Haven, 1987).

World Health Organisation, *Apartheid and Health* (Geneva, 1983).

Yudelman, D., *The Emergence of Modern South Africa. State, Capital and the Incorporation of Organized Labour on the South African Goldfields, 1902-1939* (Westport, 1983).

Zimbalist, A., *Case Studies in the Labour Process* (New York, 1979).

2. Published Articles

Batson, E., The Social Services and the Poverty of the Unskilled Worker, *Race Relations* 1939, Vol.6, No.4.

Batson, E., The Social Services: Discrimination and Counteraction, *Race Relations* 1940, Vol.7, No.2.

Burke, G. and Richardson, P., The Profits of Death: A Comparative Study of Miner's Phthisis in Cornwall and the Transvaal, *Journal of Southern African Studies* 1987, Vol.4, No.2.

Davies, R.H., Kaplan, D., Morris, M. and O'Meara, D., Class Struggle and a Periodisation of the South African State, *Review of African Political Economy* 1976, No.7.

Davenport, T.R.H., African Townsmen? South African Natives (Urban Areas) Legislation Through the Years, *African Affairs* 1969, Vol.68, No.271.

Davenport, T.R.H., The Triumph of Colonel Stallard: The Transformation of the Natives (Urban Areas) Act between 1923 and 1937, *South African Historical Journal* 1970, No.2.

Dubow, S., Holding 'A Just Balance between White and Black': The Native Affairs Department in South Africa, c.1920-1933, *Journal of Southern African Studies* 1982, Vol.12, No.2.

Duncan, D., Liberals and Local Administration in South Africa: Alfred Hoernlé and the Alexandra Health Committee, 1922-1943, *International Journal of African Historical Studies* 1990, Vol.23, No.3.

Duncan, D., The State Divided: Farm Labour Policy in South Africa, 1924-1948, *South African Historical Journal* 1991, Vol.24.

Duncan, D., State Bureaucracy and African Labour in South Africa: the Milling Workers Strike of 1944, *Canadian Journal of African Studies* 1992, Vol.25, No.3.

Duncan, D., The State and African Trade Unions, 1918-1948, *Social Dynamics* 1992, Vol.18, No.2.

First, R., Bethal Case-Book, *Africa South* 1958, Vol.2, No.3.

Jeeves, A.H., Migrant Labour and South African Expansion, 1920-1950, *South African Historical Journal* 1986, No.18.

Johannesburg Joint Council of Natives and Europeans, The Native in Industry, Memorandum No.3, 1927.

Laclau, E., The Specificity of the Political: the Poulantzas-Miliband Debate, *Economy and Society* 1975, Vol.4, No.1.

Lewin, J., The Recognition of African Trade Unions, *Race Relations* 1943, Vol.X.

Lewis, D., The South African State and African Trade Unions, 1947-53, *Africa Perspective* 1981, Vol.18.

Miliband, R., The Capitalist State: Reply to Nicos Poulantzas, *New Left Review* 1973, No.82.

Moodie, T.D., The Moral Economy of the Black Miners' Strike of 1946,

Journal of Southern African Studies 1986, Vol.13, No.1.

Moodie, T.D., The South African State and Industrial Conflict in the 1940s, *International Journal of African Historical Studies* 1988, Vol.21, No.1.

Morris, M., Apartheid, Agriculture and the State. University of Cape Town, SALDRU Working Paper No.8, 1977.

Packard, R.M., Tuberculosis and the Development of Industrial Health Policies on the Witwatersrand, 1902-32, *Journal of Southern African Studies* 1987, Vol.13, No.2.

Poulantzas, N., The Problems of the Capitalist State, *New Left Review* 1969, No.58.

Rheinallt Jones, J.D., Social Work and the Non-European, *Race Relations* 1936, Vol.3, No.4.

Saffery, A.L., African Trade Unions and the Institute, *Race Relations* 1941, Vol.VIII.

Sebris, R., Bureaucracy and Labour Relations, *Civil Service Journal* 1978, Vol.19, No.2.

Spandau, A., South African Wage Board Policy: An Alternative Interpretation, *South African Journal of Economics* 1972, Vol.40, No.4.

Swanson, M.S., The Sanitation Syndrome: bubonic plague and urban native policy in the Cape Colony, 1900-1909, *Journal of African History* 1977, Vol.XVIII, No.3.

Wolpe, H., Capitalism and Cheap Labour Power: From Segregation to Apartheid, *Economy and Society* 1974, Vol.1, No.4.

Yudelman, D. and Jeeves, A.H., New Frontiers for Old: Black Migrants to the South African Gold Mines, 1920-1985, *Journal of Southern African Studies* 1986, Vol.13 no.1.

3. Unpublished Theses and Papers

Baker, J.J., 'The Silent Crisis'. Black Labour, Disease, and the Economics and Politics of Health on the South African Gold Mines, 1902-1930 (Queen's University Doctoral Thesis, 1989).

Bell, M.M., The Politics of Administration: A study of the career of Dr. D.L. Smit with special reference to his work in the Department of Native Affairs, 1934-1945 (Rhodes University Master's Dissertation, 1978).

Bradford, H., Getting Away with Slavery: Capitalist Farmers, Foreigners and Forced labour in the Transvaal, c.1920-1950. Paper presented to the History Workshop Conference, University of the Witwatersrand, Feb. 1990.

Dubow, S., Segregation and 'Native Administration' in South Africa, 1920-1936 (Oxford University D.Phil. Thesis, 1986).

Duncan, D., 'The Mills of God': State Bureaucracy and African Labour in South Africa, 1918-1948 (Queen's University Doctoral Thesis, 1990).

Hindson, D.C., The Pass System and the Formation of an Urban African Proletariat in South Africa. A Critique of the Cheap Labour Power Thesis (University of Sussex D.Phil. Thesis, 1983).

Hirson, B., The Making of the African Working Class on the Witwatersrand: Class and Community Struggles in an Urban Setting, 1932-47 (Middlesex Polytechnic Doctoral Thesis, 1986).

James, W.G., The Group with the Flag: Class Conflict, Mine Hostels and the Reproduction of a Labour Force in the 1980s. Paper presented at the African Studies Institute, University of the Witwatersrand, Feb. 1990.

Jeeves, A.H., William Gemmill and South African Expansion, 1920-1950. Paper presented to the History Workshop Conference, University of the Witwatersrand, Feb. 1987.

Marks, S., Industrialization, Rural Health and the 1944 National Health Services Commission in South Africa. Forthcoming in S. Feierman and J. Jansen (eds.), The Social Basis of Health and Healing in South Africa (Los Angeles).

Maylam, P., The Local Evolution of Urban Apartheid: Influx Control and Segregation in Durban, c.1900-1951. Paper presented to the History Workshop Conference, University of the Witwatersrand, Feb. 1990.

Minnaar, A. de V., South African White Agriculture and the Great Depression (1929-1934) (University of South Africa Doctoral Thesis, 1988).

Nattrass, N., Wages, Profits and Apartheid: 1939-1960. Paper presented to the History Workshop Conference, University of the Witwatersrand, Feb. 1990.

Phillips, I.M., The 'Civilised Labour Policy' and the Private Sector: The Operation of the South African Wage Act, 1925-37 (Rhodes University Doctoral Thesis, 1984).

Posel, D., Influx Control and the Construction of Apartheid, 1948-61 (Oxford University D.Phil. Thesis, 1987).

Stein, M., African Trade Unionism on the Witwatersrand, 1928-1949 (University of the Witwatersrand Honours Dissertation, 1977).

Welcher, L., The Changing Relationship between the State and African Trade Unions in South Africa: 1939-1953 (University of the Witwatersrand Honours Dissertation, 1978).

INDEX